CHAMPIONS

…about bloomin' time!

THE OFFICIAL STORY OF
HOW LANCASHIRE ENDED
THEIR 77-YEAR WAIT TO
BECOME OUTRIGHT
COUNTY CHAMPIONS

WITH CONTRIBUTIONS FROM PETER MOORES, MIKE WATKINSON & GLEN CHAPPLE

GRAHAM HARDCASTLE & CHRIS OSTICK

With Forewords by Roy Tattersall, Jack Simmons and Andrew Flintoff

To/ Nigel
A year to remember!

Chris Ostick

Max Books

Part of the profits from this book are
being donated to the LCCC Foundation

First published in the UK in 2011 by Max Books in association
with Lancashire County Cricket Club

A CIP catalogue record for this title is available from the British Library

ISBN: 978-0-9562224-3-5

Cover Design by Peter Devine
Typeset and Design by Andrew Searle
Photography by Simon Pendrigh

Printed and bound by Anthony Rowe Ltd

MAX BOOKS
Epworth House
34 Wellington Road
Nantwich Cheshire CW5 7BX
Tel: 01270 625278
Email: maxcricket@btinternet.com

Contents

Acknowledgements

THE idea for this book was formed at the start of the season. I hardly dared breathe a word to anyone, but mentioned it rather tentatively to Chris Ostick and Graham Hardcastle, who cover Lancashire for the Manchester Evening News, and they agreed to start work. The book could only come out if we won the title. If we came second, no book.

After the first few wins talk in the press tent began to raise more than a murmur! Could this at last be the year? Playing with a home-grown team and on the outgrounds (renowned for results), could the 77-year wait be over? Each win made the book more of a prospect, a defeat put it further away. I used to go into the press tent and announce if the book was on or off. Others thought we were a little mad, but as the season went on, and with against-the-odds wins over Yorkshire twice and Warwickshire, it became believable. I didn't dare speak to the players.

I went down to Taunton and spent a nerve-tingling time, not only watching the match but also listening to the news from Hampshire. However, at the end of day three, the title looked to be heading Warwickshire's way. So much so, we even cancelled a meeting we had planned to discuss the book believing it wasn't going to happen. How wrong we were. The Hampshire batsmen held out and Lancashire completed a thrilling victory. As Steven Croft hit the winning runs I knew the book could now happen. As I journeyed home there were feelings of joy and relief that at last it had been achieved, but also now the responsibility of producing the book.

That it was produced so quickly and to such a high standard is due to the following. Firstly, Chris and Graham, who went to every game with their newspaper duties and have captured the excitement of this great season, and without whose enthusiasm the book would not have happened. Simon Pendrigh is Lancashire's official photographer and has provided some wonderful imagery, which perfectly illustrates this magnificent season. Additional photographs have been provided by Barry Mitchell, Joe Gardner (from the Player of the Year dinner), and Dave Bracegirdle. Paul Edwards has put together some terrific additional pieces to the book to add colour to the excitement. Andy Searle has done a sterling job putting the whole thing together under difficult circumstances, whilst the delightful dust cover was designed by Peter Devine.

At Old Trafford, Geoff Durbin and Ken Grime were very supportive, as were media manager Paul Holliday, Zoë Morgan and Treve Whitford. Roy Tattersall, Andrew Flintoff and Jack Simmons agreed to do forewords. Scorer Alan West did a very thorough job of proof-reading, so thanks to him and Darrin White, who have been a great help.

A final thanks must go to the players and coaching staff. Not only have they been extremely cooperative, they also provided something to write about. Without you, this wouldn't have been possible.

I hope you enjoy reading it as much as we have enjoyed putting it together. After all, after 77 years it's about bloomin' time!

Rev Malcolm Lorimer,
(Lancashire Chaplain & proprietor of Max Books)

Forewords

IT is a great honour to be asked to contribute a foreword to the book describing Lancashire's marvellous Championship triumph and the first thing I want to do is once again send my congratulations to Glen Chapple and his team. It's also a bit of a relief to be able to write these words because after so many near misses I was beginning to wonder when my beloved county would win the title again.

Although I can't get to games now, I still watch them very closely on television. As the final matches were being played at Worcester, Liverpool and Taunton I was struck by the similarities between the current Lancashire team and the 1950 side which shared the title with Surrey.

Both teams were well captained. Glen Chapple is both a good player and a good captain. He's a trier, who never gives in whether he's batting, bowling or fielding. Our skipper in 1950 was Nigel Howard. He was an amateur who listened to the views of the professionals and we would have done anything for him. I get the impression it's the same with this young Lancashire team because Glen never spares himself if his county needs him. I think it was sheer determination which helped him to bowl those overs with an injured hamstring in the last match against Somerset and that's something any professional respects.

Spinners were important to both sides too. I was so pleased when Simon Kerrigan took all those wickets against Hampshire at Liverpool, but I really didn't know that his were the best bowling figures for Lancashire since I took nine wickets against Notts nearly 60 years ago. We had four spinners in 1950: Bob Berry, Malcolm Hilton, Ken Grieves and me. We also had very fine close fielders like Geoff Edrich and Jack Ikin. I know the game's altered so much in the last 60 years but the basic principles like bowling a length and sharp catching haven't changed at all.

Where do Lancashire go from here? Well I'd like to challenge the current team to maintain their success in the coming years. After all, the Red Rose won the title four times in five seasons in the period 1926-1930 and I'd love this wonderful Championship win to mark the start of a great era for the team.

For now, though, I'm just so happy to repeat my thoughts when they won the title in September: Well done Lancashire!

Roy Tattersall, October 2011

I WAS so nervous during that final day of the season at Taunton that I had to turn the TV off twice! I was planning to go down to Somerset, but at the end of day three decided not to bother because I – like most people – assumed the title was heading to Warwickshire.

I haven't felt so nervous for years, but the minute Steven Croft hit those winning runs I cracked open a bottle of bubbly and I was quite drunk an hour later! Well, it has been 77 years! After waiting for so long, it will be fabulous to finally see the Championship pennant over Old Trafford.

The best captain I ever played under was Jack Bond. We had players like Clive Lloyd, Farokh Engineer, David Lloyd, Barry Wood, Peter Lever and Ken Shuttleworth in our side, but nobody was thought of as a superstar in that team because if they thought they were, Jack would tell them to go and play in the second team. There is the same feeling from this 2011 side; there are no superstars, everyone is working together and for each other and that has been great to see.

When I started playing, the Championship was the one we wanted, even though we won a host of one-day trophies. Now this group of players has finally done what we have all set out to achieve. It is an amazing achievement.

Jack Simmons, October 2011

SOME people wrote off Lancashire's chances this season, including quite a few former players, but I remember sitting down with my good mate Chappie in March and he was so excited about this group of players. He spoke so enthusiastically about them, you couldn't help but believe they were going to have a good season.

In previous years Lancashire sides have included some of the game's biggest stars, many of whom I had the pleasure of playing alongside, but they were unable to win the title for this great club. This year they've done it differently.

To have so many young Lancastrians in the side makes me really proud, and for them to go on and win the Championship after all this time is an amazing achievement. To be honest, I'm really jealous because I would have loved to have been a part of it. But I had my time. I'm just so pleased for all the lads, they deserve it.

They now have to build on this. It won't be easy. It took them 77 years to win the title, so back-to-back Championships is a big ask. But in Peter Moores and Glen Chapple they have the right men at the top to do it. England's loss was definitely Lancashire's gain where Moores is concerned and the club are reaping the rewards of the decision made by them to get rid of him.

I owe the club a lot for all the help and support they gave me during my career and they deserve the success they've had this season. Well done lads!

Andrew Flintoff, October 2011

Introduction

THIS wasn't meant to be Lancashire's year. Season after season, the county have been named among the favourites to break their County Championship duck. A host of big-name players – domestic and overseas – were drafted in over the years in a bid to finally secure the club's first outright title since 1934, but time and again, it wasn't to be as, quite often, Lancashire just came up short. They finished runners-up five times in the previous 13 years alone, and third in 2007 when they fell 25 agonising runs shy of winning the title on the last day at the Oval.

This year, however, was different. A sapping legal wrangle over the proposed £32m redevelopment of Old Trafford, married with a crunching recession, left the club in financial dire straits. So much so, they couldn't afford to go on a pre-season tour and at times they came close to not even being able to pay the players' wages.

Any plans coach Peter Moores and cricket director Mike Watkinson had of strengthening a squad which in the previous two years had finished fourth in the Championship were scuppered. Having struggled to post big first-innings totals over the past few seasons, a couple of experienced batsmen would have been on their shopping list.

The cash crisis also meant that there would be no big-name overseas players. For fans used to being enthralled by the mastery of Wasim Akram, Clive Lloyd, Muttiah Muralitharan and VVS Laxman to name just a few, it was a bit of a shock to the system. So the club began the campaign with one of their smallest squads in terms of numbers since the Second World War.

The exits of Stuart Law, Mal Loye, Iain Sutcliffe, Dominic Cork and Luke Sutton in the previous three years meant that this season the onus was on the home-grown youngsters to step up to the mark – the new generation of Lancashire stars. Although the potential of the likes of Karl Brown, Steven Croft, Luke Procter, Kyle Hogg and Gareth Cross were never in question, it was a lot to expect of them to form the backbone of a Championship-winning side.

On top of that, with the square having been turned 90 degrees at Old Trafford over the winter, Lancashire had to play all of their home Championship matches at outgrounds. Six of them were at Liverpool's Aigburth ground – which has been their second home for several years now – but the other two at Blackpool and Southport were largely unknown quantities in terms of recent first-class cricket, and with the Championship season starting as early as April 8, there were concerns over what types of wicket they would be playing on.

With all that in mind, many pundits had Lancashire down to struggle in the Championship, and some even tipped them to be relegated, but from the off the team were out to prove the doubters wrong. Time and again the players mentioned the word 'belief' when asked what was different this year. To a man, they showed a never-say-die attitude, which is an ever-present among champions. When their backs were against the wall, they came out fighting and, time and again, they turned a difficult position into a winning one.

The final, dramatic match of the season against Somerset at Taunton summed up the campaign. With title rivals Warwickshire always looking on top against Hampshire at the Rose Bowl, Lancashire's chances of ending their 77-year wait looked to be over going into the last day. While everyone else had given it up, the players themselves knew there was still a chance, and despite the weight of history hanging heavy on their shoulders, they delivered a moment every Red Rose fan will treasure as they chased down 211 to win the game – and the title.

Despite the brilliant individual performances – and there were plenty of them in this amazing, nail-biting and often unbelievable campaign – this Championship victory is a reward for team spirit. This side will not go down in history as being a team of greats, but it will be seen as a great team.

Chris Ostick & Graham Hardcastle,
October 2011

Graham would like to dedicate this book to wonderful parents, lost grandparents and his fiancée, Vicki.

Chris would like to dedicate this book to his wonderful wife Georgina, daughter Sophie, mum and dad – and grandpa, who would have loved to read it.

MATCH 1

Lancashire v Sussex

(Aigburth, Liverpool) April 8–11

DAY ONE

Skipper Glen Chapple claims the first wicket of the 2011 campaign, Chris Nash LBW for 15. Chapple went on to take nine wickets in the match

AS the new campaign started, there were several questions which still needed answering about the Lancashire side. The batting line-up was a concern, with much debate over who would be given the crucial number three spot, and there were doubts over how the pitch at Liverpool would play, especially with the season starting so early. But there was one thing which was never in doubt – that in skipper Glen Chapple Lancashire had a real gem in their ranks, even at the age of 37. And so he proved on the opening day of the season against newly-promoted Sussex.

There were a few raised eyebrows when, having won the toss, Sussex elected to bat first on what looked like an ideal day for bowling, although Chapple revealed later he would have batted first as well had he won the toss. And at lunch, it looked to have been a good call with Lancashire claiming just the one wicket in the morning session, Chapple opening his account by trapping Chris Nash lbw for 15. A half-century by Ed Joyce, and a steady knock by Luke Wells, guided the visitors safely to lunch on 108-1.

But Lancashire came to life in the afternoon session as Chapple – starting his 20th season at the club – ripped through the heart of the Sussex batting line-up. First he sent Wells' off-stump tumbling for 35, then claimed the wicket of danger man Murray Goodwin, who was caught well at point by Steven Croft for a duck. It started a collapse which saw Sussex lose three wickets in 26 balls, with Tom Smith claiming the key scalp of Joyce – who made 84 – and Rana Naved-ul-Hasan without scoring.

Oliver Newby, starting his first game since tearing the anterior cruciate ligament in his right knee at the beginning of the 2010 campaign, took his first Championship wicket since September 2009 as Ben Brown edged to Smith at second slip for one to leave Sussex reeling on 165-6 on a slow wicket.

A stubborn 56-run partnership between Joe Gatting, nephew of former England skipper Mike, and Naved Arif steadied the ship until Chapple – who else – brought it to an end. Having taken 37 balls to get off the mark, Arif fell lbw to the Red Rose skipper for six, and six overs later Chapple completed his 32nd five-wicket haul in first-class cricket and claimed his 750th first-class wicket for Lancashire as James Anyon edged him to Smith, who took a superb catch at slip. Sajid Mahmood then wiped up the Sussex tail with two wickets in three balls, including that of Gatting, who top-edged to Gareth Cross for 90, as they were all out for 243.

> *"I was a bit lucky really. I didn't feel that threatening but felt I bowled well after lunch and I am really pleased with my five wickets."*
>
> **– Glen Chapple**

Stephen Moore and Paul Horton opened the batting in Lancashire's reply. After two years of experimenting, coach Peter Moores had finally settled on the experienced duo as his opening partnership. Horton went for 17 in the 10th over as he shouldered arms to Arif, only to see the ball hit the top of his off-stump. Even then the puzzle as to who would come in at three still wasn't solved as Gary Keedy came in as night-watchman. He and Moore saw out the final few overs as Lancashire closed what was a good opening day to the campaign on 32-1.

Chapple said: "I was a bit lucky really. I didn't feel that threatening but felt I bowled well after lunch and I am really pleased with my five wickets.

"We started a bit slowly in the morning, the pitch was slower than we thought and we bowled a bit too full. But from lunch onwards I thought the lads were terrific and we have ended up having a good day.

"I didn't know I was close to claiming 750 first-class wickets, but I am really pleased. I am really enjoying my cricket and I am thankful I am still fit at my age."

CLOSE OF PLAY DAY ONE:
Sussex, having won the toss and elected to bat, 243 (JS Gatting 90, EC Joyce 84, G Chapple 5-68), led Lancashire 32-1 by 211 runs

DAY TWO

GOING into the season opener, if you had asked any Lancashire fan what their main concern about the side was, the majority would have said the batting. In the previous two seasons the team struggled to post big scores in the first innings of County Championship matches, meaning more times than not they were chasing the game as they failed to put early scoreboard pressure on teams.

In 2010, no Lancashire player passed more than 900 Championship runs for the season, and last season's two leading players in terms of averages – Shivnarine Chanderpaul and Ashwell Prince – were no longer at the club. But all those concerns were blown away on the second day of the campaign – although not without the odd minor hiccup.

Night-watchman Gary Keedy went in just the fifth over of the day for six as he was caught at silly mid-off by Joe Gatting playing forward to former England spinner Monty Panesar. When Stephen Moore, who like Keedy had just returned from playing for the MCC against 2010 champions Nottinghamshire in Abu Dhabi, went 11 overs later, playing on after mis-timing a pull to Amjad Khan for 26, Lancashire were 64-3 and the old doubts looked like they were once again beginning to surface. But, setting a tone which was to be repeated several times throughout the campaign, the Red Rose recovery came from the most unlikely of sources.

Karl Brown went into this game having played just six Championship matches for Lancashire and although in the previous season he had been prolific in the second team, his highest Championship score for the club going into the match was the 40 he scored at Aigburth against Kent in 2008. He had, however, shown enough potential for coach Peter Moores to throw him in at the deep end in the opening match of the campaign, and although he came in behind night-watchman Keedy, the Boltonian had become the man entrusted to fill the crucial number three role for the Red Rose. And he didn't let Moores, or the rest of the team, down as he blasted his maiden first-class century for the club.

He shared a brilliant 180-run fourth-wicket stand with former skipper Mark Chilton – who was also a contender for the number three spot – to put Lancashire in control of the match. Despite his inexperience at this level, Brown took the lead in the partnership with

Karl Brown celebrates his maiden first-class century in the company of Mark Chilton, who made 87, as Lancashire reached 319-5 on the second day

Chilton, punishing the Sussex attack and playing sublimely for his 114, which included 18 boundaries.

The duo saw off some probing bowling in the morning session from Panesar, then capitalised as conditions made batting easier after lunch. Chilton brought up his 38th first-class half-century in the 73rd over and, two balls later, Brown cut James Anyon for four to reach three figures for the first time.

The stand was eventually broken just after tea when Chilton was bowled by Rana Naved-ul-Hasan for 87. Just six overs later former England Under-19 batsman Brown followed as he was bowled by Anyon – but not before he had registered the highest score by a Lancashire player in a Championship game at Aigburth since Graeme Fowler's 169 in 1987.

Tom Smith (20no) and Steven Croft (37no) saw Lancashire safely to the close with a lead of 76, although just before stumps Smith had to scamper back quickly to avoid being run out having been sent back by Croft.

Brown said: "I have waited a long time for the opportunity to start, and to get a hundred in the first game is such a massive confidence boost. That would have to go down as the best knock I have ever had, especially in the circumstances – it means a lot to get my maiden first-class hundred. The fact we

> *"I have waited a long time for the opportunity to start, and to get a hundred in the first game is such a massive confidence boost."*
>
> **– Karl Brown**

have a smaller squad this season makes you train that bit harder. It gives you an incentive knowing there are spots available.

"Not having an overseas batsman could be a real positive. We have no Chanderpaul or Laxman to fall back on, they are not here so we have to go out there and do it ourselves. And being a small squad means there is tough competition for places and that will only benefit the team. If it's not competitive, people can sometimes slip into the mindset of 'oh well, I'll play in the next game anyway'.

"I felt like I was playing well before I went into the game and knew that if I didn't get a big score in the match it was going to come at some point. I didn't feel like there was any pressure on me."

CLOSE OF PLAY DAY TWO:
Sussex 243 (JS Gatting 90, EC Joyce 84, G Chapple 5-68) trailed Lancashire 319-5 (KR Brown 114, MJ Chilton 87) by 76 runs

DAY THREE

IN the whole of the 2010 campaign, Lancashire passed 400 just once in the County Championship. By lunch on day three of the opening game they had already matched that as Steven Croft, Tom Smith and Gareth Cross continued to build the Red Rose first-innings advantage over Sussex.

Croft, who was the club's leading run-scorer in 2010, brought up his half-century in the first hour of play and it included seven boundaries. But his hopes of what would have been just a second first-class century were dashed by Monty Panesar as he edged a delivery from the Ashes-winning spinner to Ed Joyce at first slip for 64, bringing to an end a 95-run partnership with Smith.

Since making his debut in 2005, Cross had spent a frustrating six years struggling to fight his way into Lancashire's County Championship side. Although during that time he became the regular first-choice wicketkeeper in Twenty20 cricket, the arrival of Luke Sutton in 2006 meant he had to take a back seat when it came to four-day cricket. With Sutton's departure to Derbyshire during the winter, Cross was given his chance to show what he could do, and he wasted little time in proving that he is right at home in the Championship team.

When Lancashire went in at lunch on 412-6, Cross had overtaken Smith. He raced to his half-century at the start of the afternoon session in just 79 balls with eight boundaries. Smith's 50 soon followed, but their 88-run stand was halted by Panesar as Cross tried to play one shot too many and was bowled for 63.

Glen Chapple came and went, edging his first ball from Panesar to Joyce at first slip. Smith batted for just over four hours for his 60 before he chopped on a delivery from Amjad Khan. When Sajid Mahmood was dismissed for 19, Lancashire were all out for 472 – their highest score for 22 Championship matches – and held a big first-innings lead of 229. Lancashire's performance with the bat was even more impressive considering Panesar caused several problems, claiming 4-105 on a wicket that, although slow, was turning, and Gary Keedy made full use of it in Sussex's second innings.

After openers Joyce and Chris Nash had taken the score to 69, the left-arm spinner forced a mistake from Joyce and he was caught at mid-wicket by Mahmood for 15. Nash, who was scoring at a run-a-ball, followed him off the last delivery before tea, trapped lbw by Oliver Newby for 43. Keedy thought he had claimed a second wicket, but Luke Wells was dropped by Croft at short leg just after the interval.

> *"There has been a bit of talk about us being relegated this year, but all the lads are so geared up to winning the title."*
>
> **– Gareth Cross**

It was, however, only a stay of execution as Keedy eventually got his man when Wells was caught by Stephen Moore at mid-wicket for 14. Murray Goodwin (28no) and Joe Gatting (27no) took Sussex on to 151-3 at the close, but they were still 78 runs behind.

Cross said: "There has been a bit of talk about us being relegated this year, but all the lads are so geared up to winning the title, especially with us playing at outgrounds. All the lads want to get 1,000 runs each and prove everyone wrong.

"I sat there for a full day wearing my pads watching other people smash it. It was good then to get out there and score a few runs. The way we batted showed the pitch is decent. There's not a lot in it for the seamers. Keeds is spinning it and he is the man to put pressure on Sussex."

CLOSE OF PLAY DAY THREE:
Sussex 243 (JS Gatting 90, EC Joyce 84, G Chapple 5-68)
& 151-3 trailed Lancashire 472 (KR Brown 114, MJ Chilton 87,
SJ Croft 64, GD Cross 63, TC Smith 60) by 78 runs

DAY FOUR

RAIN has been Lancashire's enemy far too many times over the years and it looked like it might scupper them again on the final day as the morning session was washed out. It left them with just two sessions in which to bowl Sussex out and chase any lead the visitors set. In the end, they only needed 15 overs as Glen Chapple repeated his first-innings heroics and Gary Keedy claimed five wickets as Lancashire got their campaign off to a stunning start – setting a pattern for the whole season.

Resuming on 151-3, Sussex were skittled out for 174, with seven wickets falling for just 22 runs. Chapple struck with the eighth ball of the day when he had Joe Gatting caught behind by Gareth Cross for 28. Ben Brown followed in Chapple's next over for a duck as he left alone a ball from the Lancashire skipper which cannoned into his off-stump.

Five balls later Murray Goodwin was caught by Paul Horton at first slip for 33 to give Keedy his third wicket of the innings. With the Zimbabwean's departure went Sussex's last realistic hope of salvaging a draw, although Lancashire would not have dreamt that victory would come as quickly as it did.

Rana Naved-ul-Hasan crashed Keedy down the ground for six but could only divert the spinner into the hands of Steven Croft at silly mid-off shortly afterwards as he went for 10. Naved Arif followed off the next delivery, bowled when trying to smash the ball through the off-side, leaving Keedy with figures of 5-41.

Two balls later James Anyon became the third Sussex wicket to fall with the score on 164 when he was well caught by a diving Tom Smith at second slip off Chapple. The skipper, fittingly, wrapped up an amazing win in just under an hour of play when he trapped Monty Panesar lbw for four with the penultimate ball of the 63rd over to claim 22 points.

From fearing that any chance they had of winning the game had gone down the drain with the rain, Lancashire ended up showing the rest of Division One that this year nothing was going to get in their way.

Peter Moores said: "It was a really good win which was set up really by how well we batted in the first innings. This was a proper team performance, from someone like Karl Brown coming in and getting his century backed up with a senior man in Mark Chilton.

"But you see that new breed of player – Steven Croft, Tom Smith and Gareth Cross – from the middle order coming in and playing really well. Gareth showed how he can accelerate and put pressure on people, so it was an all-round team performance.

A delighted Gareth Cross looks on as Naved Arif is bowled first ball by Keedy, one of seven wickets to tumble for 22 runs on the final morning

> *"We held the dominant end throughout the game and came out on top, so I am really pleased with the way we played."*
>
> - Peter Moores

"Sussex started well on 108-1 after the first session. The second session we got back in and they had a poor session, and I think that a sign of a good team is one that doesn't let the other side get back in. We held the dominant end throughout the game and came out on top, so I am really pleased with the way we played."

CLOSE OF PLAY DAY FOUR:
Lancashire 472 (KR Brown 114, MJ Chilton 87, SJ Croft 64, GD Cross 63, TC Smith 60) beat Sussex 243 (JS Gatting 90, EC Joyce 84, G Chapple 5-68) and 174 (G Keedy 5-41) by an innings and 55 runs

Lancashire 22pts (Batting 3, Bowling 3)
Sussex 2pts (Batting 1, Bowling 1)

LV= County Championship table April 11

	P	W	L	D	BaP	BoP	Pts
Lancashire	**1**	**1**	**0**	**0**	**3**	**3**	**22**
Yorkshire	1	1	0	0	3	3	22
Durham	1	0	0	1	5	3	11
Hampshire	1	0	0	1	2	3	8
Worcestershire	1	0	1	0	2	2	4
Sussex	1	0	1	0	1	1	2
Nottinghamshire	0	0	0	0	0	0	0
Somerset	0	0	0	0	0	0	0
Warwickshire	0	0	0	0	0	0	0

SCORECARD

Sussex first innings		Runs	Balls	Mins	4s	6s
EC Joyce	lbw b Smith	84	166	203	10	-
CD Nash	lbw b Chapple	15	15	29	2	-
LWP Wells	b Chapple	35	74	111	7	-
*MW Goodwin	c Croft b Chapple	0	9	13	-	-
JS Gatting	c Cross b Mahmood	90	123	160	11	-
+BC Brown	c Smith b Newby	1	6	5	-	-
Naved-ul-Hasan	lbw b Smith	0	11	11	-	-
Naved Arif	lbw b Chapple	6	48	60	1	-
JE Anyon	c Smith b Chapple	2	15	20	-	-
A Khan	c Horton b Mahmood	1	11	12	-	-
MS Panesar	not out	0	0	1	-	-
Extras	(3 b, 3 lb, 2 nb, 1 w)	9				
Total	(all out, 79.3 overs)	243				

Fall of wickets:
1-35 (Nash, 6.5 ov), 2-115 (Wells, 34.5 ov), 3-123 (Goodwin, 38.2 ov), 4-159 (Joyce, 49.2 ov), 5-160 (Brown, 50.2 ov), 6-165 (Naved-ul-Hasan, 53.3 ov), 7-221 (Naved Arif, 71 ov), 8-237 (Anyon, 77 ov), 9-243 (Gatting, 79.1 ov), 10-243 (Khan, 79.3 ov)

Lancashire bowling	Overs	Mdns	Runs	Wkts	Wides	No-Balls
Chapple	23	7	68	5	-	-
Mahmood	14.3	3	50	2	-	-
Newby	15	6	31	1	-	-
Smith	14	2	49	2	1	1
Keedy	13	0	39	0	-	-

Sussex second innings		Runs	Balls	Mins	4s	6s
EC Joyce	c Mahmood b Keedy	15	44	56	2	-
CD Nash	lbw b Newby	43	44	59	7	-
LWP Wells	c Moore b Keedy	14	36	49	2	-
*MW Goodwin	c Horton b Keedy	33	110	136	2	-
JS Gatting	c Cross b Chapple	28	63	71	2	-
+BC Brown	b Chapple	0	9	7	-	-
JE Anyon	c Smith b Chapple	0	10	19	-	-
Naved-ul-Hasan	c Croft b Keedy	10	8	8	1	1
Naved Arif	b Keedy	0	1	1	-	-
A Khan	not out	5	20	31	-	-
MS Panesar	lbw b Chapple	4	33	28	-	-
Extras	(16 lb, 6 nb)	22				
Total	(all out, 62.5 overs)	174				

Fall of wickets:
1-69 (Joyce, 14 ov), 2-69 (Nash, 14.3 ov), 3-105 (Wells, 27.2 ov), 4-152 (Gatting, 48.2 ov), 5-154 (Brown, 50.3 ov), 6-154 (Goodwin, 51.2 ov), 7-164 (Naved-ul-Hasan, 53.4 ov), 8-164 (Naved Arif, 53.5 ov), 9-164 (Anyon, 54.1 ov), 10-174 (Panesar, 62.5 ov)

Lancashire bowling	Overs	Mdns	Runs	Wkts	Wides	No-Balls
Chapple	19.5	5	49	4	-	-
Mahmood	5	1	27	0	-	1
Newby	8	2	35	1	-	-
Keedy	26	7	41	5	-	-
Smith	4	1	6	0	-	-

Lancashire first innings		Runs	Balls	Mins	4s	6s
PJ Horton	b Naved Arif	17	31	36	3	-
SC Moore	b Khan	26	80	109	4	-
G Keedy	c Gatting b Panesar	6	32	33	-	-
KR Brown	b Anyon	114	236	278	18	-
MJ Chilton	b Naved-ul-Hasan	87	184	216	11	-
SJ Croft	c Joyce b Panesar	64	109	143	10	-
TC Smith	b Khan	60	150	248	8	-
+GD Cross	b Panesar	63	98	101	9	-
*G Chapple	c Joyce b Panesar	0	1	1	-	-
SI Mahmood	c Joyce b Khan	13	23	29	2	-
OJ Newby	not out	0	3	6	-	-
Extras	(10 b, 12 lb)	22				
Total	(all out, 157.5 overs)	472				

Fall of wickets:
1-25 (Horton, 9.3 ov), 2-42 (Keedy, 19 ov), 3-64 (Moore, 29.5 ov), 4-244 (Chilton, 91.1 ov), 5-266 (Brown, 96.2 ov), 6-361 (Croft, 124.2 ov), 7-449 (Cross, 150.3 ov), 8-449 (Chapple, 150.4 ov), 9-467 (Smith, 156 ov), 10-472 (Mahmood, 157.5 ov)

Sussex bowling	Overs	Mdns	Runs	Wkts	Wides	No-Balls
Naved-ul-Hasan	29	8	81	1	-	-
Khan	28.5	8	94	3	-	-
Naved Arif	17	2	68	1	-	-
Panesar	47	17	105	4	-	-
Anyon	25	5	79	1	-	-
Wells	6	2	8	0	-	-
Nash	5	1	15	0	-	-

Umpires: RJ Bailey & SC Gale Scorers: DM White & MJ Charman

Gary Keedy picked up his first five-wicket haul of 2011 in the second innings of the opening game at Aigburth

Karl Brown

IT was more than fitting that Karl Brown was at the crease when Lancashire beat Somerset at Taunton to secure their first outright LV= County Championship in 77 years, because the 23-year-old from Atherton personified what the Red Rose team of 2011 was all about.

At the start of the season, nobody was quite sure how he would cope with the responsibility of batting at number three for a full first-class campaign. The talent was there, of that there was no doubt, but even coach Peter Moores admitted that until a player is put in that position you never quite know how they will deal with it. Well Moores needn't have worried, because Brown was one of the true stars of Lancashire's campaign.

For them to do well, the team needed players like Brown – young, home-grown and with little regular first-team experience – to step up to the mark and fill the void left by the lack of a big-name top-order overseas batsman. Brown, who began playing in the Lancashire age-group sides at the age of 10, duly delivered.

His impressive 114 in the opening win over Sussex gave him confidence and the knowledge that he was good enough at this level, while his 96 on a tough track in the win at Hampshire was probably the innings of the season by any Red Rose player. He impressed enough for the England selectors to start taking an interest, later naming him in the Performance Programme squad to tour Sri Lanka at the start of 2012.

Having come through the academy at Old Trafford, Brown actually made his Championship debut in 2008 after playing in the second team from the age of 15. Despite scoring runs for fun in the seconds, he struggled to break into the senior side on a regular basis. However, when the chance came this season, he took it with both hands, playing in every Championship match and forcing his way into the line-ups in both limited overs competitions.

"At the start of the season my aim was to just get in the Championship side," said Brown. "I was ready to bat anywhere, but I was really proud to start the season off batting at number three for Lancashire, and to have done well makes the feeling even better.

"I felt this was the year I could really push on following the work I had done in the winter with Peter Moores on a few technical things and also with my fitness. I felt in as good a condition as I have ever been. I was just raring to go.

"If any side worked harder than us last winter I would like to have seen it. However, I didn't expect to have as much of an impact in the side as I did. I didn't expect to play the sorts of innings I did during the season."

His maiden first-class century will always stick with Brown, who signed as a professional with Lancashire at the age of just 17, but he believes the knock at Hampshire was even better.

"To get my first first-class hundred in my first game against Sussex is something I will look at as a very proud moment and it will always stick out," he continued. "It gave me a huge amount of confidence to take into the rest of the season, but my best innings was the 96 at Hampshire. I had to play differently on a tough wicket and somehow find a way to score runs."

To be there at the end when the winning runs were scored at Taunton by good pal Steven Croft was the icing on the cake on what was a remarkable season.

"It was an amazing feeling to be out there," said Brown. "I felt nervous as I went out to bat, but it was more comfortable being out there than in the dressing room. We just wanted to get over the line.

"I still can't find the words to describe what it means as a Lancashire lad to win the title with this county after such a long time for the club, and with this set of lads. We're just a group of mates playing cricket."

CHAMPAGNE MOMENT: *"There are two for me, both Steven Croft catches. The first at Trent Bridge to get Alex Hales out and the one against Yorkshire on the final day at Aigburth in the gully to dismiss Steve Patterson. Both amazing and both very important. He sets the standards in the field we all have to try and follow."*

MATCH 2

Lancashire v Somerset

(Aigburth, Liverpool) April 20–22

DAY ONE

HAVING proved everyone wrong with their batting display in the opening win over Sussex, Lancashire had another myth to dispel when Somerset visited Aigburth – that they couldn't win without Glen Chapple. So often over the years the talismanic skipper had pulled out a little piece of magic to rescue the Red Rose, but the punishment on the body which goes along with playing 20 years of first-class cricket meant he had suffered a string of niggling injuries. And here a slight calf strain was to blame for the 37-year-old sitting out the clash with the side many tipped to win the title, having finished second in 2010.

Lancashire did have a secret weapon up their sleeve, however – a man known simply as The Roof. Farveez Maharoof had missed the opening win against Sussex because of delays with his visa. The Sri Lankan was seen as an ideal replacement for Chapple against Somerset – although little did anybody realise it would be with the bat rather than the ball that he would shine.

Having lost the toss for the second time in two matches, Lancashire faced the daunting prospect of trying to bowl out a Somerset side which included Arul Suppiah, James Hildreth, Craig Kieswetter, Jos Buttler, Peter Trego and run machine Marcus Trescothick. But they were more than up to the task as they gave an early glimpse of the destructive bowling unit which terrorised many a batting line-up during the season.

Sajid Mahmood and Gary Keedy were destroyers-in-chief with three wickets each, while Oliver Newby and Tom Smith both deserved better than the four they shared on day one as the visitors were bowled out for 268 just after tea. Although new overseas signing Maharoof didn't take a wicket, his display warranted one. On top of this, Gareth Cross wrote his name into the record books, becoming just the eighth Lancashire wicketkeeper to claim six victims in an innings in first-class cricket, with four catches and two stumpings.

Mahmood gave Lancashire the perfect start. After seeing his opening ball dispatched for four by Trescothick, he hit back with a shorter delivery which the former England opener could only nick to Cross. In an impressive opening spell, Mahmood also claimed the wicket of Suppiah, who gloved him behind.

England Lions captain Hildreth and Nick Compton gave a glimpse of their class by putting on 98 to take Somerset to 129-2 at lunch, but Lancashire struck with the fourth ball after the break as Hildreth was caught off balance and stumped by Cross for 55 off the bowling of Keedy. It started a collapse which saw Somerset lose six wickets in the session.

Compton – grandson of the England Test great Denis – was next to go as he was caught by Steven Croft at backward point off the bowling of Newby for 61. Then Smith got in on the action as Buttler was undone by an unplayable delivery which he edged to Cross for eight.

Kieswetter showed some resistance, reaching his half-century, but he began to run out of partners as Trego, on 15, skied a top-edge off Smith to Karl Brown and Gemaal Hussain became another Cross victim as he took a good catch off Keedy. When Kieswetter went for 53, stumped by Cross after advancing down the wicket to Keedy, Somerset had slumped from 129-2 to 240-8 at tea.

Mahmood returned to bowl Ajantha Mendis for 18 and Lancashire quickly wrapped up the innings when Charl Willoughby was caught by Maharoof off Newby for a duck.

A great day got even better for the Red Rose as they reached close on 70-0, with Stephen Moore unbeaten on 52 after blitzing nine boundaries in just 20 overs and Paul Horton 14.

Mahmood said: "Chappie is a top-class bowler who has performed day in, day out for Lancashire over several years now. It was a big blow when we found out he wasn't playing, but we got our heads around it. We have proven we can do well without him.

"The first session didn't go to plan for us, but we had a rethink and bowled well after lunch. We put them under pressure by stopping them scoring and are pretty pleased at keeping them to 268.

"A lot of people have been saying Somerset are favourites for this game, but the way the lads have played so far this year we can beat anyone."

Oliver Newby celebrates with his team-mates after taking the wicket of Nick Compton, the grandson of England Test legend Denis

> *"A lot of people have been saying Somerset are favourites for this game, but the way the lads have played so far this year we can beat anyone."*
>
> **– Sajid Mahmood**

CLOSE OF PLAY DAY ONE:
Somerset, having won the toss and elected to bat,
268 (NRD Compton 61, JC Hildreth 55, C Kieswetter 53)
led Lancashire 70-0 (SC Moore 52no) by 198 runs

DAY TWO

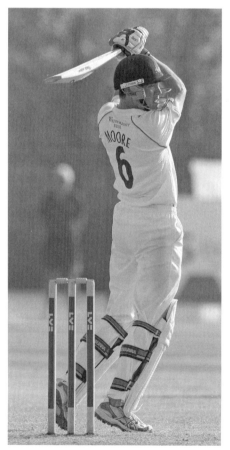

LANCASHIRE were in danger of being undone by one of their own on day two as Somerset's Steve Kirby caused a clatter of wickets in the morning session. But the seamer, who learnt his game at Central Lancashire League side Heywood, was helpless after lunch as the Red Rose took control of the match in impressive style.

Tom Smith led the way with 89, but there were also half-centuries for Stephen Moore and Gareth Cross as Lancashire claimed a 93-run lead at the end of day two. Having resumed on 70-0, they added 23 more before they lost their first wicket as Paul Horton edged Charl Willoughby to Marcus Trescothick at first slip in the 13th over of the day for 23.

Then Kirby ripped through the middle order with a spell of three wickets in just 10 balls. Moore was his first victim, caught at point by Suppiah for what was an impressive 73. And Karl Brown followed in Kirby's next over, again caught at point but this time it was Nick Compton who took a good low catch. Just

Stephen Moore began the second day undefeated on 52

— 22 —

four deliveries later Kirby struck again. This time it was Steven Croft who was caught out by the Somerset bowler's swing as, trying to drive, he edged the ball to wicketkeeper Craig Kieswetter for four.

It meant Lancashire had gone from 119-1 to 124-4, with Kirby having figures of 3-19 in his six overs before lunch. And he wasn't finished there as he struck again just after the interval when Mark Chilton, who had been trying to hold the innings together as wickets tumbled around him, was caught out by a bit of extra bounce and edged one to Trescothick at slip for 30.

It left Lancashire in a spot of bother on 169-5, but Tom Smith, Gareth Cross and Farveez Maharoof saved the day and turned the game on its head. Having opened the batting in the Championship the previous season, the fact Smith came in at six showed how deep the Red Rose line-up was. In one-day cricket, the strapping all-rounder can be as destructive as they come, but in the Championship he knows when to leave the ball, can build an innings well and is ideal to have coming in to see off the second new ball.

In Cross he had the ideal partner with the wicketkeeper always looking to go on the attack and put the fielding side under pressure. He was given a life while on 13 as Trescothick – usually the safest pair of hands in county cricket – dropped him off an Ajantha Mendis delivery. And Cross made the former England opener pay as he and Smith put on a crucial 113-run partnership. It was eventually broken by Kirby, who else, as Cross – who had reached his half-century off the previous ball – edged him to Trescothick at slip and this time he made no mistake.

Maharoof continued where Cross left off, although he gave Smith a bit of a shock as he strolled to the crease. When the pair met in the middle for a chat, instead of asking what the ball was doing, he simply said: 'I'm going to smoke Mendis!' And he certainly lived up to his claim, as his Sri Lanka team-mate – and good friend – went for 0-102 from his 23 overs!

> *"I'm going to smoke Mendis!"*
>
> – **Farveez Maharoof**

Maharoof and Smith shared a 64-run stand for the seventh wicket before Trescothick claimed his fourth victim of the innings after Smith edged Suppiah to slip while on 89 to bring to a close his impressive four-hour innings. Maharoof, however, was still there at the end of the day, just one run short of his half-century as Lancashire finished on 361-7, and in control.

Smith said: "The middle order we have now is second to none. We have Maharoof coming in at eight and he doesn't look like a lower-order batsman. Over the years we have got a bit of stick for not getting over 400 too many times. So to do it last week and now get another good score this week, the lads are flying high.

"Somerset bowled really well in the first session and didn't really give us anything to hit so we had to grind out the runs, we had to graft. Kirby bowled full and gave it a chance to swing and got his rewards. You are always in a battle against him, he is always at you. But we worked hard and in the end it is a great day for the team.

"I was disappointed not to get a hundred. But I have been in good nick all winter and it is good to bring it into the summer."

CLOSE OF PLAY DAY TWO:
Somerset 268 (NRD Compton 61, JC Hildreth 55, C Kieswetter 53) trailed Lancashire 361-7 (TC Smith, 89, SC Moore 73, GD Cross 50, MF Maharoof 49no) by 94 runs

DAY THREE

LANCASHIRE showed their title credentials by blowing Somerset away on day three. The manner of the victory was so impressive that – although many fans were still doubting the team's chances of ending the 77-year wait for an outright Championship – it left stand-in skipper Mark Chilton in no doubt that this could be the year of the Red Rose, because Lancashire didn't just beat Somerset – who remember were tipped to win the title themselves – they destroyed them as they secured victory by an innings and 20 runs.

New overseas signing Farveez Maharoof stamped his mark on the day by becoming only the sixth Lancashire player to score a century on his first-class debut as the Red Rose made 451 in their first innings, a lead of 183. He then added two Somerset wickets as the visitors' star-studded batting line-up were rolled over for 163.

Having resumed unbeaten on 49, the Sri Lankan reached his half-century in just 72 balls in the second over of the day with a cover drive. He and Sajid Mahmood took the Red Rose to 393 when Craig Kieswetter pulled off a stunning diving catch behind the stumps to bring an end to Mahmood's innings and hand Steve Kirby his sixth wicket of the innings.

The wicket seemed to spur Maharoof on as he hit Ajantha Mendis for a six and then, two overs later, three boundaries. He completed an impressive 131-ball century in the 21st over of the day with another boundary, making it a debut to remember for the new boy.

Lancashire's innings came to a sudden end when first Oliver Newby was caught by Marcus Trescothick – claiming his fifth catch of the innings – at slip off Charl Willoughby for 14. Maharoof went in the following over as he was trapped lbw on 102 while trying to sweep Arul Suppiah, leaving Lancashire all out for 451. However, he wasn't finished there

After Somerset had reached 20-0 at lunch, the Sri Lankan was handed the ball by skipper Chilton and he duly delivered. In his first over, he lured Suppiah into a rash shot and the opener edged the ball to wicketkeeper Gareth Cross. And two overs later Maharoof worked his magic again as this time Nick Compton clipped the ball to Paul Horton at slip for 10 and the floodgates opened.

Mahmood claimed the key wicket of Trescothick in the next over as Stephen Moore pulled off a good catch at cover. Then the visitors were left in real trouble on 53-4 when James Hildreth was turned back by Kieswetter while trying to complete an all-run four and was left floundering by a precise throw from Steven Croft.

Tom Smith then struck in his first over as Jos Buttler edged a swinging delivery to Cross for 10, and when he trapped Peter Trego in his fourth over lbw, Somerset were 81-6 having lost six wickets for 22 runs after lunch.

A stubborn 57-run partnership from Kieswetter and Gemaal Hussain slowed down Lancashire's victory charge, but in the end, the Red Rose were not to be denied. Newby broke the stand with the first ball after tea as Kieswetter, on 38, lofted the ball straight to Mahmood at mid-off. Hussain followed nine overs later as he was caught by Paul Horton at slip off Gary Keedy for a gusty 42 off 80 balls. Lancashire wrapped up the points in the 54th over as first Steve Kirby was run out for 14 after a great throw from Smith, and then Mendis completed a miserable match by being stumped after being deceived by Keedy.

The 22-point haul left the Red Rose proudly sitting top of Division One of the LV= County Championship, while the performance let the rest of the country know that Lancashire genuinely were title contenders.

Chilton said: "It's a very difficult Championship to win, there are a lot of very good teams, but if we produce what we have been doing so far for the rest of the season we are going to be a very tough side to beat.

"It was a fantastic performance. The whole attitude was first class against a very good team and everybody should be very proud of that performance."

A happy Lancashire team celebrate their second victory in a row

Maharoof said: "There is just one word to describe that – fantastic. I have four first-class centuries but this is the best for me because of the tough conditions, it was against a good side and against my good friend – it doesn't get any better. I got on with the boys from the first day. I feel like I am a local boy now."

> *"There is no doubt we can win the title. We thought that before we started the season, and after putting performances like this together we know the cricket we are capable of playing."*
>
> – Mark Chilton

CLOSE OF PLAY DAY THREE:
Somerset 268 (NRD Compton 61, JC Hildreth 55, C Kieswetter 53) and 163 lost to Lancashire 451 (MF Maharoof 102, TC Smith 89, SC Moore 73, GD Cross 50; SP Kirby 6-115) by an innings and 20 runs

Lancashire 22pts (Batting 3, Bowling 3)
Somerset 2pts (Batting 2, Bowling 2)

LV= County Championship table April 23

	P	W	L	D	BaP	BoP	Pts
Lancashire	2	2	0	0	6	6	44
Warwickshire	2	2	0	0	6	6	44
Nottinghamshire	2	2	0	0	3	6	41
Durham	3	1	1	1	10	9	38
Yorkshire	3	1	2	0	6	9	31
Sussex	2	1	1	0	1	4	21
Hampshire	2	0	1	1	3	6	12
Worcestershire	2	0	2	0	6	5	11
Somerset	2	0	2	0	3	4	7

SCORECARD

Somerset first innings		Runs	Balls	Mins	4s	6s
*ME Trescothick	c Cross b Mahmood	4	2	2	1	-
AV Suppiah	c Cross b Mahmood	14	27	38	1	-
NRD Compton	c Croft b Newby	61	124	180	9	-
JC Hildreth	st Cross b Keedy	55	69	82	7	-
+C Kieswetter	st Cross b Keedy	53	101	144	6	-
JC Buttler	c Cross b Smith	8	16	21	2	-
PD Trego	c Brown b Smith	15	17	19	3	-
GM Hussain	c Cross b Keedy	3	30	31	-	-
SP Kirby	not out	6	35	45	1	-
BAW Mendis	b Mahmood	18	19	21	3	-
CM Willoughby	c Maharoof b Newby	0	12	15	-	-
Extras	(3 lb, 26 nb, 2 w)	31				
Total	(all out, 73.1 overs)	268				

Fall of wickets:
1-4 (Trescothick, 0.2 ov), 2-28 (Suppiah, 8.2ov), 3-129 (Hildreth, 29.4 ov), 4-168 (Compton, 43.3 ov), 5-190 (Buttler, 48.2 ov), 6-214 (Trego, 52.4 ov), 7-235 (Hussain, 61.2 ov), 8-240 (Kieswetter, 63.2 ov), 9-263 (Mendis, 68.5 ov), 10-268 (Willoughby, 73.1 ov)

Lancashire bowling	Overs	Mdns	Runs	Wkts	Wides	No-Balls
Mahmood	22	4	72	3	-	3
Newby	13.1	2	80	2	2	3
Smith	15	2	47	2	-	3
Keedy	12	3	26	3	-	-
Maharoof	11	4	40	0	-	4

Somerset second innings		Runs	Balls	Mins	4s	6s
*ME Trescothick	c Moore b Mahmood	21	33	52	4	-
AV Suppiah	c Cross b Maharoof	7	27	31	1	-
NRD Compton	c Horton b Maharoof	10	20	16	1	-
JC Hildreth	run out	6	14	18	-	-
+C Kieswetter	c Mahmood b Newby	38	67	96	4	-
JC Buttler	c Cross b Smith	10	17	19	2	-
PD Trego	lbw b Smith	2	14	16	-	-
GM Hussain	c Horton b Keedy	42	80	75	7	-
SP Kirby	run out	14	43	50	2	-
BAW Mendis	st Cross b Keedy	2	8	18	-	-
CM Willoughby	not out	0	1	1	-	-
Extras	(1 b, 4 lb, 6 nb)	11				
Total	(all out, 53.3 overs)	163				

Fall of wickets:
1-30 (Suppiah, 8 ov), 2-42 (Compton, 12 ov), 3-46 (Trescothick, 12.5 ov), 4-53 (Hildreth, 15.5 ov), 5-71 (Buttler, 20.4 ov), 6-81 (Trego, 26.1 ov), 7-138 (Kieswetter, 40.1 ov), 8-154 (Hussain, 49.3 ov), 9-162 (Kirby, 53.1 ov), 10-163 (Mendis, 53.3 ov)

Lancashire bowling	Overs	Mdns	Runs	Wkts	Wides	No-Balls
Mahmood	9	1	22	1	-	1
Newby	11.5	3	39	1	-	1
Keedy	17.3	5	47	2	-	-
Maharoof	7	0	25	2	-	1
Smith	8.1	2	25	2	-	-

Umpires: NGC Cowley & JH Evans Scorers: DM White & GA Stickley

Lancashire first innings		Runs	Balls	Mins	4s	6s
PJ Horton	c Trescothick b Willoughby	23	108	129	2	-
SC Moore	c Suppiah b Kirby	73	116	172	11	-
KR Brown	c Compton b Kirby	16	41	50	3	-
*MJ Chilton	c Trescothick b Kirby	30	51	77	5	-
SJ Croft	c Kieswetter b Kirby	4	3	2	1	-
TC Smith	c Trescothick b Suppiah	89	205	254	13	-
+GD Cross	c Trescothick b Kirby	50	95	121	6	-
MF Maharoof	lbw b Suppiah	102	134	168	13	1
SI Mahmood	c Kieswetter b Kirby	20	46	56	2	-
OJ Newby	c Trescothick b Willoughby	14	27	40	2	-
G Keedy	not out	0	2	2	-	-
Extras	(3 b, 6 lb, 10 nb, 11 w)	30				
Total	(all out, 137.1 overs)	451				

Fall of wickets:
1-93 (Horton, 32.3 ov), 2-119 (Moore, 42.3 ov), 3-120 (Brown, 44.3 ov), 4-124 (Croft, 45 ov), 5-169 (Chilton, 62.1 ov), 6-282 (Cross, 94.2 ov), 7-346 (Smith, 111.3 ov), 8-393 (Mahmood, 126.2 ov), 9-451 (Newby, 136.4 ov), 10-451 (Maharoof, 137.1 ov)

Somerset bowling	Overs	Mdns	Runs	Wkts	Wides	No-Balls
Willoughby	32	9	90	2	1	-
Kirby	30	7	115	6	2	-
Hussain	30	6	82	0	-	1
Mendis	23	2	102	0	-	4
Trego	13	5	33	0	-	-
Suppiah	9.1	2	20	2	2	-

Tom Smith got his season off to a fine start with 89 in the win over Somerset

Farveez Maharoof

WHEN he signed for Lancashire just before the start of the 2011 season, most Red Rose fans would have been excused for not knowing too much about Farveez Maharoof. By the end of the campaign, all that had changed.

When the Sri Lankan held aloft the LV= County Championship trophy at Taunton on the final day of the season, the travelling faithful from Old Trafford broke out into a joyous chant of "The Roof, The Roof, The Roof is on fire"! It showed the affection the fans had for the man, even though he only played five Championship matches.

The tall all-rounder became an instant cult hero after a stunning debut which saw him score a century against Somerset coming in at number eight. He then cemented his name in Red Rose folklore by hitting an unbeaten 31 – and the winning runs – as Lancashire beat Yorkshire at Aigburth in the final over of what was one of the most dramatic moments of the Championship campaign. From then on, he stopped being Farveez and simply became known as The Roof!

Coming from Colombo, and as a player who has starred in 22 Tests and 95 one-day internationals as well as having graced the Indian Premier League with Delhi Daredevils, you would forgive him, having been at the club for only a matter of weeks, if he didn't fully understand the importance of Lancashire beating Yorkshire – but there was no danger of that.

"Beating Yorkshire was a fantastic moment in my career. To score the winning runs in that manner was amazing," said the 27-year-old all-rounder. "And to score a century on my debut was a dream. It's meant a lot to me to be a part of such a big club. To be a part of history, winning the title after 77 years, makes me so proud of myself and the rest of the lads."

Maharoof arrived at Lancashire on what cricket director Mike Watkinson called 'extremely modest terms'. The player himself admitted his main aim was to catch the eye of the Test selectors with Sri Lanka touring England. He did just that with his early-season performances as he was called up to play in the first and second Tests against England at Cardiff and Lord's.

When he was then summoned back to Sri Lanka to play in a domestic Twenty20 competition, it would have been easy for him to have stayed there rather than come back to Lancashire for the final part of the season having completed his initial mission to return to the Test side. But Maharoof had unfinished business. He had become a member of the team and was desperate to return and help Lancashire win the title having been inspired by the skipper.

"Glen Chapple is such a tremendous asset to the team," said Maharoof. "He's a genuine leader from the front. The way he bowled with such a bad injury in the final game of the season speaks volumes about him.

"The impact he's had for Lancashire is absolutely amazing. He's right up there among the best I've played with. I can definitely say he's a Lancashire legend and deserved to win the title."

Although he was left out of the last three Championship matches, he never once thought about going home early and fulfilled his 12th man duties at Taunton, happy just to be playing his part in helping the club to glory. It meant as much to him as to any of the other players whose association with Lancashire goes back years.

"My main priority in coming here was to put in performances that would give me a chance to get back in the national team, which I achieved," said Maharoof. "In a way, it actually broke my rhythm with Lancashire. Coming back here was not that easy, but it was all worth it. To win the Championship for our supporters can't get any better for me.

"The players are professional, and if you have that support from everyone at the club it is easy to perform. For a foreign player it is all about feeling homely and after my first game with Lancashire I felt at home.

"I will take so many good memories back with me. I am a very happy man and a complete man going back to Colombo. I'm very happy to be part of this club forever. Hopefully, I'll be able to come back."

CHAMPAGNE MOMENT: *"It's difficult for me to choose between two, so I have to have them both. Scoring a century on my debut against Somerset was just a dream, and hitting the winning runs against Yorkshire was really special."*

Match 3

Sussex v Lancashire

(The County Ground, Hove) April 26–29

DAY ONE

LANCASHIRE'S first Championship away game was always destined to be a right royal occasion, whatever the result. As the majority of the country focused their gaze on Wills and Kate, Lancashire supporters were quite happy to focus on Chappie and Chilly as they set about winning a third match on the spin.

Chappie, or Glen Chapple to be more precise, won the toss and gave his batsmen first use of a good pitch against a short boundary and a bowling attack who they had flogged for 450-plus at Liverpool just two weeks earlier. The likes of Paul Horton, Stephen Moore, who played four second-team matches for the Hove side – in 2001 – and Karl Brown didn't let him down with a commanding display in the face of some tight spin bowling from Monty Panesar.

Lancashire had Chapple back after he had missed the recent win over Somerset due to a calf strain, but were unable to call upon the services of hamstring injury victim Tom Smith. He was replaced by all-rounder Luke Procter, who would have a major influence on proceedings in his first four-day outing of the campaign.

Brown, who scored 114 in the opening-week mauling of Sussex, was the stand-out performer of the day with a superb 88 off 161 balls, including eleven fours. Murray Goodwin and his troops must have been sick of the sight of the right-hander.

Horton, the aggressor, and Moore laid the platform with an entertaining opening stand of 129 inside 37 overs, batting through until the early stages of the afternoon to take the sting out of what proved to be a lacklustre home attack until late in the day. Their stand was quite incredibly Lancashire's highest first-wicket partnership since September 2008 when Horton and Mark Chilton shared 151 in the second innings of that season's final match against Somerset at Taunton. Despite flashing and edging the odd one through or over the slips off Naved Arif and Panesar, Horton and Moore were largely in control.

Rana Naved-ul-Hasan, Amjad Khan, Arif and England one-day international Luke Wright all struggled to start with, although the former two improved and Wright got the breakthrough when he trapped Moore lbw for 49. Horton followed soon after for a 146-ball 78 – his first score above 50 of the four-day season – when he tried pull a delivery from Rana and could only top-edge it to Ed Joyce running around from slip, leaving the score at 156-2 in the 45th over.

That brought Brown and Chilton together as they really increased the Red Rose stranglehold on the contest, backing up the 180 they added for the same wicket in the first innings of the reverse fixture. They shared a more than useful 82 inside 23 overs here for the third wicket during the rest of the afternoon session, but Chilton (32) was run out by Goodwin's direct hit from mid-wicket shortly after tea following some communication issues between the pair.

The completion of Brown's half-century was sandwiched in between the departures of Chilton and Steven Croft, the latter being caught at backward short-leg by Ben Brown off Panesar, leaving the score at 266-4 in the 77th. The fact that Panesar only picked up one wicket during the first day was somewhat of a travesty, especially as the enigmatic Rana, who did improve to be fair to him, finished the day with three to his name. Sussex gifted Lancashire 42 runs in the form of 21 no-balls, including three in succession from Rana. Brown and Procter added 55 for the fifth wicket, but they had to dig in because the hosts piled the pressure on as the day drew to a close. Unfortunately for Lancashire, however, they couldn't weather the storm.

> *"There was never a question mark amongst ourselves. We always had the confidence that we were going to do well. It was just a matter of proving it. Now that we have done, everyone's even more confident than we were at the start."*
>
> **– Karl Brown**

Rana had Brown superbly caught low down at slip by Joyce before night-watchman Gary Keedy was caught behind by Andrew Hodd three balls later to dampen the visitors' spirits over dinner. Procter finished unbeaten on 26 with Gareth Cross yet to get off the mark as Lancashire had the better of the day as the wedd..sorry, a third win drew closer.

Brown said: "I felt that the ball I got out to I could have cut for four. I certainly didn't play it as well as I could have, but they bowled well for the last 15 overs, and credit to them because we couldn't get away.

"I think we're in a very good position. At the start of the day, we'd have taken 320-6. Obviously it wasn't great losing myself and Keeds late on, but we're still in a great position to go on and get 400.

"There was never a question mark amongst ourselves (about our ability at the start of the season). We always had the confidence that we were going to do well. It was just a matter of proving it. Now that we have done, everyone's even more confident than we were at the start."

CLOSE OF PLAY DAY ONE:
Lancashire, having won the toss and elected to bat,
322-6 (KR Brown 88, PJ Horton 78)

**Paul Horton set the tone on the opening day at Hove with a polished 78
as Lancashire rattled up their highest total of the season**

DAY TWO

TALK about a right royal occasion, this was a right royal batting performance from
Lancashire, who asserted their authority on the south coast by topping 450 for the third
match in a row. Gary Keedy then ended the day with two wickets as Murray Goodwin's
side were firmly put on the rack with four wickets down and their first innings score not
yet beyond 100.

While it was clear that Keedy's role in the contest during the next two days would be key, probably even pivotal, Gareth Cross and Luke Procter deserve plenty of praise as they posted career-best scores. Cross came into the season with a number of question marks hanging over him after Luke Sutton's return to Derbyshire during the winter.

Here was a lad who had impressed on his Championship debut in 2005 when Warren Hegg broke a finger to prematurely end his career, but that was the first of only 11 Championship appearances until the start of 2011. Mike Watkinson, who was cricket manager at the time, signed the experienced Sutton from Derbyshire, ahead of the 2006 season, deciding that it would be better for Cross to continue his development in the second team.

Cross has been the club's regular wicketkeeper in 20-over cricket ever since 2006, but first-team opportunities against the red ball were limited largely to friendly matches against Durham University. He may have impressed in 2006 when Sutton broke a finger, even taking Mushtaq Ahmed to the cleaners at Hove, ironically, but there was no hesitation in sending Cross back to the seconds when the more experienced man was fit. So long had Cross to wait, there were suggestions he would have to move to a new county to further his career, but he was happy to bide his time – and thank goodness he did on the evidence of this performance.

A second innings century against Hampshire at the Rose Bowl in 2010 gave an indication that he could fill the wicketkeeper-batsman's role on a long-term basis (it probably gave Sutton a nudge too). Here at Hove, Cross walloped 13 fours and five sixes as he shared a seventh-wicket stand of 129 in 35 overs with Procter, who launched his own fearsome attack on England's number two spinner Monty Panesar. The left-hander peppered the seating of the main pavilion at mid-wicket when Panesar bowled from the Sea End to post a 170-ball 89. Panesar, however, recovered well to return impressive figures of 2-133 from 50 overs, including the wicket of Procter, who said "it was massive for me to perform against a bowler of that quality" when questioned at the end of the day.

Cross also cracked Panesar straight, part-time spinner Luke Wells over wide long-on, and Naved Arif over long-on. While Paul Horton, Karl Brown and Procter had all fallen short of three figures, Cross highlighted his side's dominance by bringing up his second career ton off 176 balls. He went on to post 125 off 195 before becoming the ninth wicket to fall when he holed out to Amjad Khan at long-on off the bowling of Arif.

He had shared 86 for the eighth wicket with Farveez Maharoof, who had been the victim of a fine tumbling catch at deep backward square-leg by Wells off the bowling of Arif. Glen Chapple then clobbered five fours and two sixes in his breezy 35 not out, but saw Sajid Mahmood bowled by Arif to end the innings, which was Lancashire's 16th joint highest total in first-class cricket and their best since 2005.

Sussex openers Ed Joyce and Chris Nash then put on 46 for the first wicket, but Maharoof sparked a mini-collapse when he bowled Nash in the 16th over. Keedy then turned one sharply in the next to bowl Joyce, playing no shot, to give the Red Rose county their second wicket in the space of five balls. Then he picked up their third when Wells, also playing no shot, was lbw to leave the score at 81-3 in the 27th. Chapple finished off his side's day in style by trapping Ben Brown lbw with only nine more runs added to the total.

> *"It was an all-round performance. To get as many runs as we did, then get them four down, was a great effort. But Sussex are still quite a good batting team, so we'll have to grind them down."*
>
> **– Gareth Cross**

Cross said: "It was an all-round performance. To get as many runs as we did, then get them four down, was a great effort. But Sussex are still quite a good batting team, so we'll have to grind them down.

"It was good to get some runs. I've got a couple of fifties in the first two games, and been a bit disappointed not to get a hundred. I would settle for 50 runs a game, but to get a hundred was good for me.

"Keeds is bowling really well, and the seamers too. Saj was quite unlucky not to get a couple of wickets, while Chappie is always going to be dangerous.

"To the seamers, the wicket's still fairly flat. Unless you get a jaffer against them, you shouldn't really get out. It's just hard work for the seamers. But they've accepted their job is not to go for any runs and create pressure for Keeds at the other end."

CLOSE OF PLAY DAY TWO:
Lancashire 590 (GD Cross 125, LA Procter 89, KR Brown 88, PJ Horton 78) led Sussex 97-4 by 397 runs

DAY THREE

GARY Keedy, like Glen Chapple, is the cricketing equivalent of royalty when it comes to Lancashire fans. There can't be two players in the land, maybe even the world, who have deserved more to play for their country without ever really getting a look-in. Keedy played for the England Lions in a hastily arranged two-day match against Australia in 2009, while Chapple has a solitary one-day international cap under his belt. However, this day belonged to Keedy and his side were still in the hunt for victory at the end of it even though Sussex's batsmen fought back well.

The experienced Yorkshireman, who was poached from his home county during David Lloyd's reign as Lancashire's coach, registered his 600th first-class wicket when he had Luke Wright caught at slip by Paul Horton in the morning session. It was the left-arm spinner's third wicket of the innings following two during the latter stages of day two, and it contributed to the visitors getting a mammoth first innings lead of 300.

Keedy's maiden first-class victim was former Zimbabwe and Cambridge University all-rounder Andy Whittall in 1995 and his 400th victim, the former Kent opening batsman Dave Fulton, was present at Hove on duty for Sky Sports News.

Wright and night-watchman Amjad Khan were the only two wickets to fall in the morning session of a day that was a bit of a slog for Lancashire. Having had things their own way for the whole of the Championship season so far, this could be classed as their toughest two hours yet, but that notion proved just how dominant Chapple and company had been for the first three weeks.

Sussex went into lunch at 208-6, with the prolific Murray Goodwin en route to the 64th hundred of his first-class career. He had shared 81 for the sixth wicket with Wright (33) – playing his first game of the season after recovering from a knee injury suffered whilst on winter England duty – before wicketkeeper Andrew Hodd (28) joined him to help add 90 for the seventh as the Red Rose bowlers were forced to remain patient into the afternoon session. But then Chapple sparked a collapse when he trapped Hodd lbw to leave the score at 271-7 in the 85th.

The last three wickets fell for the addition of only 19 runs in 6.4 overs. Mark Chilton superbly caught Goodwin, forcing off the back foot, at cover in Chapple's next over before Rana Naved-ul-Hasan was trapped lbw by Sajid

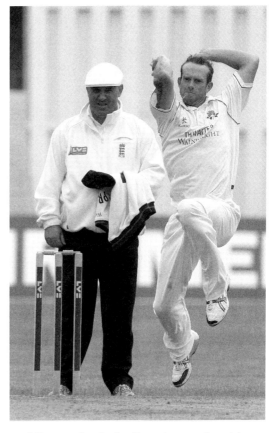

All-rounder Luke Procter made a big impression on his first outing of the season, not only by making a career-best 89, but also with his unique bowling action

Mahmood shortly afterwards. The Sussex innings was wrapped up when Naved Arif was adjudged plumb in front to Keedy at the end of the 91st over, making him the third Sussex batsman to fall not offering a shot. Chapple finished with figures of 4-63 from 24 overs and Keedy 4-101 from 29.

If you thought the day's morning session was tough going for Lancs, that was nothing compared to the evening session, which the hosts bossed from start to finish because Ed Joyce and Chris Nash both scored unbeaten fifties to help their side close on 147-0 after 38 overs of their second innings having been asked to follow-on. The pair, on 63 and 57 not out respectively, made the most of the odd nick and flick here and there to prosper against a bowling attack who were sorely in need of a good night's rest. Lancashire's evening frustrations were summed up when Sajid Mahmood bowled an unintentional beamer at Nash.

Not that you could criticize Chapple for asking the home dressing room to strap the pads on again, mind, because it was exactly the right decision given the amount of

> *"I enjoy the odd milestone, and 600 wickets is a good achievement. Since I broke my collarbone last year I've come out and played with a little bit more self belief. I'm enjoying my cricket more. As long as I'm contributing to the team, and form and fitness serve me well, I'll play as long as I can."*
>
> **– Gary Keedy**

time left in the match. It was just one of those things that can't be avoided when you're trying to bowl a side out twice on a largely flat pitch. Day four was set to be a cracker.

Keedy said: "I think we did a brilliant job to bowl them out for under 300 on that pitch in the first innings. It was a great effort by the lads. Obviously they dug in when they batted again – we always knew that it was going to be difficult – but I still think we're in a great position because they're a long way behind. If we bowl well and get some inroads, we can go from there.

"We've shown in the first innings that when you get one, you can get two pretty quickly. If we can get them six down and try to expose their tail, we're in with a chance. You've just got to hang in there.

"I enjoy the odd milestone, and 600 wickets is a good achievement. Since I broke my collarbone last year I've come out and played with a little bit more self belief. I'm enjoying my cricket more. As long as I'm contributing to the team, and form and fitness serve me well, I'll play as long as I can."

CLOSE OF PLAY DAY THREE:
Lancashire 590 (GD Cross 125, LA Procter 89, KR Brown 88, PJ Horton 78) led Sussex 290 (MW Goodwin 113) and 147-0 (EC Joyce 63no, CD Nash 57no) by 157 runs

DAY FOUR

WE KNEW this was going to be a cracker, but – jeez! – not that they were going to set aside a Bank Holiday for it. Lancashire, hoping to clinch another victory, were unfortunately left disappointed as Sussex, against all the odds, hung on for a draw.

Ed Joyce and Naved Arif, the Pakistani bowler with a Danish passport (sometimes you just couldn't dream these things up), both scored contrasting hundreds to drag their side out of the mire and secure a draw which also prevented Lancashire doing the double. It could have gone down as the earliest double in an English season had it been achieved, such was the quirk of the fixture list that threw these two sides together twice before the end of April.

It just wasn't to be for the Old Trafford side, however, who started the day like a bridegroom late for his wedding. Around about the time when William and Kate were tying the knot, the hosts were crumbling in the face of some excellent bowling from Glen Chapple, who battled through the pain barrier after jarring his knee early in the day.

Starting the day on 147-0, and 153 behind, Sussex lost four wickets for 17 runs inside eight overs, with Chapple striking twice in an over to remove Chris Nash and Luke Wells. Sussex were five down at lunch, with Murray Goodwin stumped by Gareth Cross off Gary Keedy for just eight, Ben Brown run out by Stephen Moore from cover and Luke Wright on his way after Sajid Mahmood spectacularly uprooted his leg-stump. They would have been six down had Paul Horton not unusually erred at first slip with Joyce on 104, though it didn't look like being too costly for the visitors because they kept chipping away.

Andrew Hodd was bowled shortly after lunch as he failed to cut a ball from Keedy that was too close to his body, before Rana Naved-ul-Hasan, who had clonked two sixes over long-on off the same bowler, fell as he tried to repeat the dose, handing the left-armer his third scalp of the innings. At 306-7 in the 85th over, Lancs looked well set for the win with more than a session of play left.

Joyce, who earlier brought up three figures off 176 balls, shared 60 with Arif before he fell to the off-spin of Steven Croft just before tea. Arif then opened his shoulders after the break as he closed in on a maiden career ton. He slog-swept Keedy for consecutive sixes in the midst of a last-wicket stand of 90 with Monty Panesar, who evoked memories of his famous rearguard effort at Cardiff in 2009 when he saved the first Ashes Test for England in partnership with Jimmy Anderson.

The pair took Sussex's lead beyond 150 with 12 overs left in the day, and when the Pakistani reached his ton off 131 balls by sweeping Croft for four, the players shook hands on the draw with the score at 459-9. It was frustrating to watch after tea as Arif swung and Panesar blocked with that trademark big cheesy grin on his face.

Keedy bowled an incredible 42 overs in the day with few breaks, taking 4-200 from 55 overs in all, and he can feel aggrieved that he became the first Lancashire player ever to concede 200 runs in an innings. He had been celebrating a completely different career milestone only 24 hours earlier.

The Red Rose were hamstrung by Sajid Mahmood's forced removal from the attack for bowling a second beamer at Joyce just after lunch, leaving Chapple, Keedy, Farveez Maharoof, Luke Procter and Croft to share the bowling duties. Mahmood also contributed to a Red Rose record total of 104 extras being conceded in a match. Despite the disappointment, this was still a contest which they dominated, taking 10 points.

> *"We knew the pitch was flat, but we gave it everything. The lads were terrific. We fought really hard, and we played superb cricket throughout. The result is disappointing, but we've got 10 points and we have to move on."*
>
> **– Glen Chapple**

Chapple said: "We knew the pitch was flat, but we gave it everything. The lads were terrific. We fought really hard, and we played superb cricket throughout. The result is disappointing, but we've got 10 points and we have to move on.

"To bowl them out for 290 in the first innings was a great effort. But they played well today. Joyce is a class player. They scored two hundreds in the innings, and that's what's ultimately saved them. Saj bowled really well. He just bowled two deliveries that weren't legal. We did miss him in that final session, but we don't blame him."

CLOSE OF PLAY DAY FOUR:
Lancashire 590 (GD Cross 125, LA Procter 89, KR Brown 88, PJ Horton 78) drew with Sussex 290 (MW Goodwin 113) and 459-9dec (EC Joyce 140, N Arif 100no, CD Nash 72)

Sussex 7pts (Batting 2, Bowling 2)
Lancashire 10pts (Batting 4, Bowling 3)

LV= County Championship table April 30

	P	W	L	D	BaP	BoP	Pts
Nottinghamshire	3	3	0	0	7	8	63
Durham	4	2	1	1	15	12	62
Lancashire	**3**	**2**	**0**	**1**	**10**	**9**	**54**
Warwickshire	3	2	1	0	10	8	50
Somerset	3	1	2	0	8	7	31
Yorkshire	3	1	2	0	6	9	31
Sussex	3	1	1	1	3	6	28
Worcestershire	3	0	3	0	9	8	17
Hampshire	3	0	2	1	5	7	15

SCORECARD

Lancashire first innings		Runs	Balls	Mins	4s	6s
PJ Horton	c Joyce b Naved-ul-Hasan	78	146	174	13	-
SC Moore	lbw b Wright	49	109	141	8	-
KR Brown	c Joyce b Naved-ul-Hasan	88	161	214	11	-
MJ Chilton	run out	32	76	82	4	-
SJ Croft	c Brown b Panesar	4	34	31	-	-
LA Procter	c Joyce b Panesar	89	170	204	6	5
G Keedy	c Hodd b Naved-ul-Hasan	0	3	1	-	-
+GD Cross	c Khan b Naved Arif	125	195	240	13	5
MF Maharoof	c Wells b Naved Arif	29	52	89	2	-
*G Chapple	not out	35	24	23	5	2
SI Mahmood	b Naved Arif	4	3	8	1	-
Extras	(4 b, 9 lb, 42 nb, 2 w)	57				
Total	(all out, 158.4 overs)	590				

Fall of wickets:

1-129 (Moore, 36.1 ov), 2-156 (Horton, 44.2 ov), 3-238 (Chilton, 66.3 ov), 4-266 (Croft, 76.4 ov), 5-321 (Brown, 94.2 ov), 6-321 (Keedy, 94.5 ov), 7-450 (Procter, 129.3 ov), 8-536 (Maharoof, 152.5 ov), 9-567 (Cross, 156.2 ov), 10-590 (Mahmood, 158.4 ov)

Sussex bowling	Overs	Mdns	Runs	Wkts	Wides	No-Balls
Naved-ul-Hasan	25	1	95	3	-	9
Khan	30	4	110	0	-	7
Naved Arif	24.4	1	123	3	1	1
Panesar	50	8	133	2	1	2
Wright	14	3	46	1	-	2
Nash	7	0	35	0	-	-
Wells	8	0	35	0	-	-

Glen Chapple's rapid 35 on the second morning helped Lancashire to their impressive total

Sussex first innings		Runs	Balls	Mins	4s	6s
EC Joyce	b Keedy	21	63	70	3	-
CD Nash	b Maharoof	12	38	65	1	-
LWP Wells	lbw b Keedy	19	35	44	3	-
*MW Goodwin	c Chilton b Chapple	113	212	264	11	-
BC Brown	lbw b Chapple	7	16	10	-	-
A Khan	c Horton b Chapple	4	20	17	-	-
LJ Wright	c Horton b Keedy	33	64	88	4	-
+AJ Hodd	lbw b Chapple	28	78	93	2	-
Naved-ul-Hasan	lbw b Mahmood	6	17	23	1	-
Naved Arif	lbw b Keedy	9	15	19	1	-
MS Panesar	not out	0	3	5	-	-
Extras	(1 b, 1 lb, 30 nb, 6 w)	38				
Total	(all out, 91 overs)	290				

Fall of wickets:

1-46 (Nash, 15.5 ov), 2-48 (Joyce, 16.3 ov), 3-81 (Wells, 26.2 ov), 4-90 (Brown, 29.5 ov), 5-100 (Khan, 35.1 ov), 6-181 (Wright, 58.4 ov), 7-271 (Hodd, 84.2 ov), 8-278 (Goodwin, 86.4 ov), 9-288 (Naved-ul-Hasan, 89.3 ov), 10-290 (Naved Arif, 91 ov)

Lancashire bowling	Overs	Mdns	Runs	Wkts	Wides	No-Balls
Chapple	24	3	63	4	2	-
Mahmood	17	3	56	1	-	7
Keedy	29	0	101	4	-	-
Maharoof	15	2	56	1	-	7
Procter	6	1	12	0	-	1

Sussex second innings (following on)		Runs	Balls	Mins	4s	6s
EC Joyce	c Horton b Croft	140	256	386	13	1
CD Nash	b Chapple	72	152	168	12	-
LWP Wells	c Horton b Chapple	0	3	1	-	-
*MW Goodwin	st Cross b Keedy	8	15	15	1	-
BC Brown	run out	0	10	10	-	-
LJ Wright	b Mahmood	7	22	33	-	-
+AJ Hodd	b Keedy	16	52	53	1	-
Naved-ul-Hasan	c Brown b Keedy	32	42	44	2	2
Naved Arif	not out	100	131	128	8	4
A Khan	lbw b Keedy	1	10	6	-	-
MS Panesar	not out	17	66	74	2	-
Extras	(11 b, 15 lb, 34 nb, 1 w, 5 pen)	66				
Total	(9 wkts, dec. 124.2 ovs)	459				

Fall of wickets:

1-169 (Nash, 43.1 ov), 2-169 (Wells, 43.4 ov), 3-184 (Goodwin, 48.1 ov), 4-186 (Brown, 50.2 ov), 5-207 (Wright, 59.4 ov), 6-250 (Hodd, 74.3 ov), 7-306 (Naved-ul-Hasan, 85 ov), 8-366 (Joyce, 98 ov), 9-369 (Khan, 100.3 ov)

Lancashire bowling	Overs	Mdns	Runs	Wkts	Wides	No-Balls
Chapple	24	3	64	2	-	-
Mahmood	14.1	2	64	1	-	6
Keedy	55	7	200	4	-	1
Procter	6	0	18	0	1	2
Maharoof	13.5	2	47	0	-	4
Croft	11.2	3	35	1	-	-

Umpires: MA Gough & SJ O'Shaughnessy Scorers: MJ Charman & DM White

Gareth Cross

WHEN Gareth Cross talks about ornaments, memories of his amusing faux pas during the 2010 Player of the Year dinner at Old Trafford come flooding back. The 27-year-old wicketkeeper had been awarded the Champagne Moment gong for hitting a six off the penultimate ball of a Twenty20 match to beat Warwickshire. Upon receiving the glass trophy, however, Cross dropped it in front of a packed audience in The Point, who looked on aghast as it smashed into smithereens.

It was a good job HRH Prince Philip didn't know that when he met Cross just over 12 months on as part of the county champions' reception in one of the lavish function rooms at Buckingham Palace. He need not have worried, though, because Cross had only been recognised as having the safest pair of hands in county cricket for 2011 just a few weeks earlier by the Professional Cricketers' Association.

Visiting the Palace proved to be a special day for the excellent Bury-born gloveman, who was, quite ironically, greeted by his predecessor Luke Sutton in the first-class carriage of the train on the way back up to Manchester after the Derbyshire captain had been in London himself for the day.

"It was all a bit surreal really," he said. "You're in the Palace, but you don't actually believe it. You're stood there with all the ornaments around that are probably worth millions and not 100 percent sure what to do. It's something that hasn't massively interested me before, but it did when I was there. Everyone was really excited, more so the girls than the lads. When we got there, it was amazing to see the guards and all the things that go on behind the scenes.

"The Duke just said 'well done'. He asked who I was and I said 'the keeper'. That was it. I don't know what I would have said to him had he said a bit more to me, but it was all really good, and it was an experience that you'd love to repeat. It was a day to remember and to push us on to win more."

Cross was exceptional during the summer, although he admitted he would have liked more than the 557 runs he scored from 16 matches. He hardly put a foot wrong behind the stumps, having started the season with a few question marks as to how he would fare during a full season of county cricket after biding his time in the seconds since 2005.

He dispelled those fears quickly with scores of 63, 50, a career-best 125 and 44 in his first four Championship knocks, and finished with an enviable total of 46 catches and 10 stumpings. In fact, he played in every game but one across all three competitions.

"I started off really well, although I'd have liked to have kicked on," continued the former second-team skipper. "I didn't get quite as many runs as I'd have liked. Looking back on it, though, we've won the Championship in my first full season. It's more about the team than me.

"I had four or five years in the seconds when I thought that I should have been playing, and I had a big point to prove when I got my chance. Mooresy put a lot of faith in me to play by not getting a back-up keeper. I needed to play well, and I thought that I did that, especially in the first four or five games."

Cross's 125 – his second Championship ton after the one at Hampshire in 2010 – came against Sussex at Hove in the drawn match.

"It was a really good wicket," he recalled. "Scoring a hundred is something that I aimed to do, and it worked out. I'd got a couple of fifties in the games before and I was desperate to push on."

In terms of runs, Cross had a fixture to forget when Yorkshire visited Liverpool in May. In what has been described by a number of people as one of the most fiery Roses fixtures in recent memory, he got a first ball duck. As he explains, it couldn't have come at a worse time. He added: "It was one of the spiciest games I've played in and I was getting a bit of stick from their batters about that when I was keeping.

"But you have to try and get involved and stick up for a few people. It was a difficult situation to try and keep it in the spirit of the game. We just went hard at them because we wanted the points. They were on the wrong end of the result, which they wouldn't have liked. As far as I was concerned, it was definitely a fair contest."

CHAMPAGNE MOMENT: *"Chasing down the runs against Yorkshire was unbelievable. We had so much momentum, and we went top of the league as well. I can't look beyond that."*

Match 4

Warwickshire v Lancashire

(Edgbaston, Birmingham) May 4–6

DAY ONE

AFTER commanding early-season performances, Lancashire's batsmen were largely the architects of their own downfall after Glen Chapple had won the toss. The visitors should have posted more than 250, even though there were signs that bowlers would enjoy themselves against the backdrop of a new £32m stand being constructed at the Old Pavilion End of the ground.

The pitch was generally sluggish, and a handful of visiting players will have been disappointed at the manner of their dismissals. Karl Brown and Steven Croft, bowled and lbw, offered no shot to Rikki Clarke, Mark Chilton loosely edged Chris Woakes to second slip and Gareth Cross chopped Clarke onto his stumps.

Despite impressive displays with the ball from Clarke and lofty Irishman Boyd Rankin, Lancashire still managed to chisel out something to bowl at thanks to valuable contributions from Stephen Moore, Brown and Cross. Moore's 67, against one of his suitors when he decided to leave Worcestershire in the winter of 2009, was a determined effort. He looked strong square of the wicket, taking advantage of a drop in the slips on 45. It also enhanced an already impressive record in Championship cricket at Edgbaston. It was his sixth score above 50 in 10 innings there, also including two centuries for his former county in 2007 and 2008.

After the early departures of Paul Horton and Brown, Moore shared a calming 63 for the third wicket with Chilton to take the visitors beyond lunch without any further alarms. It was just a shame, therefore, that the latter fell shortly after the break to undo their good work, and he ended up being one of three wickets to fall for 30 runs, including Croft and Moore.

There was still hope for Lancashire because that brought together Luke Procter and Cross, who had shared 129 for the seventh wicket in the first innings of the previous game away at Sussex, scoring 89 and 125 respectively. They added crucial runs yet again – 90 of them to be precise – to clinch a batting bonus point and seemingly tip the balance in their side's favour at 219-5.

An entertaining alliance was brought to an end when Procter prodded outside off-stump at five-wicket star Rankin. It was the first sign of uncertainty from the left-hander, described as the King of Royton by Peter Moores later in the summer. His departure sparked a dramatic collapse as five wickets fell for eight runs in 40 balls. Within that,

Rankin even got Jimmy Anderson, Chapple and Gary Keedy within the space of five balls to prevent the visitors claiming a second batting point, something which had looked certain only half an hour earlier. The only plus regarding the collapse, from Lancashire's point of view, was that it at least gave them 16 overs to bowl before close.

The pitch may not have been at its most lively, but it was definitely showing signs of sideways movement, while there had also been some swing on offer for Rankin, Clarke et al. So, Warwickshire openers Varun Chopra and William Porterfield, Ireland's World Cup captain, would not have relished the prospect of lining up against Chapple and Anderson with the new ball in their hands, even though Chopra had already got two double hundreds to his name during the first month of the season.

> *"They'll be quite happy to go in only one down, but we know that we're in the game. We're very hopeful that we can restrict them to a low score."*
>
> **– Glen Chapple**

Chopra survived to ensure he would return the following morning for take two of the stringent examination, but Porterfield didn't. Anderson rapped him on the pads with one that nipped back, leaving the score at 9-1 in the fifth. You can only imagine Anderson having a wry little chuckle at getting the left-hander, who led the Irish to that remarkable win in Bangalore less than two months earlier.

This was still Warwickshire's day, but only just. Chopra and England's Ian Bell, captaining the hosts due to Jim Troughton's shoulder injury, would certainly have not slept easily overnight.

Chapple said: "We've played on three very good batting tracks so far this season, but this was tricky. Having said that, we would have liked more runs. You can say there were a few loose shots, but the ball's doing a bit. It's a bit two-paced, and there's plenty in it for the seamers if we get it in the right area.

"If we bowl well in the morning, we should get more than the one wicket we got. The wicket's a bit under-prepared. It's quite soft, but very dry. Without the heavy roller, it's not going to flatten out. I would imagine that it's not going to get any better to bat on. They'll be quite happy to go in only one down, but we know that we're in the game. We're very hopeful that we can restrict them to a low score."

CLOSE OF PLAY DAY ONE:
Lancashire, having won the toss and elected to bat, 227 (SC Moore 67; WB Rankin 5-57) led Warwickshire 39-1 by 188 runs

DAY TWO

THIS was the day when Lancashire seized control of the contest as they went in search of their third win from four, and it wasn't just Jimmy Anderson and Glen Chapple who starred with the ball. Yes, they shared five wickets between them as they again bowled expertly with the new ball on a now deteriorating pitch, but it was the attack's third seamer who rammed home the advantage and earned the bulk of the plaudits.

Luke Procter, a fast medium-paced bowler with an eye-catching whippy action that runs in his family, had starred twice already with the bat in his breakthrough summer, including on day one of this clash with an important 46. He further stamped his authority on proceedings with the wickets of Mohammad Yousuf, Rikki Clarke and Chris Woakes. Pakistani Yousuf, a former Lancashire overseas player and a prolific run-scorer at international level, was understandably his prized wicket, even though it came with a hint of fortune as the right-hander dragged a wide ball back onto his stumps as he aimed an expansive drive through the off-side.

Incidentally, Procter, who took advantage of exaggerated uneven bounce, had made his Championship debut on this ground 12 months earlier, but he was substituted out of the game when Anderson returned from England's successful World Twenty20 campaign to get some red-ball practice ahead of the summer Tests.

Mo Yo, as we abbreviated him on Twitter, was the sixth Warwickshire batsman to fall with only 102 on the board, and they lost Woakes before lunch. Jonathan Trott and Ian Bell had been amongst the early departures, Trott caught at second slip by Moore off Chapple and Bell caught behind by Cross off Simon Kerrigan's ever-improving left-arm spin. It was a little over 12 months before when Kerrigan claimed Bell as his maiden first-class wicket in the season opener at Old Trafford when the England man lap-swept him around the corner, only for Mark Chilton to run around from short-leg and take the catch with a superb piece of anticipation.

Wicketkeeper Tim Ambrose and ex-Lancashire youngster Keith Barker, a former striker with Blackburn Rovers and Rochdale, then held Lancashire up for an hour or so after lunch with a plucky partnership of 56 inside 15 overs. Ambrose counter-attacked with effect, while Barker went toe-to-toe in a mid-pitch confrontation with Anderson for one reason or another. Anderson later trapped Ambrose in front for 43 before bowling Boyd Rankin, while Kerrigan had Barker caught at deep cover by a tumbling Chapple to complete the innings as Warwickshire were all out for 172. Procter finished with 3-33 from nine overs.

> *"Being that third seamer really helped Luke. In the last game, he was the fourth seamer trying to hold up an end. But, with the ball doing a bit here, it gave him a bit more responsibility."*
>
> **– Jimmy Anderson**

Lancashire started their second innings in the latter half of the afternoon session with a commanding 55-run lead, but not a game-clinching one just yet. There was still more than enough in this pitch to suggest Bell and his boys could turn the tables. That feeling was enhanced within 11 overs because Woakes, Clarke and Barker had all struck to get rid of Paul Horton, Karl Brown and Stephen Moore with only 27 runs added. The latter two were rapped on the pads, while Horton flicked down the leg-side to Ambrose behind the stumps.

That brought Chilton and Steven Croft together as they looked to repair the damage, which they did with a stand of 61, but they had more than their share of luck as Trott spilled two straightforward chances at first slip off Rankin. Chilton was reprieved on 18 and Croft on 31, while the latter had already been dropped by Rankin at mid-on off the bowling of Woakes on 10. But you could argue that they

Steven Croft finished the second day unbeaten on 53

earned the luck with a passage of brave batting, taking the odd blow on the body to ensure Lancashire's good work during the first day and a half wasn't squandered.

Chilton may have fallen before close when he was trapped lbw by Woakes, leaving the score at 88-4, but Croft, having reached his half-century in the last over of the day, remained unbeaten on 53.

Anderson said: "I thought we did well and scrapped hard. There's a bit in the wicket, but they've got some quality players in their line-up. Chilly and Crofty put on a good partnership, and we're pleased to have a few wickets left in the tent.

"It's not as if it's an impossible wicket. With the new ball, there's a bit (of lateral movement). It looked like it swung a bit for Woakes, Clarke and Barker when they bowled. They're going to come hard at us in the morning with their main bowlers. If we can get through that period, hopefully we can push on towards a lead of 300.

"Being that third seamer really helped Luke. In the last game, he was the fourth seamer trying to hold up an end. But, with the ball doing a bit here, it gave him a bit more responsibility."

CLOSE OF PLAY DAY TWO:
Lancashire 227 (SC Moore 67; WB Rankin 5-57) and 118-4 (SJ Croft 53no) led Warwickshire 172 by 173 runs

DAY THREE

THE decision to play spin twins Gary Keedy and Simon Kerrigan was justified after all as the Red Rose moved top of Division One with a third win from four. 16 wickets fell in all on a day that proved to be a statistician's dream. Fans, members, media and even players, some more than others, all love a good stat, and this day provided more than you could shake a stick at.

It also proved to be a memorable day for Preston-born Kerrigan, who recorded stunning figures of 5-7 in seven overs to bowl his side to a thumping win well before tea. It was all the more remarkable as Kerrigan wouldn't have even played in the game had any of Sajid Mahmood, Farveez Maharoof or Kyle Hogg been fit. The latter rolled his ankle playing football in practice the day before the game.

On his first outing of the season Simon Kerrigan produced the remarkable figures of 5-7 to help Lancashire defeat Warwickshire well before tea. He was to produce an even more devastating spell of bowling later in the season as the Red Rose men honed in on the Championship title

Lancashire resumed with a 173-run lead. Steven Croft continued his determined effort for the first 10 overs of the day with help from Luke Procter, but Croft was the first of five wickets to fall for seven runs in 23 balls as the visitors slipped from a position of strength at 147-4 to one of peril at 154-9, bringing the game back into the balance. In fact, maybe it had even gone a little bit further than that and swung into Warwickshire's favour.

Croft edged Chris Woakes to bucket hands Rikki Clarke (anybody who saw his catch to get rid of Paul Collingwood on the boundary in a televised Twenty20 match later in the summer will vouch for that) before Gareth Cross was trapped lbw for a golden duck by the same bowler. Procter then holed out to Will Porterfield off Boyd Rankin, who also bowled Glen Chapple and trapped Kerrigan lbw.

That brought Keedy, massively under-rated as a batsman, and Jimmy Anderson

> *"Keggsy's a very talented cricketer. There's no reason why he can't play Test cricket. He's a phenomenal talent. He's got the variation, he's a fast learner, and he's proved that he can get good players out regularly. What else do you need? Just an opportunity."*
>
> **– Gary Keedy**

together as Lancashire desperately needed a partnership. They counter-attacked superbly to share 35 for the last wicket, swinging the pendulum back in their side's favour.

With players like Jonathan Trott and Ian Bell in opposition, it was difficult to describe the Red Rose as racing certs for the win, but they were clear favourites on a pitch which had planted seeds of doubt in many a batsman's head throughout the first two and a bit days.

Lancashire were given the chance to have a three-over burst with the new ball before lunch, which proved ideal. Will Porterfield would have been hoping to sit down for his cheese ploughman's (that's just a guess, but it won't have been fish and chips, would it Flat Jack?) with the prospect of an innings to play after lunch. Instead, the Irishman could take his time to eat because he fell to Chapple 12 balls into the innings, caught behind by Cross.

Even though nine wickets still had to fall, you got the feeling that it was game over three balls into the afternoon when Bell fell in a rather extraordinary way to the Lancs skipper. As he was trying to play a regulation flick through the leg-side, he advanced down the track, the ball got big on him, and the shot ended up looking rather ugly as he spooned a catch to Karl Brown at mid-wicket. It left Warwickshire reeling at 14-2.

Then Kerrigan, watched by England team director Andy Flower and Lions coach David Parsons, started his memorable wicket-taking spree. He had Chopra caught behind with only his third ball after striking as early in the first innings too. He then got Mohammad Yousuf stumped to leave the score at 86-4 in the 22nd over.

Keedy then trapped Trott lbw before Kerrigan had Clarke in identical fashion shortly afterwards. Next, Kerrigan had Tim Ambrose caught at first slip by Anderson and Keith Barker caught at short-leg by Croft with successive deliveries in the 28th over, leaving the score at 93-8. Keedy then put the icing on the cake with the scalps of Woakes and Maurice Holmes, both lbw, to ensure the capture of 20 points and finish with super figures of 3-2 from 4.2 overs himself as Warwickshire were bowled out for just 97.

Keedy said: "I've said before that I hadn't seen the 7-22 we got in the Sussex game at Liverpool too often. But to get what we've just got now, I've never seen anything like it. Keggsy's a very talented cricketer. There's no reason why he can't play Test cricket. He's a phenomenal talent. He's got the variation, he's a fast learner, and he's proved that he can get good players out regularly. What else do you need? Just an opportunity."

Kerrigan said: "You have to pinch yourself when you walk back down to fine-leg and look at the scoreboard and see that you've just got somebody like Ian Bell out. I've bowled in little bursts as well as that on wickets not as helpful and not got the results, but I've never bowled as well as that for as consistent a spell."

CLOSE OF PLAY DAY THREE:
Lancashire, 227 (SC Moore 67; WB Rankin 5-57) and 189
(SJ Croft 67) beat Warwickshire 172 and 97 (SC Kerrigan 5-7)
by 147 runs

Warwickshire 3pts (Bowling 3)
Lancashire 20pts (Batting 1, Bowling 3)

LV= County Championship table May 6

	P	W	L	D	BaP	BoP	Pts
Lancashire	**4**	**3**	**0**	**1**	**11**	**12**	**74**
Nottinghamshire	3	3	0	0	7	8	63
Durham	4	2	1	1	15	12	62
Somerset	4	2	2	0	11	10	53
Warwickshire	4	2	2	0	10	11	53
Yorkshire	3	1	2	0	6	9	31
Sussex	3	1	1	1	3	6	28
Worcestershire	4	0	4	0	10	11	21
Hampshire	3	0	2	1	5	7	15

SCORECARD

Lancashire first innings		Runs	Balls	Mins	4s	6s
PJ Horton	c Ambrose b Woakes	7	13	10	1	-
SC Moore	lbw b Rankin	67	138	202	9	-
KR Brown	b Clarke	13	33	39	3	-
MJ Chilton	c Clarke b Woakes	24	66	81	2	-
SJ Croft	lbw b Clarke	0	8	13	-	-
LA Procter	c Clarke b Rankin	46	113	145	7	-
+GD Cross	b Clarke	44	67	96	7	-
*G Chapple	c Ambrose b Rankin	2	15	30	-	-
JM Anderson	c Clarke b Rankin	5	17	20	-	-
SC Kerrigan	not out	1	1	5	-	-
G Keedy	c Ambrose b Rankin	0	2	2	-	-
Extras	(5 b, 3 lb, 10 nb)	18				
Total	(all out, 78 overs)	227				

Fall of wickets:
1-10 (Horton, 2.4 ov), 2-36 (Brown, 12.3 ov), 3-99 (Chilton, 33.3 ov), 4-104 (Croft, 36.3 ov), 5-129 (Moore, 49 ov), 6-219 (Procter, 71.3 ov), 7-219 (Cross, 72.4 ov), 8-226 (Anderson, 77.2 ov), 9-227 (Chapple, 77.4 ov), 10-227 (Keedy, 78 ov)

Warwickshire bowling	Overs	Mdns	Runs	Wkts	Wides	No-Balls
Woakes	14	2	45	2	-	-
Barker	16	5	39	0	-	-
Clarke	21	5	42	3	-	-
Rankin	17	3	57	5	-	5
Trott	5	0	14	0	-	-
Holmes	5	1	22	0	-	-

Lancashire second innings		Runs	Balls	Mins	4s	6s
PJ Horton	c Ambrose b Woakes	3	11	9	-	-
SC Moore	lbw b Barker	12	26	42	1	-
KR Brown	lbw b Clarke	12	22	28	3	-
MJ Chilton	lbw b Woakes	23	66	95	3	-
SJ Croft	c Clarke b Woakes	67	149	176	10	-
LA Procter	c Porterfield b Rankin	18	70	93	2	-
+GD Cross	lbw b Woakes	0	1	1	-	-
*G Chapple	b Rankin	2	7	14	-	-
JM Anderson	not out	18	27	49	2	-
SC Kerrigan	lbw b Rankin	0	6	3	-	-
G Keedy	c Clarke b Holmes	12	31	34	1	-
Extras	(5 b, 7 lb, 10 nb)	22				
Total	(all out, 68.3 overs)	189				

Fall of wickets:
1-4 (Horton, 2.2 ov), 2-27 (Brown, 9.4 ov), 3-27 (Moore, 10.1 ov), 4-88 (Chilton, 34.2 ov), 5-147 (Croft, 56.2 ov), 6-147 (Cross 56.3 ov), 7-149 (Procter, 57.2 ov), 8-152 (Chapple, 59.1 ov), 9-154 (Kerrigan, 60 ov), 10-189 (Keedy, 68.3 ov)

Warwickshire bowling	Overs	Mdns	Runs	Wkts	Wides	No-Balls
Woakes	23	9	40	4	-	-
Clarke	13	1	47	1	-	-
Barker	9	3	18	1	-	-
Rankin	19	3	58	3	-	5
Holmes	3.3	0	10	1	-	-
Trott	1	0	4	0	-	-

Warwickshire first innings		Runs	Balls	Mins	4s	6s
V Chopra	lbw b Chapple	21	55	68	1	-
WTS Porterfield	lbw b Anderson	2	15	16	-	-
*IR Bell	c Cross b Kerrigan	33	89	127	3	-
IJL Trott	c Moore b Chapple	9	23	34	-	-
Mohammad Yousuf	b Procter	26	47	71	3	-
R Clarke	c Moore b Procter	0	8	12	-	-
+TR Ambrose	lbw b Anderson	43	79	78	7	-
CR Woakes	c Cross b Procter	4	6	7	1	-
KHD Barker	c Chapple b Kerrigan	25	52	74	3	-
WB Rankin	b Anderson	0	4	9	-	-
MG Holmes	not out	1	2	10	-	-
Extras	(1 b, 6 lb, 1 w)	8				
Total	(all out, 63.2 overs)	172				

Fall of wickets:
1-9 (Porterfield, 4.4 ov), 2-43 (Chopra, 17.1 ov), 3-57 (Trott, 25.1 ov), 4-76 (Bell, 35.3 ov), 5-83 (Clarke, 38.1 ov), 6-102 (Mohammad Yousuf, 42.4 ov), 7-106 (Woakes, 44.4 ov), 8-162 (Ambrose, 58.5 ov), 9-168 (Rankin, 61 ov), 10-172 (Barker, 63.2 ov)

Lancashire bowling	Overs	Mdns	Runs	Wkts	Wides	No-Balls
Anderson	23	5	57	3	-	-
Chapple	22	7	56	2	-	-
Procter	9	4	33	3	1	-
Kerrigan	9.2	3	19	2	-	-

Warwickshire second innings		Runs	Balls	Mins	4s	6s
V Chopra	c Cross b Kerrigan	29	52	72	6	-
WTS Porterfield	c Cross b Chapple	0	5	7	-	-
*IR Bell	c Brown b Chapple	3	5	5	-	-
IJL Trott	lbw b Keedy	39	54	79	6	-
Mohammad Yousuf	st Cross b Kerrigan	10	15	15	2	-
R Clarke	lbw b Kerrigan	3	15	12	-	-
+TR Ambrose	c Anderson b Kerrigan	0	12	15	-	-
CR Woakes	lbw b Keedy	1	9	12	-	-
KHD Barker	c Croft b Kerrigan	0	1	1	-	-
WB Rankin	not out	2	4	10	-	-
MG Holmes	lbw b Keedy	0	10	6	-	-
Extras	(6 b, 4 lb)	10				
Total	(all out, 30.2 overs)	97				

Fall of wickets:
1-2 (Porterfield, 2 ov), 2-14 (Bell, 3.3 ov), 3-68 (Chopra, 17.3 ov), 4-86 (Mohammad Yousuf, 21.4 ov), 5-88 (Trott, 23 ov), 6-92 (Clarke, 25.1 ov), 7-93 (Ambrose, 27.3 ov), 8-93 (Barker, 27.4 ov), 9-93 (Woakes, 28.2 ov), 10-97 (Holmes, 30.2 ov)

Lancashire bowling	Overs	Mdns	Runs	Wkts	Wides	No-Balls
Anderson	7	1	31	0	-	-
Chapple	8	3	17	2	-	-
Procter	4	0	30	0	-	-
Kerrigan	7	1	7	5	-	-
Keedy	4.2	3	2	3	-	-

Umpires: NJ Llong & RT Robinson   Scorers: DE Wainwright & DM White

James Anderson

WHEN Jimmy Anderson hangs up his bowling boots and looks back at his career, surely nothing will be able to beat 2011. 2010 ended on a personal high note as his wife Daniella gave birth to their second daughter, Ruby, in December, with Anderson flying 10,000 miles to be at the birth having helped England take a 1-0 lead in the Ashes series in Australia. Just days later he was back there playing in the third Test, and by the first week of January he had become part of English cricket history as Andrew Strauss's men won the Ashes Down Under for the first time in 24 years.

Anderson finished the series, which England claimed 3-1, as the leading wicket-taker with 24, dispelling the myth he would struggle in Australian conditions. The exertions of winning that series left him drained, however, and it showed in the World Cup which followed almost immediately. He was left out of the England side for their final two matches as they crashed out to Sri Lanka in the quarter-finals.

A rejuvenated Anderson, however, put it quickly behind him as he played a key role in the 1-0 Test series win over the Sri Lankans at the start of the summer. He then terrorised Sachin Tendulkar and the star-studded Indian batting line-up, claiming 21 wickets as England became the best Test team in the world with a comprehensive 4-0 series win. In doing so, he reached number two in the official ICC Test bowling rankings.

In August he was granted a benefit for 2012 by the club. In between it all, he played a part in Lancashire winning their first outright County Championship in 77 years. Beat that! Choosing the greatest achievement out of what was an amazing eight months for the Burnley Express would be impossible. But for Anderson, collecting a Championship-winners medal from the Duke of Edinburgh at Buckingham Palace with the club he grew up supporting is right up there.

"I've got such strong ties with Lancashire and have an awful lot to thank them for because they have given me a lot of help over the years," said the 29-year-old. "I supported them as a kid and played all of my age-group cricket here. I love playing for the county. Every chance I get to play for them is a real honour. Because of my situation with England, I never know when I am next going to play for Lancashire, so I always give it my all.

"It's hard to describe the feeling having been part of a Championship-winning side but, if I'm honest, I was more happy for everyone else associated with the club, people like Glen Chapple and Peter Moores, who has done a fantastic job since he joined the club three years ago. I'm delighted for the players because I know how much effort they put in."

Anderson only played two Championship matches during the summer, but Lancashire won them both – at home to Yorkshire and against Warwickshire at Edgbaston. He knew then they were capable of winning the title.

"It's always hard to come into the side for just a couple of matches," said Anderson. "I just start to feel a part of the team and then I have to go again. It was difficult to leave the lads after the win over Yorkshire because you could tell something special was happening.

"I think the lads were underestimated by a lot of people at the start of the season, but when you have young players coming through the ranks, they are always keen to show what they can do in the first team, so I wasn't surprised we won the title. I was more surprised by how many people had the side down to be relegated. Nobody in the squad even gave that a second thought.

"To win the title you need a number of players to have good seasons, and we had that. Kyle Hogg claimed 50 wickets for the first time in his career, and you had Paul Horton and Stephen Moore giving the team a solid base at the top of the batting order. Chappie is one of the best bowlers in the country, if not the world. He is so skilful and as a captain he's been fantastic.

"The spirit of the side showed through simply by the number of tight games we won during the season. You look at the two matches I played in, we never gave up and were rewarded for it. It is something Mooresy is big on. He constantly tells us teams don't like playing against sides that scrap right to the end. That's what we did all season. When we needed 121 from 15 overs to beat Yorkshire, nobody in the dressing room thought at any stage that we weren't going to do it."

CHAMPAGNE MOMENT: *"Watching Chappie hobbling around the field at Taunton one minute, and then steaming in with the ball in hand and taking wickets the next! It was amazing stuff from my good mate."*

MATCH 5

Lancashire v Yorkshire

(Aigburth, Liverpool) May 18–21

DAY ONE

**A large and expectant crowd gathered at Aigburth in sunny
weather for the first Roses clash of the season**

THERE weren't many times during 2011 that Jimmy Anderson's bowling was overshadowed – but this was one of them. The seamer spent most of the summer terrorising India's batting line-up and helping England become the best Test team in the world. But on the opening day of the first Roses battle of the season – Anderson's second and last Championship appearance for Lancashire in the campaign – it was Farveez Maharoof and Gary Keedy who stole the limelight.

The Aigburth clash also saw another rarity in 2011 – as Lancashire won the toss for the only time at home all season. It proved to be a crucial one as skipper Glen Chapple invited the visitors to have a bat, and then reaped the rewards as wickets tumbled. In fact, Yorkshire's last five batsmen fell in just nine overs after tea while adding only 12 to the score as the White Rose wilted to 141 all out.

An opening strike-force of Chapple and Anderson would give most county batsmen a few sleepless nights. Chapple, who was born in Yorkshire, showed why in his opening spell as he made an early breakthrough, trapping Adam Lyth lbw in the fourth over. In his

> *"I didn't expect to come on so early, and I certainly didn't expect to bowl 23 overs on the first day."*
>
> **– Gary Keedy**

incredible six-over opening burst, Chapple bowled three maidens and conceded just five runs, while Anderson was just as miserly as his eight overs went for just 15 as Yorkshire struggled for runs.

After such a tight start from the seamers, it came as a surprise – to the bowler himself as well as to the watching crowd – when Chapple turned to spinner Keedy in the 14th over. He maintained the pressure on the visitors with his seven-over spell going for just 10 runs. It was Maharoof, however, who claimed the only other wicket before lunch as he trapped Joe Root lbw as Yorkshire reached the interval on 57-2. The all-rounder was in good form, having played for Sri Lanka in their warm-up match against Middlesex the previous week ahead of the Test series with England.

Joe Sayers and Andrew Gale looked to be building a strong partnership for the visitors, with Sayers bringing up his half-century in 130 balls. Having done all the hard work in getting through the tough opening session, he was undone by a stunning one-handed diving catch from Steven Croft at backward point which changed the course of the game as Anderson picked up his only wicket of the innings.

It was the start of an amazing collapse. Skipper Gale quickly followed, bowled around his legs by a smart delivery from Keedy, who also accounted for Gary Ballance in his next over, caught by Mark Chilton at silly point. It left Yorkshire in real trouble on 106-5 at tea – but worse was to come for the White Rose. Simon Guy was bowled by Maharoof in the 65th over, Adil Rashid was caught and bowled by Keedy in the next and then, when Steve Patterson was trapped lbw by the Sri Lankan, Yorkshire had lost three wickets for just one run.

Maharoof finished with 4-35 as he bowled Moin Ashraf to finish a spell in which he took three wickets for seven runs, and Keedy – playing in his 20th Roses match – ended the innings with 4-44 when Oliver Hannon-Dalby was out lbw for a duck. Having at one stage been 95-2 and with Sayers and Gale looking comfortable, all of a sudden Yorkshire were 141 all out and Lancashire were well and truly on top of their rivals from over the Pennines.

Although Stephen Moore was out lbw for just a single in the fifth over of Lancashire's reply, an unbeaten 39 from Paul Horton saw them reach 56-1 at the end of an extraordinary day.

Keedy said: "I didn't expect to come on so early, and I certainly didn't expect to bowl 23 overs on the first day.

"Playing in a Roses game does feel special. The rivalry had gone slightly a few years ago because of the Kolpak players coming in. Some of the traditions were lost and people representing the two sides weren't fully tuned into what these matches are all about, but now, credit to both clubs, they have brought through a lot of young players. They have their traditions back again."

CLOSE OF PLAY DAY ONE:
Yorkshire, having lost the toss and been invited to bat, 141 (JJ Sayers 53) led Lancashire 56-1 by 85 runs

DAY TWO

FORMER Lancashire skipper Mark Chilton is renowned for building partnerships. He and one-time opening partner Iain Sutcliffe hold the record for the highest first-wicket stand for Lancashire against Yorkshire for their 223 against the old enemy at Old Trafford in 2005. When coach Peter Moores took over at the club, he introduced 'the wall'. Players get their name on 'the wall' every time they make a century partnership – and nobody appears more on the list than Chilton.

So with all that in mind, it was no surprise when Chilly put the White Rose to the sword again on day two as he shared in two crucial partnerships. He and Paul Horton came together with nine overs gone in the day after Karl Brown was out lbw to Steve Patterson for 19 and with Lancashire on 69-2. The stand should have been quickly nipped in the bud when Horton edged Adil Rashid while on 73, but stand-in wicketkeeper Simon Guy – playing his first match for two years having been drafted in at short notice to replace the injured Gerard Brophy – dropped the chance.

It proved expensive as Horton and Chilton guided Lancashire safely past Yorkshire's first innings total of 141. In the end they put on a more than useful 81 for the third wicket before Guy finally got his man when Horton edged Rashid again and this time the wicketkeeper made no mistake.

Starting an unwanted trend for the season, Horton was out in the nineties as he fell just seven short of what would have been his first century for Lancashire in the Championship for 13 months. Chilton, who reached his half-century in 124 balls, hadn't finished as he and Steven Croft took Lancashire into a commanding lead. They reached tea untroubled on 225-3 and the duo built the second substantial stand in the Red Rose innings.

With Lancashire 99 runs ahead, Chilton's knock came to an end as he was caught by Adam Lyth at slip off Moin Ashraf for 77 off 174 balls, ending a 90-run fourth-wicket stand. Although he deserved a century, he had more than done his job in putting Lancashire in a commanding position.

His wicket, however, did start a mini-collapse. Croft followed him back to the pavilion just three overs later as he chopped a Joe Root delivery onto his own stumps for 41. Then Gareth Cross suffered the unenviable stat of being out for successive golden ducks when

Mark Chilton on his way to 77 as Lancashire took command

he was trapped lbw by spinner Root without scoring as the Red Rose slipped from 240-3 to 244-6. Farveez Maharoof and Luke Procter steadied the ship as they put on a 55-run partnership to strengthen Lancashire's stranglehold over their rivals.

The Roof made 34 in just 42 balls before his stumps were sent flying by an angry Ryan Sidebottom, but that just made way for a little piece of Red Rose history. Glen Chapple became just the fifth Lancashire player to take 700 wickets and score 7,000 runs in first-class cricket for the club on his way to making 18 – the others being RG Barlow, Johnny Briggs, Jack Simmons and current cricket director Mike Watkinson. The Lancashire skipper became Sidebottom's second victim when he was lbw to a full toss, but the Red Rose ended a good day on 327-8, a lead of 186.

Horton said: "I am disappointed I didn't get a big score, but in the context of the game it is nice to have a knock like that, and it's not about personal milestones, it's about winning games of cricket for Lancashire. If I get past 60 or so I should be making big hundreds and this is just as much a disappointment as if I get out early doors.

"We're very happy with the way the two days have gone. We'll have to work, Yorkshire are a good side and are not going to roll over, but if at the start someone had offered us going into the third day that we would be almost 200 ahead we would have taken that."

Chilton said: "I'm playing really nicely and I felt in total control out there. I should have gone on to get a hundred because the way I'm batting I should be getting centuries really, but I hope it's a significant contribution to the game."

> *"If I get past 60 or so I should be making big hundreds and this is just as much a disappointment as if I get out early doors."*
>
> **– Paul Horton**

CLOSE OF PLAY DAY TWO:
Yorkshire141 (JJ Sayers 53) trailed Lancashire 327-8 (PJ Horton 93, MJ Chilton 77) by 186 runs

DAY THREE

JUST when things looked rosy for Lancashire as they aimed to wrap up their fourth Championship win of the season, the old enemy returned. Not Yorkshire – but the rain! For years – some would say 77 of them – the weather has been one of the deciding factors in Lancashire's failure to win the County Championship. Time and again, they have been scuppered by downpours at Old Trafford while in the south the sun has been shining on their rivals.

This year, as if fate was smiling on the Red Rose at long last, was different. On more than one occasion during the season, as it rained at Old Trafford and around other areas of the North West, it seemed like Lancashire's home away from home at Aigburth had a micro-climate of its very own as the players took to the field. When the rain did come, it seemed to fall when Lancashire had a week off and their title rivals suffered instead. On this third day, it felt like the old luck had returned as 44 overs were washed out.

Lancashire's first innings was over in a flash as they lost their last two wickets within the opening 10 balls of the day. Luke Procter was out lbw to Steve Patterson for his overnight 23 facing his first delivery of the day. Gary Keedy followed four balls later as he was bowled for a duck by Patterson, who finished with 4-51, leaving Jimmy Anderson unbeaten on five and Lancashire on 329 – a very healthy lead of 188.

Glen Chapple then produced an extraordinary spell with the new ball. After bowling three successive maidens, he then accounted for Yorkshire opener Adam Lyth for the second time in the match, this time with a fine caught and bowled. Chapple then finished his spell with another maiden, leaving him with astonishing figures of 5-5-0-1!

Farveez Maharoof started the day with some doubt over his future availability for Lancashire. Having done well playing for Sri Lanka against Middlesex the previous week, there was talk he might be called up by the national side to play in the Test series against England, which was due to start the following week. There was also a chance he could be selected in the Sri Lanka A side, which was also touring the country in July and August, and if not it looked certain he would have to return home to play in the inaugural Sri Lankan Twenty20 Premier League, which was expected to start on July 19 and run for three weeks. All the uncertainty didn't seem to phase The Roof, as he just got on with the job in hand in his usual laid-back style. Having dismissed Joe Root lbw in the first innings, he repeated the trick in the second as Yorkshire went in at lunch on 48-2.

It was a longer break than expected as the rain came down, and when they did eventually get back on the field with more than a session lost, Yorkshire launched a fightback. It was led by Joe Sayers, who earlier had survived a barrage of short-pitched deliveries, and a few verbals, from Anderson. He brought up his half-century in 141 balls, and Gale saw the visitors safely to the close on 131-2, trailing still by 57 runs. Not even a brave streaker, who jumped over the stumps while wearing a paper bag over his head, failed to disrupt the White Rose fightback.

Gareth Cross said: "It was frustrating that we lost a session to have a go at them. They played well at the end, but hopefully we can knock them over tomorrow.

"We're just hoping to bowl them out and chase whatever we need. We still have quite a decent lead, and they have quite a long tail. The pitch is still flat and hard work for the seamers."

Maharoof said: "I am pushing hard to get back in to the Sri Lanka squad. There is a Sri Lanka A team tour coming up in July and August and the Sri Lanka Premier League as well, so it is up to the selectors where they want me. I am contracted to my country to leave Lancashire whenever they need me.

"I did pretty well last week with the national side, both bowling and scoring runs. I did what I wanted to do and I am pretty happy. Whatever happens, it won't happen overnight."

> *"I am looking forward to playing for Lancashire and helping them to reach the top of their game before I leave."*
>
> **– Farveez Maharoof**

CLOSE OF PLAY DAY THREE:
Yorkshire 141 (JJ Sayers 53) and 131-2 (JJ Sayers 57no) trailed Lancashire 329 (PJ Horton 93, MJ Chilton 77) by 57 runs

DAY FOUR

SOME people say County Championship cricket is boring. Some say there is never any drama, excitement or thrills. Some say Twenty20 cricket is the only way forward and that the four-day game is dying. Those people should have been at Aigburth on May 21, 2011, because the final day of the Roses match had it all. Two bitter rivals, battling it out to the end for the pride of their county. One fighting for survival, the other gunning for glory. Plot twists until the very last moment when a hero emerged to claim the day! It was a script made for Hollywood!

The drama started early as Jimmy Anderson continued his verbal jousting with Joe Sayers, forcing Yorkshire skipper Andrew Gale to complain to the umpires, who had a chat with the England bowler. However, it was victory for Anderson as he claimed the catch at slip off Gary Keedy to end Gale's resistance on 60, and he celebrated with gusto. It brought to an end what had been a frustrating 115-run partnership for Lancashire. The Red Rose also claimed a bit of luck as well just before lunch as Sayers, on 75, swept Keedy, the ball hitting Mark Chilton and looping up for Paul Horton to take the catch at leg slip.

Anderson's verbal jousting with Joe Sayers in his final appearance for the Red Rose in 2011 created an atmosphere which continued into the return fixture

Any chance of a Lancashire victory looked to have gone in the afternoon session as Adil Rashid and Gary Ballance put on 88 for the fifth wicket and put Yorkshire into the lead. Even when the off-spin of Steven Croft broke the partnership, with Rashid stumped by Gareth Cross for 52, the visitors were 278-5 and looking favourites to bat out the day. But Keedy, who started his career at Yorkshire, had another script.

Having had Simon Guy caught by Anderson just before tea, he then produced a stunning spell which saw him take three wickets in seven balls after the interval to leave the White Rose struggling on 301-9. First he produced an absolute beauty, which Ballance, on 57, left and then watched in horror as it clattered his leg-stump. The left-arm spinner then bowled Ryan Sidebottom three balls later and followed that by trapping Moin Ashraf for a duck. Yorkshire had lost five wickets for just 23 runs and Lancashire were on the charge. It also gave Keedy his 31st five-wicket innings haul and seventh 10-wicket match haul as he claimed 6-133.

As in all good movies, the bad guys hadn't finished yet. Oliver Hannon-Dalby and Steve Patterson batted out 14 overs for the final wicket before Croft pulled off a stunning catch at gully off the bowling of Jimmy Anderson to dismiss Patterson, with Yorkshire finishing on 308. That last-wicket partnership, although adding just seven runs, had taken enough time out of the game to leave Lancs with what looked like a tough ask – 121 runs in 15 overs for victory. In a Twenty20 match, that would be a fair chase, but in the Championship – with no fielding restrictions, no limitations on how many overs bowlers could send down or strict rules on wides – it would take some getting.

With the light closing in, and the field spread, Paul Horton and Stephen Moore struggled to find boundaries, and when both openers went to successive Rashid deliveries in the sixth over, Lancs were 39-2 and struggling. 28 off just 19 balls by Croft, which included a six that sailed out of the ground off Rashid, and a crucial 11 from just six deliveries by Cross put Lancashire back in the hunt.

As the temperature plummeted and with the crowd on the edge of their seats, the game swung away from the Red Rose again as Cross went in the eighth over, caught by Patterson, and then Croft followed in the 12th, caught by Ballance off Sidebottom. It left Lancashire needing 18 from the dramatic final two overs.

Two huge sixes from Farveez Maharoof, who changed his bat to the one he uses in Twenty20 cricket, took them to the verge before he scored the winning runs with amazingly just four balls to spare. The Aigburth crowd chanted, "The Roof, The Roof, The Roof is on fire!" and the man himself celebrated as if he had helped Lancashire win the title there and then. In hindsight, he could well have done just that!

The Sri Lankan had smashed 31 off just 19 balls and written his name in Red Rose folklore. He then happily rode off into the sunset to join up with the Sri Lanka Test squad. The six-wicket victory put Lancashire top of the table, with a game in hand. Nobody was in doubt about their title aspirations now.

Anderson said: "This side can definitely win the Championship. The squad is as strong as any other in the competition. We beat Yorkshire without Simon Kerrigan, Tom Smith, Sajid Mahmood and Oliver Newby. The side is getting stronger all the time, and you need that to win the Championship.

"Being top of the table with a game in hand is a good position to be in. If I am honest, most of the lads thought time had run out for us because it was a big ask. But we were all on our feet when we won, it was an amazing feeling."

Maharoof said: "I'll be honest with you, I thought it would be a big ask for us to get the runs because it's a big boundary and they've got good bowling, but we approached it in the right manner and spirit, and we were positive when we went out to bat.

**Farveez Maharoof and Karl Brown
celebrate a stunning victory**

"I tried to get settled at the crease before freeing myself to clear the boundary, which I managed to do on a couple of occasions. The bat was a Twenty20 bat made by my sponsor, it was a bit thicker and more woody."

> *"I will miss not being with the lads, there's something really special happening here."*
>
> – Jimmy Anderson

CLOSE OF PLAY DAY FOUR:
Lancashire 329 (PJ Horton 93, MJ Chilton 77) and 121-4 beat Yorkshire 141 (JJ Sayers 53) and 308 (JJ Sayers 75, AW Gale 60, GS Ballance 57, AU Rashid 52; G Keedy 6-133) by six wickets

Lancashire 22pts (Batting 3, Bowling 3)
Yorkshire 2pts (Bowling 2)

LV= County Championship table May 21

	P	W	L	D	BaP	BoP	Pts
Lancashire	**5**	**4**	**0**	**1**	**14**	**15**	**96**
Durham	6	3	1	2	21	16	91
Warwickshire*	6	4	2	0	18	17	91
Nottinghamshire	6	3	2	1	12	16	79
Sussex	6	3	1	2	9	13	76
Somerset	6	2	3	1	17	16	68
Yorkshire	6	1	3	2	12	17	51
Hampshire	5	0	2	3	10	11	30
Worcestershire	6	0	6	0	12	16	28

* Warwickshire deducted eight points for poor pitch

SCORECARD

Yorkshire first innings		Runs	Balls	Mins	4s	6s
A Lyth	lbw b Chapple	4	7	12	1	-
JJ Sayers	c Croft b Anderson	53	148	181	3	-
JE Root	lbw b Maharoof	4	35	51	-	-
*AW Gale	b Keedy	31	109	133	2	-
GS Ballance	c Chilton b Keedy	6	31	28	-	-
AU Rashid	c and b Keedy	14	33	47	2	-
+SM Guy	b Maharoof	8	30	30	-	-
RJ Sidebottom	not out	7	22	38	-	-
SA Patterson	lbw b Maharoof	1	9	10	-	-
MA Ashraf	b Maharoof	4	16	16	-	-
OJ Hannon-Dalby	lbw b Keedy	0	1	2	-	-
Extras	(6 b, 3 lb)	9				
Total	(all out, 73.3 overs)	141				

Fall of wickets:
1-9 (Lyth, 3.1 ov), 2-30 (Root, 17 ov), 3-95 (Sayers, 48.1 ov), 4-105 (Gale, 53.4 ov), 5-106 (Ballance, 55.4 ov), 6-129 (Guy, 64.3 ov), 7-129 (Rashid, 66 ov), 8-130 (Patterson, 68.4 ov), 9-140 (Ashraf, 73 ov), 10-141 (Hannon-Dalby, 73.3 ov)

Lancashire bowling	Overs	Mdns	Runs	Wkts	Wides	No-Balls
Anderson	16	6	27	1	-	-
Chapple	11	5	9	1	-	-
Keedy	23.3	4	44	4	-	-
Maharoof	16	4	35	4	-	-
Procter	7	1	17	0	-	-

Yorkshire second innings		Runs	Balls	Mins	4s	6s
A Lyth	c and b Chapple	9	20	28	2	-
JJ Sayers	c Horton b Keedy	75	232	285	4	-
JE Root	lbw b Maharoof	15	46	51	-	-
*AW Gale	c Anderson b Keedy	60	117	149	6	-
GS Ballance	b Keedy	57	142	180	1	1
AU Rashid	st Cross b Croft	52	98	100	5	-
+SM Guy	c Anderson b Keedy	7	12	10	1	-
RJ Sidebottom	b Keedy	8	22	19	1	-
SA Patterson	c Croft b Anderson	2	51	49	-	-
MA Ashraf	lbw b Keedy	0	3	4	-	-
OJ Hannon-Dalby	not out	6	43	39	1	-
Extras	(2 b, 9 lb, 6 nb)	17				
Total	(all out, 130.3 overs)	308				

Fall of wickets:
1-13 (Lyth, 7.3 ov), 2-48 (Root, 21 ov), 3-163 (Gale, 63.1 ov), 4-190 (Sayers, 77.2 ov), 5-278 (Rashid, 105.2 ov), 6-287 (Guy, 108.3 ov), 7-300 (Ballance, 114.1 ov), 8-301 (Sidebottom, 114.4 ov), 9-301 (Ashraf, 116.1 ov), 10-308 (Patterson, 130.3 ov)

Lancashire bowling	Overs	Mdns	Runs	Wkts	Wides	No-Balls
Anderson	25.3	8	50	1	-	1
Chapple	14	7	22	1	-	-
Keedy	54	10	133	6	-	-
Maharoof	9	2	39	1	-	2
Croft	26	8	41	1	-	-
Procter	2	0	12	0	-	-

Lancashire first innings		Runs	Balls	Mins	4s	6s
PJ Horton	c Guy b Rashid	93	199	209	9	-
SC Moore	lbw b Patterson	1	9	17	-	-
KR Brown	lbw b Patterson	19	52	78	2	-
MJ Chilton	c Lyth b Ashraf	77	174	213	7	-
SJ Croft	b Root	41	101	112	3	-
LA Procter	lbw b Patterson	23	77	109	1	-
+GD Cross	lbw b Root	0	1	1	-	-
MF Maharoof	b Sidebottom	34	42	54	3	-
*G Chapple	lbw b Sidebottom	18	21	25	3	-
JM Anderson	not out	5	11	15	-	-
G Keedy	b Patterson	0	4	2	-	-
Extras	(9 b, 5 lb, 4 nb)	18				
Total	(all out, 114.5 overs)	329				

Fall of wickets:
1-9 (Moore, 4.2 ov), 2-69 (Brown, 25 ov), 3-150 (Horton, 56.4 ov), 4-240 (Chilton, 87.2 ov), 5-244 (Croft, 90.3 ov), 6-244 (Cross, 90.4 ov), 7-299 (Maharoof, 105.3 ov), 8-321 (Chapple, 111.2 ov), 9-329 (Procter, 114.1 ov), 10-329 (Keedy, 114.5 ov)

Yorkshire bowling	Overs	Mdns	Runs	Wkts	Wides	No-Balls
Patterson	24.5	8	51	4	-	-
Sidebottom	21	7	48	2	-	-
Rashid	30	4	94	1	-	1
Ashraf	11	2	50	1	-	1
Hannon-Dalby	13	1	37	0	-	-
Root	15	4	35	2	-	-

Lancashire second innings		Runs	Balls	Mins	4s	6s
PJ Horton	c Lyth b Rashid	18	18	26	1	-
SC Moore	c and b Rashid	19	18	28	1	-
SJ Croft	c Ballance b Sidebottom	28	19	27	-	2
+GD Cross	c Patterson b Rashid	11	6	11	-	1
MF Maharoof	not out	31	19	30	1	2
KR Brown	not out	6	7	15	-	-
MJ Chilton	did not bat					
LA Procter	did not bat					
*G Chapple	did not bat					
JM Anderson	did not bat					
G Keedy	did not bat					
Extras	(1 b, 2 nb, 5 w)	8				
Total	(4 wickets, 14.2 overs)	121				

Fall of wickets:
1-39 (Horton, 5.4 ov), 2-39 (Moore, 5.5 ov), 3-64 (Cross, 8 ov), 4-85 (Croft, 11.1 ov)

Yorkshire bowling	Overs	Mdns	Runs	Wkts	Wides	No-Balls
Sidebottom	7	0	58	1	1	1
Patterson	4	0	28	0	-	-
Rashid	3.2	0	34	3	-	-

Umpires: NL Bainton & RK Illingworth Scorers: DM White & JT Potter

Mark Chilton

AS a professional sportsman, calling time on your career is always a difficult decision, but if you're going to go, the best way to do it is when you are at the top. That is exactly what Mark Chilton did. Just a week after Lancashire lifted the LV= County Championship trophy, Chilly announced he was retiring from professional cricket. Having gone close to winning the trophy several times during his 15 seasons with Lancashire, it was more than fitting that he left the game having finally played a part in ending the 77-year wait for the outright title.

"While I've been at the club I've always been the nearly man, so to be a part of what we've achieved as a team this season is the perfect way to end my career," said 35-year-old Chilton, who made his Red Rose debut in 1997. "The time seemed right and I could never see myself playing anywhere else. I always said being captain of Lancashire was the proudest thing I have ever done."

Chilton, who followed in the footsteps of former Manchester Grammar School pupils Mike Atherton, John Crawley and Gary Yates into the Old Trafford first team, scored over 14,000 runs in all forms of the game for the club, including 26 centuries. He captained the side to promotion back up to Division One in 2005 in his first year in the role following Warren Hegg's retirement, and then took them to the C&G Trophy final at Lord's the following year.

In 2007, Chilton led the team to within 25 agonising runs of the title when they lost out to Sussex. It was the closest any captain had taken Lancashire to the title since they shared it in 1950 with Surrey, and was a bitter blow to the team and the skipper, who was pictured in tears on the balcony at The Oval as the final Red Rose wicket fell along with their Championship hopes. It was his last match as Lancashire captain, but heartbreak like that makes the good times even sweeter. After a disappointing season with the bat the following year, he came back in 2009 to be named the club's Player of the Year, and his dedication, commitment and sheer love of Lancashire was rewarded by the club, who granted him a benefit in 2011.

Chilton started the campaign in good form, sharing a 180-run partnership with Karl Brown in the opening match of the season against Sussex at Aigburth, and captained the side to victory against Somerset in the absence of the injured Glen Chapple, after which he stated Lancashire were capable of winning the title. How right he was. Crucial knocks at Sussex and against Warwickshire followed before he played a leading role in another key partnership, this time with Paul Horton, on the second day of the Roses match at Aigburth. A drop in form, however, saw Chilton lose his place for three of the final four games, but he still had an influence on the young squad as the title battle heated up.

"I believe I set the right example as a senior player throughout my last season. I am not one for moaning about things, I get on with the job," said Chilton. "The way the senior pros act can have a significant impact on the younger players because they tend to look up to them as an example of how things are done. I can honestly say that every day of my career I threw everything in to my game. I hope people recognise the professionalism I've shown and the significant contribution I've made on and off the field. It's not all about stats on paper. I've had highs and lows throughout my career, as everybody does. The thing I'm most proud of is that I always gave 100 percent for the club and my team-mates and I believe that is the way sport should be played. I made a commitment every day to the game and to the team."

After years of coming so close to dominating the domestic scene, Chilton believes the title is just the start for this Lancashire squad. "We deserve all the success we've had this year. Under Peter Moores and Glen Chapple an awful lot of good things are happening at this club, and winning the Championship is proof of that," he said. "When you win something, you start to build belief. I think you will see this team go from strength to strength. Although I won't be part of it going forward, having played a role in a Championship-winning Lancashire side, I retire a proud man."

Chilton could have a burgeoning second career in the offing. At the club's Player of the Year dinner, he took to the stage with his guitar to sing two Oasis songs and a Paul Weller classic in front of 700 people. It went down well as the crowd demanded an encore. "I was petrified," said Chilly. "I was less nervous facing 90mph bowling than I was up on stage!"

CHAMPAGNE MOMENT: *"It has to be that run chase in the Roses match at Aigburth. There is nothing sweeter than beating your nearest rivals, but it was even more special because at one point it looked as if the chance to win the game had gone."*

MATCH 6

Hampshire v Lancashire

(The Rose Bowl, Southampton) May 24–26

DAY ONE

THE opening day gave glimpses into Lancashire's recent past and into their future as Dominic Cork and Karl Brown starred. Cork, Hampshire's captain, returned figures of 4-78 from 24.5 overs as the Red Rose were bowled out for 328 in the day's last over on a green-tinged pitch showing signs of variable bounce. Brown, however, put the odd snorter to the back of his mind, backing up an opening week 114 against Sussex at Liverpool with a 174-ball 96, including 14 fours. His excellent knock underpinned a more than useful total after Cork had elected to bowl first in his attempt to end a five-match winless streak. Steven Croft, Sajid Mahmood and Kyle Hogg chipped in with scores in the thirties for the visitors, who were without the injured Glen Chapple, England's Jimmy Anderson and Farveez Maharoof, who had been called up to the Sri Lankan side ahead of the first Test at Cardiff.

Give Cork his due, he was excellent as he moved to 983 first-class wickets. There's a strong argument to say that Lancashire wouldn't be where they are now had Cork not trodden the same exit route out of Old Trafford as Stuart Law did in 2008, but Cork was still one heck of a performer, even during his final season in the game! Those who saw the way he orchestrated his field, ramped up the pressure and then delivered the final over in the Friends Life t20 semi-final against Somerset at Edgbaston in August to secure his side an unlikely tie will no doubt agree. He may have lost that zip, but he took advantage of some help off the pitch during this particular day to remove Paul Horton with the new ball, Brown during the late afternoon, Tom Smith after tea and Gary Keedy with the day's penultimate ball.

It was just a good job that Brown was up to the task for the majority of his innings. Having seen Horton fend Cork's sixth ball to James Vince in the slips, Brown and opener Stephen Moore also looped balls over the cordon in the early stages. Moore failed to survive much longer, however, and he was one of three wickets to fall inside 23 overs when he slashed behind to Nic Pothas off the speedy David Griffiths.

Mark Chilton, standing in as skipper, fell in a similar fashion to Horton, fending another snorter from Griffiths to Danny Briggs at cover, leaving the score at 65-3. At that stage, Cork's decision to bowl first looked vindicated, but Brown steadied the ship in partnership with Croft, the pair adding 100 for the fourth wicket inside 30 overs before the latter fell for 37 as he tried to sweep Briggs' left-arm spin mid-way through the afternoon.

Mark Chilton and Karl Brown (right) meet mid-wicket during their 180-run partnership on the second day of the opening fixture of the season at Aigburth. Brown went on to record his maiden first-class century, while Chilton's 87 was to be his highest score of the summer.

Gary Keedy (below) celebrates his first five-wicket haul of a prolific summer with his Lancashire team-mates on the morning of the final day against Sussex. Keedy was the Red Rose's leading wicket-taker in 2011 with 61 victims.

Lancashire's two elder statesmen lead the team off after the innings and 55-run victory over Sussex in the opening game. Gary Keedy finished with 5-41 in Sussex's second innings, which followed skipper Glen Chapple's 5-68 in the visitors' first innings. They set the example which the rest of the bowling attack were to follow.

Oliver Newby didn't quite make the impact he would have liked in 2011, but in the second game at Aigburth against Somerset he took the important wickets of Nick Compton in the first innings and Craig Kieswetter in the second just as they were threatening to launch a revival.

Farveez Maharoof is a picture of concentration as he prepares to make his debut for the Red Rose – and what a debut it was! 'The Roof', as he was to be affectionately christened, became only the sixth Lancashire player to score a century on debut in first-class cricket as he smashed 102 in 134 balls across the second and third days of the Somerset game. His performances were to attract the attention of the touring Sri Lankans' selectors and his initial appearances for Lancashire were brief, but spectacular.

Maharoof and Tom Smith run between the wickets. Smith also made a great start to the season, scoring 89 in Lancashire's innings and taking four wickets in the match against Somerset. His all-round contribution with the bat, ball and in the field was to be crucial to the Red Rose's success in 2011.

Jimmy Anderson was to play just two Championship games in 2011 due to his international commitments. The last one was the Roses game at Aigburth, where he gave Yorkshire opener Joe Sayers a working over with the ball.

Anderson gives Sayers a telling look after the Yorkshireman's dismissal in the second innings. The verbal jousting between the two prompted the umpires to speak to the England fast bowler and the atmosphere that confrontation created was to spill over into the return match at Headingley.

If 'The Roof' had already endeared himself to the Lancashire faithful with his century on debut, then his remarkable innings to snatch victory on the final afternoon in the Roses match was to bestow on him legendary status. He scored 31 in just 19 balls as the Red Rose chased down 121 in 15 overs with just four balls to spare.

Peter Moores and the players celebrate the victory over Yorkshire in what was to be one of several thrilling finishes during the 2011 season. One of the features of the Lancashire side was the camaraderie, which was largely as a result of most of the side growing up together through the Lancashire Academy.

Lancashire's other overseas import, Junaid Khan, in action against Durham at Aigburth. He didn't have the same impact as Maharoof in the County Championship, but his miserly bowling played a huge role in the Red Rose's march to Twenty20 Finals Day.

Luke Procter was one of several of the contingent of young Lancastrians to make their mark in 2011. He topped the Lancashire batting averages and in the Durham game at Aigburth scored his second half-century of the season against a bowling attack considered by some as the finest in the County Championship. The young all-rounder from Royton also weighed in with some useful wickets and looks to have a great future.

Kyle Hogg's first half-century of the season came in the return Roses game at Headingley, where his partnership with Sajid Mahmood was crucial in setting Yorkshire a target from which the Red Rose emerged victorious by just 23 runs in a pulsating match. Hogg's superb bowling and more than useful batting marked him out as an all-rounder of real substance.

Despite the efforts of Kyle Hogg, who took 5-28 in Nottinghamshire's first innings – including the wicket of former team-mate Steven Mullaney (above) – and Glen Chapple (below), who claimed 6-70 in the second, Lancashire suffered defeat at Trafalgar Road, Southport. It was thought that the outgrounds would prove a fortess for the Red Rose in 2011, but this was their second successive home reverse. The batting, which had shown such resilience thus far in the season, proved Lancashire's undoing as no player scored more than 37 in the match.

But for Tom Smith and Stephen Moore, who scored 31 and 76 respectively, Lancashire's batting woes could have continued in their next home game against Warwickshire. Despite their efforts, the Red Rose still conceded a 91-run first-innings defecit, although the match ended in a rare draw.

History was made at Aigburth as Warwickshire's Rikki Clarke entered the record books. The 29-year-old claimed seven catches to equal the world record for the number of catches made by a non-wicketkeeper in a first-class innings, set by both Mickey Stewart in 1957 and Tony Brown in 1966. If he hadn't dropped Stephen Moore in the first innings, he would have made it 10 for the match to equal Wally Hammond's world record for a game, which was set in 1928!

Tom Smith snaffles Warwickshire skipper Jim Troughton on the final afternoon at Aigburth to have the visitors reeling at 92-4 and give the Red Rose an outside chance of victory. Thanks to the efforts of former England wicketkeeper Tim Ambrose, Warwickshire survived an exciting finale as Gary Keedy and Steven Croft, who had completed his first century of the season the day before, almost spun Lancashire to victory. It was, however, a third consecutive home game without a win and meant Durham extended their lead at the top of the LV= County Championship to six points.

Blackpool Tower looms large in the background as the Red Rose attempt to get back to winning ways. Visits to the seaside resort were stopped following the abandonment in 2008 when not a ball was bowled in the match against Surrey because of a damp outfield, even though it didn't rain during the four days.

'The Roof' made his return to the Lancashire fold at Stanley Park, and although his contribution wasn't as spectacular as in the games with Somerset and Yorkshire earlier in the season, he did make a vital breakthrough when he dismissed Gareth Andrew, with Steven Croft taking a superb one-handed catch at gully, as Andrew and Ben Scott were threatening a Worcestershire recovery. As well as his brilliant fielding and catching, Croft had made his second successive century the day before.

Kyle Hogg can't quite believe it as another appeal is turned down against Vikram Solanki, whose century on the third day left Worcestershire in sight of victory on the final morning at Stanley Park. This innings was one of the rare occasions in the season that Hogg remained wicketless, while Solanki fell shortly before the close, caught by Paul Horton off Gary Keedy (below), to put the Red Rose in the box seat to force victory on the final morning. Horton's catch was one of 32 he snaffled, mostly at slip, the third highest total in the 2011 Championship.

Glen Chapple and Kyle Hogg added 116 for eighth wicket against Hampshire at Aigburth as Lancashire rattled up 388 in the first innings. Chapple, who led from the front with ball and bat throughout the campaign, fell three runs short of what would have been a well-deserved century, while Hogg completed his second half-century of the season.

Stephen Moore produced Lancashire's highest individual innings of the season, 169 not out, in the Red Rose's second innings against Hampshire to set up a declaration and the astonishing finish to the match. South African-born Moore passed 1,000 Championship runs for the campaign in the final match at Taunton.

With just four minutes to go and the Red Rose's title challenge hanging by a thread, Simon Kerrigan bowls to Neil McKenzie, who edges towards Tom Smith at slip. McKenzie was to play an even more important role the following week.

Smith takes the catch and turns in jubilation, realising the importance of the moment, while Gareth Cross, Paul Horton and Stephen Moore race to congratulate Kerrigan, who has claimed his ninth wicket to become the first Lancashire player to do so since Roy Tattersall in 1953.

The players, with Kerrigan at the forefront, descend on Smith as pandemonium ensues. Smith and Kerrigan (below) are engulfed by their delighted team-mates as Lancashire take the title race down to the wire.

Steven Croft and Karl Brown celebrate clinching the title. After Paul Horton and Stephen Moore had both scored brisk half-centuries to put Lancashire in sight of victory, and with Hampshire having held out at the Rose Bowl, the pair added an undefeated 88 to pass their target of 211. It was the culmination of a fantastic season for the Red Rose.

Batting conditions seemed easier after lunch with the ball softening, and that allowed Brown to play with confidence on both sides of the wicket. He failed to reach a second hundred when Cork dug one in 58 overs into the day and had the right-hander caught behind by Pothas running backwards as the ball looped towards short fine-leg.

Smith (17) followed in the second over after tea, guiding Cork to Jimmy Adams at slip, and Lancashire were six down just shy of 200. Gareth Cross, who scored a maiden century in a draw at the Rose Bowl the previous August, was one of eight men to make it into double figures as he helped to secure a first batting bonus point. Having survived a huge lbw shout from Briggs just before tea, he played a couple of eye-catching shots off the seamers through the covers and mid-wicket before scooping yet another short ball from Kabir Ali behind with 228 on the board.

> *"If you're going on the wickets we've played on, I think this one was a far better knock than Sussex. I fell four runs short, but I'd have taken 96 before I went out."*
>
> **– Karl Brown**

At that stage, there was a fear that Lancashire would fail to capitalise on the good work of Brown, in particular, but, as happened on numerous occasions through the season, Hogg and Sajid Mahmood (32) returned useful lower order contributions. They shared 68 in 12.1 overs for the eighth wicket, counter-attacking against the new ball. Hogg often scythed through the off-side on the way to 38 off 46 balls, including eight fours.

The pair fell to successive deliveries at the end of the 85th and start of the 86th overs, Mahmood bowled by Griffiths and Hogg trapped lbw by Kabir, but Oliver Newby and Gary Keedy nudged, nurdled, edged and flicked their way to a 32-run stand for the last wicket before the latter was trapped lbw by former team-mate Cork after a third batting point had been secured.

Brown said: "If you're going on the wickets we've played on, I think this one was a far better knock than Sussex. I fell four runs short, but I'd have taken 96 before I went out. It was a tricky pitch. It's done a bit all day, even with the older ball. When I got in, I wanted to cash in.

"We feel like we've got a good score. It's definitely something to bowl at. If we bowl in good areas tomorrow, we can cause some problems. We ended up putting a couple of good partnerships together."

CLOSE OF PLAY DAY ONE:
Lancashire, having lost the toss and been invited to bat, 328 all out (KR Brown 96)

DAY TWO

KYLE Hogg's seven up helped Lancashire fizz as Hampshire crumbled to hand over the initiative during another fast and furious day of Championship cricket. Career-best figures of 7-28 from the former England Under-19 player confirmed what most of us had suspected - that Lancashire's first day total of 328 was worth closer to 400, even 450. He took advantage as uneven bounce was still obvious from short of a length and late movement was on offer when the ball was pitched up. The home side were bowled out for just 133 inside 42 overs.

Hogg, whose previous best haul of wickets in a first-class season stood at 34 in 2009, then saw Sajid Mahmood strike a triple blow as Hampshire closed on 161-5 from 51.5 overs in their second innings after Mark Chilton had enforced the follow-on.

> *"I believe Chappie was upstairs saying 'he best not get eight because I've only ever got seven'. If I'd known that, I would've been even more desperate to get eight."*
>
> **– Kyle Hogg**

Dominic Cork's reported decision to ask groundsman Nigel Gray to produce a result pitch will have produced as many laughs from Red Rose followers as news of a fluffed major police operation close to this ground had just a few days earlier. A passer-by thought he or she had spotted a white tiger in a field adjacent to Hampshire's ever improving home, alerting the local zoo and police, who advised the delay of an Academy match at the ground. Police swept in with a helicopter and heat detection equipment, only to find it was just a cuddly toy.

Hogg's display, sparked by the capture of Bordeaux-born debutant Benny Howell 13 balls into the day, was anything but cuddly, definitely more tigerish and had a certain *joie de vivre*.

Despite Howell's duck, Jimmy Adams and Johann Myburgh shared 55 for the second wicket to ensure Hampshire's start was a respectable one, but the latter fell when he was bowled shouldering arms to Oliver Newby. When Adams was caught behind for 35 as he drove at a wide one from the same bowler, Lancashire held the whip-hand with their opponents at 73-3 in the 22nd over.

Chilton's side tightened their stranglehold on the contest as Hogg blew the home side away with six more wickets for just six runs in 28 balls after they had been loitering on 98-3 just before lunch. Neil McKenzie edged behind to Gareth Cross in the last over of the morning, James Vince edged to Paul Horton at second slip a little over three overs later, Dimitri Mascarenhas feathered behind as he shouldered arms like Myburgh had, Cork was trapped lbw for a three-ball duck, Nic Pothas was strangled down the leg-side in Hogg's next and Danny Briggs continued the procession when he was trapped lbw.

That left the score at 121-9 in the 39th over, and it was all over Red Rover (or should that be Red Roser?) when Sajid Mahmood had big mate Kabir Ali caught and bowled shortly afterwards.

Despite playing second fiddle to Kyle Hogg, both Gareth Cross and Sajid Mahmood made important contributions to the victory at the Rose Bowl, Cross with his five first-innings catches and Mahmood by ripping out Hampshire's middle order in the second innings

Hogg's previous best haul came on his county debut back in 2002, and they were the best figures by anybody in English cricket at that stage of the season and the best by a Lancashire bowler since Peter Martin's 8-32 against Middlesex in 1997.

Tom Smith and Newby then heightened the prospect of a two-day finish when they struck inside the first 10 overs of Hampshire's second innings, with Smith getting Adams caught behind one-handed by Cross and Newby forcing Myburgh to edge to a tumbling Horton at first slip. Howell at least gave Hampshire some French Connection with a determined 71 off 177 balls, including a huge six off Gary Keedy over the ropes at long-on. He shared 48 in 16 overs with McKenzie, but after a couple of glorious cover drives and short-arm pulls, the latter was trapped lbw by Mahmood for 35 to leave the score at 79-3.

Howell and Vince then shared 82 inside 24 overs for the fourth wicket to ensure the game crept over into a third day, the former completing a 110-ball half-century with a punch to point off Keedy. They made batting look pretty easy as the demons in the pitch briefly disappeared and Lancashire's bowlers maybe tired a touch.

But fear not, because Mahmood struck twice in the closing stages of the day. He had Vince superbly caught by a diving Steven Croft at gully, the ball looping off the shoulder of the bat. Then night-watchman Briggs was pouched by Karl Brown in the slip cordon with the penultimate ball of another excellent day.

Hogg said: "With Jimmy missing, Chappie injured and The Roof gone, once you get in this side you have to prove your worth. We just bowled well today, Saj probably better than anyone. There was a lot of help for the bowlers, but you've just got to put the ball in the right areas. Some days you get the nicks behind, some days you don't.

"We've got three international class players missing, yet we're still in a great position to win the game. I believe Chappie was upstairs saying 'he best not get eight because I've only ever got seven'. If I'd known that, I would have been even more desperate to get eight."

CLOSE OF PLAY DAY TWO:
Lancashire 328 (KR Brown 96) led Hampshire 133 (KW Hogg 7-28) and 163-5 (BAC Howell 68no) by 32 runs

DAY THREE

THEY say that every Hogg has his day... but Kyle had two in a row! What a way to mark your first start of the season after thigh and ankle injuries had frustrated the keen music fan. The Saddleworth seamer (sounds more like a train that winds its way through Shaw and Milnrow rather than the description of a county's fast bowler) polished off Hampshire with four more wickets at a cost of only seven runs, bowling the hosts out for 201 in their second innings. That left openers Paul Horton and Stephen Moore with the easy task of knocking off the seven runs required for the 22 points that went with a third win on the spin following successes over Warwickshire and Yorkshire.

Such was the manner of their victory, the following line headed the day's match report in the Manchester Evening News: "Pinch yourself. It really is happening. Lancashire are on course to win their first outright title since 1934".

Polishing off the match in double-quick time also enabled the Lancashire squad an extra day's rest before their gruelling 315-mile trek from Southampton to Durham ahead of a Sunday start to their next four-day match. With Hampshire still 32 runs behind with half their side back in the pavilion, a Lancashire win was expected on day three, but it wasn't expected to come quite as easily as it did.

Hampshire slumped from 163-5 to 201 all out in 15 overs to cement their position at the foot of the table and leave them contemplating a drop in divisions even at this early stage in the campaign. Captain Dominic Cork, one of only four men to reach

> *"This start hasn't just been about good luck. We've been working towards it for a long time. From the time we got together in December, Peter Moores has been extremely efficient, especially with the bowlers. Every ball has been monitored, and we've worked incredibly hard on being consistent and disciplined."*
>
> **– Mark Chilton**

double figures in the innings, even stormed out to his car 20 minutes after the last ball had been bowled. Having also seen an expected deluge of rain arrive as he started the engine, the former Derbyshire man left home coach Giles White to face the waiting media, who described their dressing room as "a sad place". The contrast in mood in the camps was stark as stand-in captain Mark Chilton spoke about the strength in depth within Lancashire's squad and about how the hard work during the winter months was reaping rewards.

Hogg's four-for during the third morning made it a career-best match haul of 11-59 from 31 overs. Wicketkeeper Nic Pothas was first to go just five balls into the day when he edged to Horton at first slip before Benny Howell was bowled off an inside edge as he shouldered arms for 71, leaving the score at 167-7 in the 57th over. Cork then took three boundaries and an emphatically pulled six off a Sajid Mahmood over to delay the inevitable... but not for long.

Hogg's 10th wicket of the match came as Dimitri Mascarenhas was caught on the crease and adjudged lbw before Cork attempted and failed to clear the ropes for a second time a couple of overs later. Gary Keedy was perfectly placed at long-on, and Hogg was in eleventh heaven. Keedy then wrapped up the innings himself when he nicked the top of David Griffiths' off-stump four-and-a-half overs later.

It took Horton, who hit Cork for two boundaries, just three balls to knock off the runs required to secure for his side their second 10-wicket win in six-and-a-half seasons.

Chilton said: "I don't think that morning session could have gone any better, but we started the match so well. 328 on the first day was a brilliant effort. Karl Brown's 96 was one of the best knocks I've seen for a long time. For Kyle to come in and bowl that well in his first Championship appearance of the summer speaks volumes for the quality we have in our group.

"This start hasn't just been about good luck. We've been working towards it for a long time. From the time we got together in December, Peter Moores has been extremely efficient, especially with the bowlers. Every ball has been monitored, and we've worked incredibly hard on being consistent and disciplined."

CLOSE OF PLAY DAY THREE:
Lancashire 328 (KR Brown 96) and 8-0 beat Hampshire 133
(KW Hogg 7-28) and 201 (BAC Howell 71) by 10 wickets

Hampshire 3pts (Bowling 3)
Lancashire 22pts (Batting 3, Bowling 3)

LV= County Championship table May 26

	P	W	L	D	BaP	BoP	Pts
Lancashire	6	5	0	1	17	18	118
Durham	6	3	1	2	21	16	91
Warwickshire*	6	4	2	0	18	17	91
Nottinghamshire	6	3	2	1	12	16	79
Sussex	6	3	1	2	9	13	76
Somerset	6	2	3	1	17	16	68
Yorkshire	6	1	3	2	12	17	51
Hampshire	6	0	3	3	10	14	33
Worcestershire	6	0	6	0	12	16	28

* Warwickshire deducted eight points for poor pitch

SCORECARD

Lancashire first innings		Runs	Balls	Mins	4s	6s
PJ Horton	c Vince b Cork	5	4	3	1	-
SC Moore	c Pothas b Griffiths	18	34	50	1	-
KR Brown	c Pothas b Cork	96	174	220	14	-
*MJ Chilton	c Briggs b Griffiths	7	31	36	1	-
SJ Croft	lbw b Briggs	37	86	114	5	-
TC Smith	c Adams b Cork	17	53	47	2	-
+GD Cross	c Pothas b Ali	28	36	58	4	-
SI Mahmood	b Griffiths	32	49	83	4	-
KW Hogg	lbw b Ali	38	46	54	8	-
OJ Newby	not out	9	36	42	2	-
G Keedy	lbw b Cork	15	28	40	1	-
Extras	(9 b, 3 lb, 14 nb)	26				
Total	(all out, 95.5 overs)	328				

Fall of wickets:

1-6 (Horton, 1 ov), 2-41 (Moore, 12.5 ov), 3-65 (Chilton, 22.5 ov), 4-165 (Croft, 52.1 ov), 5-183 (Brown, 57.5 ov), 6-196 (Smith, 66 ov), 7-228 (Cross, 72.5 ov), 8-296 (Mahmood, 85 ov), 9-296 (Hogg, 85.1 ov), 10-328 (Keedy, 95.5 ov)

Hampshire bowling	Overs	Mdns	Runs	Wkts	Wides	No-Balls
Cork	24.5	8	78	4	-	1
Ali	23	2	79	2	-	-
Griffiths	21	5	82	3	-	2
Mascarenhas	17	1	52	0	-	-
Briggs	10	1	25	1	-	-

Hampshire first innings		Runs	Balls	Mins	4s	6s
JHK Adams	c Cross b Newby	35	66	92	6	-
BAC Howell	c Cross b Hogg	0	3	10	-	-
JG Myburgh	b Newby	28	45	57	5	-
ND McKenzie	c Cross b Hogg	16	46	51	1	-
JM Vince	c Horton b Hogg	12	27	39	1	-
+N Pothas	c Cross b Hogg	9	15	33	1	-
AD Mascarenhas	c Cross b Hogg	1	7	7	-	-
*DG Cork	lbw b Hogg	0	3	2	-	-
K Ali	c and b Mahmood	9	16	33	1	-
DR Briggs	lbw b Hogg	2	14	10	-	-
DA Griffiths	not out	4	10	13	1	-
Extras	(5 b, 8 lb, 4 nb)	17				
Total	(all out, 41.4 overs)	133				

Fall of wickets:

1-1 (Howell, 2.1 ov), 2-56 (Myburgh, 16 ov), 3-73 (Adams, 21.5 ov), 4-98 (McKenzie, 29.2 ov), 5-108 (Vince, 32.3 ov), 6-112 (Mascarenhas, 34.1 ov), 7-112 (Cork, 34.4 ov), 8-117 (Pothas, 36.1 ov), 9-121 (Briggs, 38.5 ov), 10-133 (Ali, 41.4 ov)

Lancashire bowling	Overs	Mdns	Runs	Wkts	Wides	No-Balls
Hogg	14	5	28	7	-	-
Mahmood	12.4	1	50	1	-	2
Smith	7	1	13	0	-	-
Newby	5	0	26	2	-	-
Keedy	3	1	3	0	-	-

Hampshire second innings (following on)		Runs	Balls	Mins	4s	6s
JHK Adams	c Cross b Smith	3	15	17	-	-
BAC Howell	b Hogg	71	177	223	7	1
JG Myburgh	c Horton b Newby	5	18	20	1	-
ND McKenzie	lbw b Mahmood	35	41	60	8	-
JM Vince	c Croft b Mahmood	39	71	88	4	-
DR Briggs	c Brown b Mahmood	1	11	8	-	-
+N Pothas	c Horton b Hogg	0	2	3	-	-
AD Mascarenhas	lbw b Hogg	2	17	31	-	-
*DG Cork	c Keedy b Hogg	20	14	24	3	1
K Ali	not out	8	20	26	-	-
DA Griffiths	b Keedy	2	17	16	-	-
Extras	(1 b, 10 lb, 4 nb)	15				
Total	(all out, 66.5 overs)	201				

Fall of wickets:

1-14 (Adams, 4.3 ov), 2-31 (Myburgh, 9.5 ov), 3-79 (McKenzie, 25.5 ov), 4-161 (Vince, 49.4 ov), 5-163 (Briggs, 51.5 ov), 6-164 (Pothas, 52.4 ov), 7-167 (Howell, 56.5 ov), 8-188 (Mascarenhas, 60.2 ov), 9-195 (Cork, 62.1 ov), 10-201 (Griffiths, 66.5 ov)

Lancashire bowling	Overs	Mdns	Runs	Wkts	Wides	No-Balls
Hogg	17	5	31	4	-	-
Mahmood	18	2	59	3	-	-
Smith	11	4	28	1	-	-
Newby	9	1	49	1	-	2
Keedy	11.5	4	23	1	-	-

Lancashire second innings		Runs	Balls	Mins	4s	6s
PJ Horton	not out	8	3	2	2	-
SC Moore	not out	0	0	2	-	-
KR Brown	did not bat					
*MJ Chilton	did not bat					
SJ Croft	did not bat					
TC Smith	did not bat					
+GD Cross	did not bat					
KW Hogg	did not bat					
SI Mahmood	did not bat					
OJ Newby	did not bat					
G Keedy	did not bat					
Extras		0				
Total	(no wicket, 0.3 overs)	8				

Hampshire bowling	Overs	Mdns	Runs	Wkts	Wides	No-Balls
Cork	0.3	0	8	0	-	-

Umpires: PK Baldwin & RA Kettleborough Scorers: AE Weld & DM White

Kyle Hogg

KYLE Hogg ended 2011 with 50 Championship wickets to his name and only captain Glen Chapple and Gary Keedy above him in the club's list of wicket-takers. Even better than that, the laid-back seamer's average of 18.80 topped anybody else in the entire division who had taken over 50 wickets. There was a point in the summer, however, when Hogg, a former England National Academy player, doubted whether he would play at all.

Hogg tore a thigh muscle during the first-class friendly against Oxford University at the Parks in early April, which ruled him out of action for five weeks. He then rolled his ankle playing football in the build-up to the clash with Warwickshire at Edgbaston, and he could only sit and watch as his team-mates started their four-day campaign like a train with four wins from five.

"I was watching from the sidelines and we were hammering teams," he said. "All the bowlers were bowling well, the batters were scoring runs, and I wondered whether I'd get a game. I remember watching the Sussex game at Liverpool and thinking 'I'll do well to play here'. Then, all of a sudden, I've played eleven games in a row and ended up doing well.

"This year my mental approach has been different. I've gone into every game thinking I want to win it for Lancashire, and, more often than not, I've done pretty well. During the winter I realised how lucky I am to be playing cricket when I did some of the hardest work I've ever done in my life with SJM (the music promoters), and I wanted to make the most of the game." And make the most of it he did. Career-best figures of 7-28 in his first four-day match of the season against Hampshire at the Rose Bowl came his way, contributing to a match haul of 11 wickets, and he added two more five-wicket hauls against Yorkshire and Notts.

He continued: "When I've bowled well, it's generally seemed to be three or four for 20, but it was just one of those days at Hampshire. When you listen to Chappie or someone like Corky talk about their big hauls, they just say that the batsmen seem to just nick it. I was always like 'yeah, yeah', but that happened that day for me. It will probably happen just once in my career, 7-20, and it was very surreal."

That wasn't the only surreal moment that Hogg can recall. Messages of congratulations came into Old Trafford from far and wide at the end of the season, but it was one from a little bit closer to home that blew the 28-year-old from Saddleworth away. He explained: "I was in my local pub going to the bar when Paul Scholes came up to me and shook my hand. He said that he'd been following our season closely. To know that legends in football have been following how you've been doing is fantastic. I ended up chatting to him for about half an hour just about cricket. All he wanted to talk about was cricket, but all I wanted to talk about was football. It was absolutely mental.

"He's played at Middleton in their seconds before. I knew he was interested, but his knowledge was brilliant. All he was interested in was what Mooresy was like as a coach and why did I think I'd bowled so well this season in particular. All I wanted to talk was Beckham, Ronaldo and Rooney."

Hogg was one of the first men to run onto the field to start the celebrations with Steven Croft and Karl Brown after the victory over Somerset at Taunton had sealed Championship glory, but ask him what happened in the run chase, and he wouldn't have a clue. That's because he didn't watch a ball.

"I didn't see one shot played," he chuckled. "Everybody had their set positions in the dressing room when we started the run chase. I was just playing games on my phone at the back of the dressing room. I didn't move. I saw the lads clapping, and knew we had lost a wicket when I saw somebody walk out with a bat. Some of us are terrible at watching, and I'm one of them. It's just the way we are. When we won at Nottinghamshire earlier in the season, I didn't see a ball of that innings either. I was just in the back room lying down."

CHAMPAGNE MOMENT: *"The way we celebrated after that Yorkshire game at Headingley was something that will stick with me for a long time. The majority of the team just piled on Keeds when he took that wicket. There was just so much relief after the game had swung this way and that for three and a half days."*

MATCH 7

Durham v Lancashire

(Chester-le-Street) May 29–June 1

DAY ONE

THERE'S no I in Team. This was one of the phrases that summed up Lancashire's season, and the win against Hampshire at the Rose Bowl just a couple of days earlier was the perfect example. Their pace bowling quartet of Kyle Hogg, Sajid Mahmood, Tom Smith and Oliver Newby hadn't played in either of the two previous wins against Warwickshire or Yorkshire, yet they still managed to come up trumps and put clear daylight between their side and the chasing pack at the top of the Division One table.

But the Red Rose's mettle would be severely tested in the North East by Phil Mustard's Durham, who had won the title twice in the last three years and had started this season well, too, thanks to four wins from their first seven matches. Notable performances had come from Dale Benkenstein, Ben Stokes and Graham Onions amongst others and, as it turned out, the trio would have a pretty big influence on the outcome of this clash too.

Lancashire's players may have come into the match on the back of that thumping win against rock-bottom Hampshire, many's pre-season tip for a title challenge incidentally, but they had also just completed an unenviable seven-hour coach ride from the south coast. The Durham game, their seventh Championship match of the season, was slap bang in the midst of a run of three four-dayers, two CB40s and three Twenty20s in the space of 22 days. In that period, there were journeys from Manchester to Taunton and back, Manchester to Southampton, Southampton to Durham, Durham to Derby, Derby to Manchester and Manchester to Leicester and back.

Therefore, it was to Lancashire's credit that they put in yet another solid performance to make an acceptable start to this fixture, having been invited to bat by Mustard and reduced to 9-2 when Stephen Moore fell in Callum Thorp's first over and Karl Brown to England hopeful Onions, who was being watched by selector James Whitaker.

Paul Horton, having survived a first-ball lbw appeal from Onions and a dropped catch in the slips on one, was the visiting star of the day with 94 off 176 balls, including 15 fours, to fashion a recovery in tricky conditions, none more so than on the first morning when Onions, Thorp and Mitch Claydon were enjoying seaming conditions.

Horton featured in a battling stand of 77 for the third wicket with Mark Chilton, who edged Benkenstein's medium pace to Michael Di Venuto at first slip on the stroke of lunch. As was said earlier, Chilton is renowned for building partnerships, which he did with some effect here. He may have only scored 12 runs, but he faced 60 balls in allowing the excellent Horton to compile more at the other end. It was just unfortunate for Chilly that his dismissal came as a result of a stroke of luck for the hosts, the ball rebounding to Di Venuto off Mustard's gloves behind the stumps.

Talking about partnerships, Horton, whose emphatic cut off Onions just after lunch was a shot to remember, was doing his bit during the opening day. He added 72 for the fourth wicket with Steven Croft (38). It was just a shame that Stokes gained revenge for conceding three boundaries in one over when he shaped one in and rocked back Horton's off-stump, leaving the batsman stranded in the nineties and his side at 158-4 in the 55th over.

An entertaining fifth-wicket alliance of 33 inside seven overs between Croft and Smith followed, but the former edged Ian Blackwell's left-arm spin to a juggling Di Venuto at slip. Blackwell also accounted for Gareth Cross,

> *"We're quite happy, although you can never gauge what a good score is until both sides have batted. We were put in last week at Hampshire as well and 328 was a really good score. We'll have to wait and see what 313 is like."*
>
> **– Paul Horton**

stumped, to leave the score at 215-6 before Smith was trapped lbw by leggie Scott Borthwick's third ball with only 10 more runs added.

There would no doubt have been a little bit of added pressure on Luke Procter when he strode to the crease having been preferred to Sajid Mahmood, who had bowled impressively at Hampshire. He soon shoved that to one side as he notched an important 45, looking strong either side of the wicket as he and captain Glen Chapple, another man returning to the side – in place of Newby – added 87 in 17 overs for the eighth wicket to clinch a third batting point.

Chapple, who bettered Procter by one run, even lofted Thorp back over his head for a stunning straight six, but he fell soon after when he found Borthwick at third-man as he tried to uppercut Claydon. Unfortunately, he was the first of three wickets to fall for just one run in 19 balls to end the innings. Procter was caught behind off the same bowler before Hogg was bowled by Blackwell.

Horton said: "We're quite happy, although you can never gauge what a good score is until both sides have batted. We were put in last week at Hampshire as well and 328 was a really good score. We'll have to wait and see what 313 is like.

"It did a little bit early on with the new ball, and they bowled quite well with it. The new ball's extremely helpful here because it sits in the wicket and seams a little bit more than usual. Hopefully our bowlers can get as much out of it as they did."

CLOSE OF PLAY DAY ONE:
Lancashire, having lost the toss and been invited to bat, 313 all out (PJ Horton 94)

DAY TWO

IT'S a funny old game. Less than a week earlier, Lancashire made 328 on the first day at Hampshire having been inserted, and it was reasonably clear that they were on top in the contest. Here, however, having made 313 after Glen Chapple had lost the toss, things were different. Conditions had been tough for batting during the first morning, yes, but it got easier as the day went on. There was just a nagging feeling that the visitors might well have been under par.

Rain and bad light had severely interrupted the morning session, accounting for the loss of 25 overs. Much talked about all-rounder Ben Stokes underpinned his side's score of 279-3 with a brilliant unbeaten hundred. He was helped out by fifties from Gordon Muchall and Dale Benkenstein, who remained not out before close.

The hosts recovered from 6-1 in the third over and 94-3 in the 25th, with Stokes and Benkenstein adding an unbroken 185 for the fourth wicket. While those two bossed proceedings and made Lancashire toil, Muchall was pretty fortunate to post a 63-ball 54. The right-hander edged through or over the slip cordon with regularity, no less than three times in Luke Procter's first over. The fact that Procter's opening six balls cost him 17 runs was unjust to say the least, with three edges finding the third-man fence.

Muchall added 84 for the second wicket with Will Smith after Chapple had removed Michael Di Venuto, caught behind as the opener failed to get his gloves out of the way as he left alone outside off. A brief delay for bad light proved advantageous to the visitors, who then struck twice in six balls shortly after the resumption.

Procter was rewarded for a probing start when Smith feathered a drive behind to Gareth Cross in the 24th over before Muchall was rapped on the pads five balls later to leave the score on 94-3. That, however, was as good as it got for quite some time for the Lancashire attack, who chased leather until the end of the day.

Stokes is widely regarded as one of the hottest young properties in English cricket. Along with Yorkshire's Jonny Bairstow, Somerset's Jos Buttler and even Lancashire's Simon Kerrigan, the New Zealand-born player is one to watch. Unfortunately from Lancashire's point of view, it was the worst time to prove why.

A powerful and fearless left-handed batsman who bowls medium pace, Stokes turned 20 three days after this match finished, and he picked up an early birthday present in the form of a fifth Championship ton. He became only the second man in the history of the competition to post three figures five times before the age of 20. Denis Compton being the other.

An obvious statement maybe, but anybody who hits five sixes in one over, as he did against Hampshire left-arm spinner Liam Dawson earlier in the campaign, can take the game away from you in a flash. While he still played crisply on both sides of the wicket (particularly through the covers off the back foot), he batted with plenty of gumption against an in-form attack. That was highlighted by his reaching his half-century off 94 balls, exactly the same as Benkenstein did shortly afterwards. The pair's 185 and counting was Durham's highest partnership for any wicket against Lancashire in Championship cricket.

This was also the day that Farveez Maharoof and his Sri Lanka colleagues collapsed to 84 all out inside just 25 overs to hand England an improbable victory on the final day of the first Test at Cardiff (Sorry, Roofy!). With England selector James Whitaker sitting in the press box and, understandably, getting more and more fixated by events on the TV screens, you couldn't help but think that Stokes had picked the wrong time to perform. But, as all good players generally do, he still had something else in his locker with which to catch the eye of Whitaker. Against Steven Croft's off-spin bowling, he found the cover fence expertly off the very last ball of the day to reach his century and move his side within 34 of first innings parity with seven wickets still in hand.

Smith said: "Credit to Stokes and Benkenstein, they played very well. We had our game-plans to each batter, but they combated them quite well. We spoke before the game and said that we've played somewhere around 60 sessions of cricket this year and dominated nearly all of them. This wasn't our day, but we definitely created chances. It was a tough day, but we're fighters, we'll come back strong.

"When we rocked up on the first morning there was a green tinge to the pitch. It seems to have flattened out now, and is quite nice to bat on. But, on another day, we might have got a few more wickets because we beat the bat on a number of occasions."

> *"We spoke before the game and said that we've played somewhere around 60 sessions of cricket this year and dominated nearly all of them. This wasn't our day, but we definitely created chances."*
>
> **– Tom Smith**

CLOSE OF PLAY DAY TWO:
Lancashire 313 (PJ Horton 94) led Durham 279-3 (BA Stokes 100no, DM Benkenstein 67no, GJ Muchall 54) by 34 runs

DAY THREE

SOMETIMES you just have to stand back and applaud even though it may be through gritted teeth. Ben Stokes and Dale Benkenstein, at either end of their respective careers, put on a batting masterclass to take this game away from the Red Rose, sending records tumbling in the process.

Then, with their tails up, Durham's bowling attack prospered to leave Lancashire tottering at 69-3 from 25 second innings overs. Graham Onions removed Paul Horton and Stephen Moore, while Karl Brown fell to Callum Thorp. Horton fell in the day's penultimate over to round off what had been a pretty miserable day for him and his team. Born in Sydney, Australia and brought up in the leafy Liverpudlian suburb of Sefton Park, Horton generally grabs the headlines for his solid contribution of runs against the new ball season after season. It's his work in the slip cordon that has been just as important this campaign. Unfortunately, things didn't go quite as planned during this particular day.

Lancashire were hamstrung by five dropped catches, with three of them going to Horton at first slip either off the pace bowlers or the spin of Gary Keedy. Stokes gave chances on 84 (late on day two off Keedy), 108 and 167, and, while two of them could only be classed as half chances, Horton will have expected to take them.

The one late on day two, which thudded into his outstretched left hand, was followed 24 runs later by another sharp one off Keedy's bowling. This time the ball just hit Horton on his left shoulder before he could react. But the third, Horton should have grabbed. Luke Procter can count himself unlucky not to have had more success, and he was the victim as Horton failed to hold a ball that went straight in and straight out, showing that even the best make mistakes.

That came after Stokes, who finished with 185 off 272 balls, had slog-swept Steven Croft for the first of two gigantic sixes over the pavilion and into the car park at mid-wicket, the second coming in the same over he was bowled by the off-spinner. With Benkenstein already out, caught behind off Procter, that left the score at 461-5 in the 113th over. Ian Blackwell was bowled by Kyle Hogg shortly afterwards and Horton went some way to making up for his early troubles by pouching Scott Borthwick off Glen Chapple's bowling.

Phil Mustard (61 off 63 balls) and Thorp, dropped at second slip by Tom Smith off Chapple, then shared 73 inside 12 overs for the eighth wicket to further frustrate the Red Rose in good batting conditions, the former hitting three sixes. Smith did pick up the wicket of Thorp, caught behind, before Keedy had Mustard caught at short fine-leg by Hogg and bowled Mitch Claydon to finally end the innings.

How many times do you see it? One team makes batting look as easy as ABC before the other, having been flogged around the park, makes the same discipline look about as tough as Pythagoras's Theorem. Onions, in particular, was causing problems. He was keen to impress the watching James Whitaker now that he knew a place in the England team was up for grabs with Jimmy Anderson ruled out of the second Test against Sri Lanka with a side strain. And he did a pretty good job of it late in the day as Moore was pinned lbw on the back foot and Horton was caught behind off a bottom edge. Sandwiched in between was Brown's departure, lbw to Thorp.

The only downside of the day for Durham was a nasty injury to Stokes's right index finger. He failed to hold on to a full-blooded Horton cut at point, and it transpired that he would miss nine weeks, have two operations and a pin inserted. The blood stains on the pavilion steps were still there when Peter Moores did his post-day interviews.

Moores said: "If we can come out of this with a draw, it will feel like a win. It was a tough day, there's no doubt about that, but we've played good cricket all year. The team have got to find a way of batting three sessions.

"They've proved that you can put a partnership together. The odd ball is doing a bit, but you've just got to hope that you don't nick it. We knew that once we had got a session in, we were going to be trying to save the game."

CLOSE OF PLAY DAY THREE:
Lancashire 313 (PJ Horton 94) and 69-3 trailed Durham 586 (BA Stokes 185, DM Benkenstein 137, P Mustard 61, GJ Muchall 54) by 204 runs

DAY FOUR

LANCASHIRE'S unbeaten start to the season was ended as Durham moved top of the table with a clinical performance, wrapping up their fifth win of the season with close to two sessions to spare. Graham Onions and Ian Blackwell were their stars, sharing seven wickets between them to clinch the maximum haul of 24 points.

The Red Rose county succumbed inside 35 overs on day four, despite fourth-wicket pair Mark Chilton and night-watchman Gary Keedy resisting for close to an hour. But Chilton's departure was the death knell because he was the first of five wickets to fall for 22 runs, with the visitors slipping from 94-3 in the 39th over to 116-8 in the 50th. Paul Horton, out late on day three, top-scored with 34, while Chilton (25) was the only other man to make it into the twenties.

This was the third match on the spin that Durham had claimed 24 points, and it was understandable that they were immediately installed as title favourites by the majority of pundits due to the depth and quality within their squad. Neither Paul Collingwood nor Steve Harmison played in this clash.

Chilton was the first Lancashire wicket to fall on day four following a 15-over alliance with Keedy, failing to evade a rising delivery from Mitch Claydon and edging to Gordon Muchall at first slip. With the score still on 94, Keedy fell less than three overs later when he was enticed into attempting a slog-sweep by Blackwell's left-arm spin and was bowled.

Steven Croft and Tom Smith had managed to take the score beyond 100 by the time Croft was adjudged lbw to Onions, then Gareth Cross was bowled trying to cut a straight Blackwell ball, leaving the score at 109-7 in the 46th over. When Smith was the second man out trying to sweep Blackwell, caught at first slip by Michael Di Venuto, Lancashire were eight down and in tatters.

Luke Procter, unbeaten on 15, and Glen Chapple batted for close to eight overs to delay the inevitable until after lunch, with Chapple even top-edging and cutting Onions for a couple of boundaries. The game was up within 28 balls of the post-lunch resumption when Chapple uppercut Claydon to Dale Benkenstein at deep backward point and Kyle Hogg was bowled by the skilful Blackwell as Lancashire were dismissed for 148.

With the humdrum of the Friends Life t20 starting a little over 24 hours later, under lights against Derbyshire at the County Ground, this was Lancashire's last Championship outing for two and a half weeks. And, despite this defeat handing Durham a 17-point lead at the top of the tree (they had played one more match), anybody in their right mind would have taken five wins, a draw and a loss after seven matches had it been offered at the start of the season. A setback? Yes! A knockout blow? Pull the other one!

Chapple said: "We've played a very good team playing good cricket, and I think our standards probably dropped a bit as well. We need to brush up on some of the things we

> *"They're the best team we've played against all year, without doubt."*
>
> — Glen Chapple

did in this game and get back to how we were playing previously.

"We've got to take it on the chin because we were out-played. It was just that 10 percent in all areas. We still competed. The effort was superb throughout, but the quality of our bowling wasn't as good as it has been, mine included.

"It's one performance, one loss, and that's all. We're still confident because we've had a fantastic start to the year. You're not going to go through a season without losing a game. They're playing the best cricket at the moment. We had to come with our best game and we didn't do that. They're the best team we've played against all year, without doubt."

CLOSE OF PLAY DAY FOUR:
Lancashire 313 (PJ Horton 94) and 148 lost to Durham 586 (BA Stokes 185, DM Benkenstein 137, P Mustard 61, GJ Muchall 54) by an innings and 125 runs

Durham 24pts (Batting 5, Bowling 3)
Lancashire 4pts (Batting 3, Bowling 1)

LV= County Championship table June 1

	P	W	L	D	BaP	BoP	Pts
Durham	8	5	1	2	31	22	139
Lancashire	**7**	**5**	**1**	**1**	**20**	**19**	**122**
Somerset	7	3	3	1	22	19	92
Warwickshire∗	7	4	3	0	18	18	92
Sussex	7	3	1	3	13	16	86
Nottinghamshire	7	3	3	1	13	19	83
Yorkshire	8	1	4	3	18	19	62
Worcestershire	7	1	6	0	13	19	48
Hampshire	6	0	3	3	10	14	33

∗ Warwickshire deducted eight points for poor pitch

SCORECARD

Lancashire first innings		Runs	Balls	Mins	4s	6s
PJ Horton	b Stokes	94	176	210	15	-
SC Moore	c Borthwick b Thorp	4	6	8	1	-
KR Brown	c Di Venuto b Onions	4	11	11	1	-
MJ Chilton	c Di Venuto b Benkenstein	12	60	91	2	-
SJ Croft	c Di Venuto b Blackwell	38	90	114	4	-
TC Smith	lbw b Borthwick	32	65	68	5	-
+GD Cross	st Mustard b Blackwell	15	21	23	2	-
LA Procter	c Mustard b Claydon	45	77	94	9	-
*G Chapple	c Borthwick b Claydon	46	52	59	6	1
KW Hogg	b Blackwell	1	8	11	-	-
G Keedy	not out	0	0	1	-	-
Extras	(4 b, 8 lb, 10 nb)	22				
Total	(all out, 93.3 overs)	313				

Fall of wickets:
1-4 (Moore, 2 ov), 2-9 (Brown, 5 ov), 3-86 (Chilton, 28 ov), 4-158 (Horton, 54.1 ov), 5-191 (Croft, 60.2 ov), 6-215 (Cross, 67 ov), 7-225 (Smith, 73.3 ov), 8-312 (Chapple, 90.3 ov), 9-313 (Procter, 93 ov), 10-313 (Hogg, 93.3 ov)

Durham bowling	Overs	Mdns	Runs	Wkts	Wides	No-Balls
Onions	17	4	55	1	-	-
Thorp	15	2	47	1	-	-
Claydon	17	5	55	2	-	4
Stokes	14	2	64	1	-	-
Benkenstein	4	1	17	1	-	1
Blackwell	22.3	7	57	3	-	-
Borthwick	4	2	6	1	-	-

Lancashire second innings		Runs	Balls	Mins	4s	6s
PJ Horton	c Mustard b Onions	34	78	97	5	-
SC Moore	lbw b Onions	10	19	25	2	-
KR Brown	lbw b Thorp	6	15	23	-	-
MJ Chilton	c Muchall b Claydon	25	87	109	4	-
G Keedy	b Blackwell	12	45	72	1	-
SJ Croft	lbw b Onions	6	14	22	1	-
TC Smith	c Di Venuto b Blackwell	12	27	26	2	-
+GD Cross	b Blackwell	3	7	5	-	-
LA Procter	not out	15	44	48	1	-
*G Chapple	c Benkenstein b Claydon	13	16	22	2	-
KW Hogg	b Blackwell	0	8	10	-	-
Extras	(5 b, 2 lb, 4 nb, 1 w)	12				
Total	(all out, 59.4 overs)	148				

Fall of wickets:
1-19 (Moore, 6.2 ov), 2-30 (Brown, 12 ov), 3-69 (Horton, 24 ov), 4-94 (Chilton, 39 ov), 5-94 (Keedy, 41.2 ov), 6-106 (Croft, 44.2 ov), 7-109 (Cross, 45.4 ov), 8-116 (Smith, 50 ov), 9-139 (Chapple, 56.4 ov), 10-148 (Hogg, 59.4 ov)

Durham bowling	Overs	Mdns	Runs	Wkts	Wides	No-Balls
Onions	19	5	56	3	-	-
Thorp	8	2	24	1	-	-
Claydon	15	7	27	2	1	2
Blackwell	16.4	7	34	4	-	-
Borthwick	1	1	0	0	-	-

Umpires: MJD Bodenham & JW Lloyds Scorers: B Hunt & DM White

Durham first innings		Runs	Balls	Mins	4s	6s
MJ Di Venuto	c Cross b Chapple	6	8	9	1	-
WR Smith	c Cross b Procter	30	76	87	4	-
GJ Muchall	lbw b Smith	54	63	83	9	-
BA Stokes	b Croft	185	272	332	20	2
DM Benkenstein	c Cross b Procter	137	250	304	15	-
ID Blackwell	b Hogg	21	23	36	2	1
*+P Mustard	c Hogg b Keedy	61	63	108	2	3
SG Borthwick	c Horton b Chapple	6	20	19	1	-
CD Thorp	c Cross b Smith	22	42	45	4	-
ME Claydon	b Keedy	18	23	22	3	-
G Onions	not out	1	4	2	-	-
Extras	(9 b, 23 lb, 9 nb, 4 w)	45				
Total	(all out, 140 overs)	586				

Fall of wickets:
1-6 (Di Venuto, 2.1 ov), 2-90 (Smith, 23.5 ov), 3-94 (Muchall, 24.4 ov), 4-425 (Benkenstein, 108 ov), 5-461 (Stokes, 112.5 ov), 6-476 (Blackwell, 116.2 ov), 7-485 (Borthwick, 121.2 ov), 8-558 (Thorp, 132.5 ov), 9-585 (Claydon, 139.1 ov), 10-586 (Mustard, 140 ov)

Lancashire bowling	Overs	Mdns	Runs	Wkts	Wides	No-Balls
Chapple	28	7	97	2	1	-
Hogg	28	7	88	1	-	3
Smith	26	2	112	2	2	1
Procter	22	0	101	2	1	-
Keedy	28	2	101	2	-	-
Croft	8	0	55	1	-	-

Skipper Glen Chapple was philosophical about Lancashire's first defeat of the season

Luke Procter

AT the start of the campaign, Luke Procter just wanted to get a slot in Lancashire's one-day squad. By doing so, if he earned a call-up to the four-day side, then all well and good. But he did far better than even he could have hoped for. The 23-year-old finished the campaign having played seven County Championship matches, topping the club's batting averages and with a winners' medal on the mantelpiece. Procter also ended the season with a raft of new fans, with former England and Lancashire coach David Lloyd among them.

Procter is not your run-of-the-mill cricketer. He wears a diamond stud in one ear and has a tattoo of Jesus on his arm. He also has one of the most unusual bowling actions you are ever likely to see. Although it looks at first sight as if he is bowling off the wrong foot, he actually isn't. Many a coach has tried to tinker with it, but to no avail. In the end, as the old saying goes, if it isn't broken don't fix it, and it certainly isn't broken as he claimed some crucial wickets in the title race, including three during the first innings in the win over Warwickshire at Edgbaston.

"I bowl off the right foot but I jump off the wrong foot," explained Procter, who became a dad for the first time just weeks before the start of the season following the birth of his son Albie. "It's just natural to me and I've always bowled that way. People have tried changing it, and I can bowl just as well when I do change my action, but this way is just more natural to me."

Procter made his Championship debut in 2010 against Warwickshire as a stand-in for Jimmy Anderson, who was flying back from the Twenty20 World Cup at the time the game started but was allowed to take Procter's place when he landed back in England. Having sat out the first two matches of this season, he showed his talent with an impressive 89 in his first Championship knock of the campaign at Sussex and never looked back.

"At the start of the year I aimed just to get into the one-day squad and hoped that would give me a chance to get into the Championship side," said Procter. "I ended up playing seven matches and was over the moon with that. I also averaged 42. Before the start of the season I didn't really know if I was good enough to play at this level. There was a doubt at the back of my mind because I've only really played second team cricket. I didn't know if I was capable of making that big step up into first-class cricket.

"Peter Moores and Glen Chapple gave me so much confidence by first of all picking me to play in the side when there are so many good players in the squad, and then by sticking by me and keeping me in the team. It makes you feel like you're doing well when they do that and it gives you the confidence to carry on doing what you're doing.

"For the last game at Taunton they left out Mark Chilton – one of the most experienced players in the squad – and Sajid Mahmood, who has played Test matches and one-day internationals for England, and picked me. It was a great boost."

Procter admits, however, that he is still getting used to playing at the highest level in the domestic game. He said: "There were times just as I was going out to bat I remember thinking 'crikey, I'm facing Graham Onions here', or whoever it was I was facing, but once I got in and got relaxed, I didn't think about it. It was just a case of playing the ball as I saw it no matter who was bowling."

Procter started his career playing for Central Lancashire League side Oldham, following in his father's footsteps, before joining Royton when he was 17 and taking the job there as pro at 19. Having come through the Academy at Lancashire, he signed professional forms ahead of the 2010 season.

"My dad was a good player," said Procter. "He is over the moon about me being part of a Lancashire side which has won the Championship. My mum passed away last year, and up until then she used to watch every game, coming to support me. She was a big cricket fan and would have loved to have seen this.

"It feels brilliant to be part of the side which has finally won the Championship. People who I don't really know that well have stopped me in the street wanting to talk about cricket, saying they've seen me on the TV. It's mad really."

CHAMPAGNE MOMENT: *"Getting that last wicket against Hampshire with just four minutes left. I thought we had no chance of winning the game at that stage, and then we got the wicket we needed."*

Match 8

Nottinghamshire v Lancashire

(Trent Bridge, Nottingham) June 20-23

DAY ONE

HAVING already done it against Somerset at Liverpool and Hampshire at the Rose Bowl, Lancashire had proved that they could win without Glen Chapple. Now they would have to go and do it for a third time against the reigning champions because their captain had been forced to sit out close to six weeks with a mystery hip injury.

Chapple had been on the sidelines since pulling up whilst bowling in the North Division Twenty20 opener against Derbyshire on June 2, only returning in the same competition on July 15, three weeks after the visit to Trent Bridge. It was only then that he revealed the exact problem.

"The doctors said they have never seen a cricketer do it before," said the 37-year-old old explaining he had damaged something called the Iliacus. "But it's a muscle, and it has every right to be pulled."

> 'The Iliacus is a flat, triangular muscle, which lies deep within in the pelvis. It attaches from the pelvis to the thigh bone (femur). Its primary action is to flex and rotate the thigh. It is considered one of the muscles that make up the hip flexors; a group of muscles that bring the legs and trunk together in a flexion movement'.
>
> Dictionary definition, www.about.com

Step up Sajid Mahmood. The 29-year-old fast bowler had been on the sidelines himself for three weeks until shortly before the trip to Trent Bridge, suffering from a hip flexor injury of his own, but he had returned to action with a couple of encouraging Twenty20 performances, and it was clear that he was ready and raring to go.

He formed an impressive alliance with in-form Kyle Hogg, who had taken 12 wickets in his first two four-day appearances of the summer. The pair shared nine wickets on day one, with Mahmood clinching his first five-wicket haul since the previous April and only the eighth of a career which has seen him play eight Tests for England, including three in the famous whitewashed Ashes series of 2006/7.

Having reduced Notts to 138-6 after losing the toss, this looked likely to be a stunning day for the Red Rose. Alex Hales and Samit Patel both scored half-centuries, but Neil Edwards, Riki Wessels, David Hussey and Steven Mullaney all fell cheaply. However, there was a sting in the tail in the form of Chris Read, Paul Franks and Andre Adams, the trio helping to add a frustrating 188 runs for the last four wickets, including 47 for the last, to wrestle the momentum back during an enthralling opening day.

Notts' Achilles heel during the last couple of seasons has been their opening partnership. The fact that Franks, coming in at eight here, did the job the previous season pretty much tells you all you need to know. That continued because Hogg and Mahmood accounted for Edwards and Wessels within the first six overs.

Mahmood claimed the wickets of Wessels, Hussey, Patel, Read and Franks, lbw (the only man in the innings not out caught), harnessing hostility with accuracy on a pitch showing plenty of signs of uneven bounce, while Hogg was metronomic with his line and length, taking advantage of help off the pitch, mainly in the form of uneven bounce. He had Edwards caught behind by Gareth Cross, Hales (51) caught at short extra cover by stand-in skipper Mark Chilton and former team-mate Mullaney caught by Paul Horton at first slip to put the visitors in control.

> *"To come away with an economy rate just over five doesn't seem to do Saj justice. I thought he bowled a great spell after lunch in particular, and he was pretty fierce."*
>
> **– Mark Chilton**

Mahmood had Wessels caught at long-leg by Farveez Maharoof, Patel caught by Horton for 52 and Australian Hussey, making his only Championship appearance of the season, caught behind before the home recovery began. There were only three partnerships during the innings that topped 20. Having seen Hales and Patel share 88 for the third wicket, Read and Franks added a counter-attacking 135 inside 46 overs for the seventh. They hit 14 fours and a six between them to take their side within sight of 300, which had never looked likely just after lunch.

Within the space of five deliveries and with the new ball in hand, Mahmood returned and got Read caught behind for 58 with a sharp lifter (a carbon copy of Hussey's dismissal) and Franks lbw for an innings top-score of 69. When Hogg had Luke Fletcher caught and bowled, the 2010 champions had lost three in eight balls to fall to 279-9 in the 86th over, putting Lancs back in the box seat.

The only problem was that Adams, a notoriously fearsome striker of the ball, was still there with nothing to lose and a licence to thrill. As Lancashire subsequently found out, that is a potent concoction. The New Zealander battered five sixes on his way to 43 off just 27 balls in a little less than 40 minutes at the crease before holing out to Horton in the deep off Tom Smith to end the innings with Notts all out for 326. He was the main reason why Mahmood conceded 112 runs in 22 overs. Openers Horton and Moore had no problem surviving the final two overs left in the day's play.

Chilton said: "It was a good and bad day. I feel a bit deflated really because it's never a nice scenario to go through when somebody's smashing a few towards the end. A score of 280 or 290, we'd have been really happy with.

"To come away with an economy rate just over five doesn't seem to do Saj justice. I thought he bowled a great spell after lunch in particular, and he was pretty fierce."

CLOSE OF PLAY DAY ONE:
Nottinghamshire, having won the toss and elected to bat, 326 (PJ Franks 69, CMW Read 58, SR Patel 52, AD Hales 51; SI Mahmood 5-112) led Lancashire 7-0 by 319 runs

DAY TWO

PAUL Horton, Lancashire's unruffled opening batsman, wouldn't have known whether to laugh or cry at the halfway stage of this match after his 99 anchored a steady first innings display from the Red Rose side as they responded to the home side's 326. Horton, who scored exactly 2,000 Championship runs in seasons 2007 and 2008 combined, struggled to match that kind of consistency in the next two campaigns, but he had started well this time around.

The only problem was the lack of a hundred. Three times since April, including this, he had failed to convert scores in the nineties into three figures. His last Lancashire hundred had come against Essex at Chelmsford in 2010, although he had posted three hundreds during a winter spell in Zimbabwe.

Horton, understandably, loves to spend his winters abroad, going back to his native Australia to play grade cricket in Perth for the Gosnells club up until last winter when he decided to leave his comfort zone and take up an offer from ex-Derbyshire coach Dave Houghton to open the batting for the Matabeleland Tuskers in the ever-improving Zimbabwean domestic competition.

Despite initial fears about security, Horton loved his time in the troubled African country, both on and off the field. Off it, he enjoyed the beautiful scenery, the "lovely" people, and even said there were times when he had felt less safe in Manchester than he had done in Bulawayo. On the field, he prospered too, scoring his first two Twenty20 half-centuries and three first-class hundreds, including a career-best 209.

At Trent Bridge, meanwhile, his failure to raise his bat should not detract from what was a mightily impressive knock, accrued off 184 balls and including eleven boundaries and plenty of scampering between the wickets. Having faced two overs and taken seven runs the night before, he and Stephen Moore shared 82 in 27 overs for the first wicket, the pair taking advantage of some wayward bowling from Andre Adams, the competition's leading wicket-taker the previous season.

When Moore slashed seamer Luke Fletcher behind to Chris Read, it sparked a loss of six wickets for 115 runs to give the home side the upper hand in the early stages of the evening session. Karl Brown was caught at first slip by Alex Hales off Fletcher before Mark Chilton (24) dragged Paul Franks back onto his stumps, leaving the score at 146-3 in the 47th.

Horton had reached his half-century off 103 balls just after lunch, but he lost another partner with only 10 more runs added to the total when Steven Croft miscued the same bowler to Neil Edwards at short mid-wicket. Tom Smith followed, edging Franks behind shortly afterwards, with 174 on the board.

Then came the jaw-dropping moment of the day. The nearest Horton came to perishing was when he flashed hard at Samit Patel's left-arm spin and edged between wicketkeeper and first slip, but, with just one run required to celebrate his century, he nicked a probing delivery from Franks, the day's best bowler by a distance, behind to add a second 99 to his stats after the one against Essex at Old Trafford in 2005.

Farveez Maharoof and Gareth Cross quickly followed Horton back to the pavilion, both caught by David Hussey at second slip off Charlie Shreck and Fletcher respectively, to put Lancashire in danger of not passing 250. But fear not because Sajid Mahmood and Kyle Hogg, as they had done on day one with the ball, united with some effect to bat through until close to prevent any further alarms. They shared an unbroken 50 in eleven overs to clinch the second batting point and put a third within striking distance. They took advantage of the new ball being taken by hitting seven fours between them.

> *"There's not really that much difference between 99 and a hundred. I felt I deserved a hundred, but that's life. I may look back in 20 years time and tell my kids that I got a lot of nineties!"*
>
> **– Paul Horton**

It also became clear as the day went on that Notts all-rounder Patel, who had been called up to the England one-day party for the forthcoming series against Sri Lanka, would miss the final day of the game to link up with the squad for training at Bristol. Notts would be able to name a like-for-like replacement for day four, which ended up being youngster Sam Wood.

Horton said: "This is the third time I've made 90 this season, and people may look differently at you if you have three hundreds. There's not really that much difference between 99 and a hundred. I felt I deserved a hundred, but that's life. I may look back in 20 years time and tell my kids that I got a lot of nineties! I'd have settled for that at the start of the day.

"There wasn't a great deal I could do. Some of the balls have been unplayable. If it hits either side of a crack, it goes up your nose. That's part of this wicket. It's just a shame that I managed to glove it.

"It was a shame we couldn't push on earlier, but it was a good last 45 minutes. It's going to be an interesting game over the next two days. The wicket won't get any better. The cracks will open up as the game goes on, and the pitch will get more uneven."

CLOSE OF PLAY DAY TWO:
Nottinghamshire 326 (PJ Franks 69, CMW Read 58, SR Patel 52, AD Hales 51; SI Mahmood 5-112) led Lancashire 293-8 (PJ Horton 99) by 33 runs

Ten wickets in the match for Sajid Mahmood

DAY THREE

NOT for the first time this season, and certainly not the last, Lancashire were involved in another action-packed day of Championship cricket, which ended with them bang on course in their pursuit of a victory target of 237 against the reigning champions.

However, at the start of the day, Lancashire's first innings was quickly wrapped up for 306, a deficit of 20. Luke Fletcher completed figures of 5-82 from 25.4 overs by trapping Kyle Hogg lbw for 22 and forcing Sajid Mahmood to edge to David Hussey at slip for 46.

But, as they had done with the ball on day one, the visiting pair continued a productive alliance. They shared nine wickets to restrict the Notts first innings to 326, with Mahmood taking five of them. And that was exactly the same again during a thrilling third day.

Notts failed to cope with yet more hostile bowling from Mahmood – most evident when he sent David Hussey's off-stump cartwheeling – and yet more nagging accuracy from Hogg before the first of two rain delays after lunch helped them regroup and set up a tense fourth day.

Mahmood took three of the four wickets to fall before lunch, rapping Neil Edwards and Samit Patel (he could now stop off for lunch on the way to Bristol if he wanted) on the pads and doing Hussey for pace, while Hogg had Steven Croft to thank as the score was reduced to 40-4 in the 12th over. Alex Hales, who scored 51 in the first innings, absolutely murdered a short ball towards point, where Croft took the latest in his series of stunning catches.

Riki Wessels and Steven Mullaney steadied the ship, taking their side into lunch at 79-4, but that was most definitely the calm before the storm as three wickets fell for two runs in 13 balls immediately after the resumption, with all three of them going to Hogg. Mullaney and Chris Read were adjudged lbw, while Wessels was caught behind for 35 in between.

Continuing the theme of players who shone on day one doing it again on day three, Paul Franks and Andre Adams dug their side out of a huge hole, building on a lead that stood at just 100 with only three wickets in hand. Lancashire were soon on the back foot, struggling to cope with a tide that had suddenly turned.

Like a crazed lumberjack, Adams wielded and scythed his way to a 47-ball half-century that included three sixes – one off Hogg and two off Mahmood – and five fours, while Franks was more cautious as he continued to be a thorn in the Red Rose side. His innings top-score of 57 was the sixth time in his last seven knocks against Lancashire that he had posted 40 or more. The pair even took 22 off one Farveez Maharoof over, the 39th of the innings. Maharoof went through the match without a wicket.

A partnership of 119 in 19 overs for the eighth wicket was broken when Adams, trying to heave a fourth six, could only glove Mahmood through to Gareth Cross, leaving the score at 200-8 in the 44th over and his side with a lead of 220. Then came the day's second rain delay, which accounted for the loss of 16 overs, but this time it was Lancashire who benefitted.

After the resumption, Gary Keedy had Franks superbly stumped by Cross a little under four overs after Adams had departed, the ball spinning sharply through the gate. It was a cracking piece of work from Cross, the type that proves why he was rated as the best keeper in the country by the Professional Cricketers' Association come the end of the season. It was the only wicket of the match to fall to spin.

Then, with the score still on 216, the innings was wrapped up by Mahmood's fifth scalp, that of Fletcher, who skewed a short ball to Maharoof at mid-off. Mahmood finished with second innings figures of 5-74 from 14.1 overs and match figures of 10-186, only the second 10-wicket haul of his first-class career.

More importantly, it also set Lancashire a very gettable target, even though the pitch was still helpful. You could have argued a case for suggesting that either side was favourite to clinch

> "If you'd have said at the beginning that we'd be chasing 240 to win in a day and a bit whatever happens, we'd have taken it."
>
> – Kyle Hogg

the 16 points, but there were more erring on the side of the visitors come the end of the day as Paul Horton and Stephen Moore safely navigated the 13 remaining overs, reducing the target by 32 runs.

Hogg said: "That was the perfect ending to the day. Horts and Moorey batted really well because it was a very tough time to bat. Once Andre Adams gets going, as he's done in both innings, he can be quite hard to stop. He can make this ground look very small. If you'd have said at the beginning that we'd be chasing 240 to win in a day and a bit whatever happens, we'd have taken it."

CLOSE OF PLAY DAY THREE:
Nottinghamshire 326 (PJ Franks 69, CMW Read 58, SR Patel 52, AD Hales 51; SI Mahmood 5-112) and 216 (PJ Franks 57, AR Adams 52; SI Mahmood 5-74) led Lancashire 306 (PJ Horton 99; LJ Fletcher 5-82) and 32-0 by 204 runs

DAY FOUR

STEPHEN Moore had scored hundreds against the very best during his career, but a maiden Lancashire LV= County Championship century had eluded him for a season and a half since arriving at Old Trafford. Until now! As a Worcestershire player, he established himself alongside Michael Carberry as the next in line for an England Test place should anything happen to Alastair Cook or Andrew Strauss, partly thanks to a superb 120 for the England Lions in a four-day warm-up match against the touring Australians at New Road in 2009. The Aussie attack included Brett Lee, Mitchell Johnson, Stuart Clark and off-spinner Nathan Hauritz, but Moore combated them with 15 fours and two sixes in a 176-ball knock that was only ended when he edged Lee behind to Brad Haddin.

To be fair to Moore, he missed the second half of last season with a badly dislocated shoulder. He had already proved his worth with a number of eye-catching displays in one-day cricket, including a debut 40-over ton against Surrey at Whitgift School and a match-winning 20-over half-century against the old enemy Yorkshire. Even he would have agreed that he was due a three-figure score against the red ball. After all, he had only notched four half-centuries in 29 innings prior to this one since moving to the North West. Ironically, his last one was for Worcester against Lancashire at Old Trafford in July 2009 (he was bowled by Kyle Hogg for 107). It must have been influential in convincing Peter Moores to offer him a two-year contract that winter.

With the rain-filled clouds circling Trent Bridge, Moore and Paul Horton were quick to build a platform at the start of day four, the pair posting their second half-century partnership of the match. Moore had copped a couple of nasty blows on his right index finger from Luke Fletcher and Andre Adams late on day three, which forced him to spend part of that evening with his digits in a glass of iced water, but he was soon dishing out some of his own punishment in the form of boundaries. Having lost Horton, caught at second slip by David Hussey off Charlie Shreck's bowling with the score on 64, and Karl Brown, trapped lbw playing across the line to the same bowler, Moore provided a presence at the crease that gave all Lancashire followers confidence that their team were still on track. He reached his half-century before lunch, when Lancashire were 115-2, needing another 122 to win.

The game-breaker came immediately after lunch when, without adding to his 57, he was given a huge let-off by Riki Wessels, the South African who qualifies as a Kolpak thanks to a visa loophole. Wessels, formerly of Northants and the son of former Australia and South Africa batsman Kepler, can keep wicket, but he failed to demonstrate his catching prowess at deep backward point off the bowling of Paul Franks. It was a dolly!

Moore and Mark Chilton went on to score quickly for the next 45 minutes, the former even taking two fours and a pulled six off Luke Fletcher, and that was pretty much that. The pair added 90 inside 24 overs for the third wicket, taking the score to 176, before the latter was trapped lbw by Adams for 35. The pair may have just fallen short of a place on Peter Moores's wall for century partnerships, but this was just as important. If only Mooresy had a wildcard system!

> *"That hundred is going to be right up there with the best centuries I've scored, purely based on the fact that it was a fourth day wicket which was doing a bit and there was a game to be won."*
>
> **– Stephen Moore**

Another good partnership followed. Moore and Steven Croft shared 50 for the fourth wicket inside 15 overs, taking their side to within 11 runs of victory. Unfortunately for Croft, however, he was unable to see it through, edging to Hussey at second slip to hand Shreck his third wicket. Still, there was no need to panic because Moore, who had earlier brought up three figures off 185 balls, sealed the points as he finished unbeaten on 124. The only disappointment for the visiting dressing room was the confirmation of a docked point for a slow over-rate during the first three days.

Moore said: "To lose the toss and go on and win shows great character from the lads. The way we fought with the ball and with the bat was great. We're a team of very happy lads after that. There's a lot of cricket still to be played, but we're in a very good position now.

"There aren't many times when you get the opportunity to go out there to bat to win a four-day game. Thankfully I was the one in at the end and able to see the guys home. That hundred is going to be right up there with the best centuries I've scored, purely based on the fact that it was a fourth day wicket which was doing a bit and there was a game to be won."

CLOSE OF PLAY DAY FOUR:
Lancashire 306 (PJ Horton 99; LJ Fletcher 5-82) and 240-4
(SC Moore 124no) beat Nottinghamshire 326 (PJ Franks 69,
CMW Read 58, SR Patel 52, AD Hales 51; SI Mahmood 5-112) and
216 (PJ Franks 57, AR Adams 52; SI Mahmood 5-74) by six wickets

Nottinghamshire 6pts (Batting 3, Bowling 3)
Lancashire 21pts (Batting 3, Bowling 3*)
*Lancashire deducted 1pt for slow over rate

LV= County Championship table June 23

	P	W	L	D	BaP	BoP	Pts
Durham	9	5	1	3	36	25	150
Lancashire**	8	6	1	3	23	22	143
Warwickshire*	8	5	3	0	22	21	115
Somerset	8	3	4	1	24	20	95
Nottinghamshire	8	3	4	1	16	22	89
Sussex	7	3	1	3	13	16	86
Worcestershire	8	2	6	0	18	22	72
Yorkshire	9	1	4	4	18	21	67
Hampshire	7	0	4	3	11	16	36

* Warwickshire deducted eight points for poor pitch
** Lancashire deducted one point for slow over rate

SCORECARD

Nottinghamshire first innings		Runs	Balls	Mins	4s	6s
NJ Edwards	c Cross b Hogg	2	14	12	-	-
MH Wessels	c Maharoof b Mahmood	4	14	27	1	-
AD Hales	c Chilton b Hogg	51	87	100	8	-
**SR Patel	c Horton b Mahmood	52	92	133	4	-
DJ Hussey	c Cross b Mahmood	5	15	24	-	-
SJ Mullaney	c Horton b Hogg	5	9	6	1	-
*+CMW Read	c Cross b Mahmood	58	134	182	5	1
PJ Franks	lbw b Mahmood	69	156	172	9	-
AR Adams	c Horton b Smith	43	27	38	2	5
LJ Fletcher	c and b Hogg	1	3	3	-	-
CE Shreck	not out	4	13	31	1	-
Extras	(6 lb, 26 nb)	32				
Total	(all out, 91.5 overs)	326				

Fall of wickets:
1-4 (Edwards, 2.3 ov), 2-12 (Wessels, 6 ov), 3-100 (Hales, 27.5 ov), 4-117 (Hussey, 34.3 ov), 5-124 (Mullaney, 35.5 ov), 6-138 (Patel, 38.5 ov), 7-273 (Read, 84.1 ov), 8-278 (Franks, 84.5 ov), 9-279 (Fletcher, 85.2 ov), 10-326 (Adams, 91.5 ov)

Lancashire bowling	Overs	Mdns	Runs	Wkts	Wides	No-Balls
Hogg	22	4	75	4	-	4
Mahmood	22	1	112	5	-	5
Smith	14.5	2	51	1	-	1
Maharoof	17	1	55	0	-	3
Keedy	15	3	26	0	-	-
Croft	1	0	1	0	-	-

Nottinghamshire second innings		Runs	Balls	Mins	4s	6s
MH Wessels	c Cross b Hogg	35	71	98	6	-
NJ Edwards	lbw b Mahmood	0	3	6	-	-
AD Hales	c Croft b Hogg	1	11	13	-	-
**SR Patel	lbw b Mahmood	8	11	12	2	-
DJ Hussey	b Mahmood	13	16	16	2	-
SJ Mullaney	lbw b Hogg	18	24	40	3	-
*+CMW Read	lbw b Hogg	2	5	9	-	-
PJ Franks	st Cross b Keedy	57	88	99	6	-
AR Adams	c Cross b Mahmood	52	51	79	5	3
LJ Fletcher	c Maharoof b Mahmood	5	10	17	1	-
CE Shreck	not out	0	1	4	-	-
Extras	(8 b, 17 nb)	25				
Total	(all out, 47.1 overs)	216				

Fall of wickets:
1-4 (Edwards, 1.3 ov), 2-9 (Hales, 4.4 ov), 3-22 (Patel, 7.5 ov), 4-40 (Hussey, 11.4 ov), 5-79 (Mullaney, 22.1 ov), 6-80 (Wessels, 22.5 ov), 7-81 (Read, 24.1 ov), 8-200 (Adams, 43.1 ov), 9-216 (Franks, 46.5 ov), 10-216 (Fletcher, 47.1 ov)

Lancashire bowling	Overs	Mdns	Runs	Wkts	Wides	No-Balls
Hogg	12	3	44	4	-	-
Mahmood	14.1	0	74	5	-	6
Smith	6	1	30	0	-	-
Maharoof	8	1	46	0	-	2
Keedy	7	1	14	1	-	-

Lancashire first innings		Runs	Balls	Mins	4s	6s
PJ Horton	c Read b Franks	99	184	253	11	-
SC Moore	c Read b Fletcher	42	83	99	7	-
KR Brown	c Hales b Fletcher	10	18	21	1	-
*MJ Chilton	b Franks	24	49	50	3	-
SJ Croft	c Edwards b Franks	2	15	13	-	-
TC Smith	c Read b Franks	6	21	22	1	-
+GD Cross	c Hussey b Fletcher	21	101	106	4	-
MF Maharoof	c Hussey b Shreck	13	40	51	2	-
SI Mahmood	c Hussey b Fletcher	46	59	81	6	-
KW Hogg	lbw b Fletcher	22	44	54	2	-
G Keedy	not out	2	4	8	-	-
Extras	(9 lb, 4 nb, 6 w)	19				
Total	(all out, 102.4 overs)	306				

Fall of wickets:
1-82 (Moore, 27 ov), 2-100 (Brown, 32.5 ov), 3-146 (Chilton, 46.2 ov), 4-156 (Croft, 50.3 ov), 5-174 (Smith, 56.5 ov), 6-197 (Horton, 68.5 ov), 7-227 (Maharoof, 83.3 ov), 8-243 (Cross, 87 ov), 9-299 (Hogg, 100.4 ov), 10-306 (Mahmood, 102.4 ov)

Notts bowling	Overs	Mdns	Runs	Wkts	Wides	No-Balls
Shreck	22	5	65	1	1	-
Fletcher	25.4	3	82	5	1	2
Mullaney	1	0	1	0	-	-
Adams	17	3	69	0	-	-
Franks	22	4	50	4	-	-
Patel	15	3	30	0	-	-

Lancashire second innings		Runs	Balls	Mins	4s	6s
PJ Horton	c Hussey b Shreck	30	73	96	3	-
SC Moore	not out	124	208	280	17	1
KR Brown	lbw b Shreck	17	27	27	3	-
*MJ Chilton	lbw b Adams	35	78	91	6	-
SJ Croft	c Hussey b Shreck	21	51	49	3	-
TC Smith	not out	1	11	10	-	-
+GD Cross	did not bat					
KW Hogg	did not bat					
MF Maharoof	did not bat					
SI Mahmood	did not bat					
G Keedy	did not bat					
Extras	(2 b, 2 lb, 8 nb)	12				
Total	(4 wickets, 74 overs)	240				

Fall of wickets:
1-64 (Horton, 24.3 ov), 2-86 (Brown, 32.5 ov), 3-176 (Chilton, 56.2 ov), 4-226 (Croft, 70.4 ov)

Notts bowling	Overs	Mdns	Runs	Wkts	Wides	No-Balls
Shreck	17	5	54	3	-	-
Fletcher	18	6	63	0	-	3
Adams	15	2	62	1	-	-
Franks	12	3	33	0	-	1
Mullaney	8	1	16	0	-	-
Wood	4	1	8	0	-	-

Umpires: JW Lloyds & P Willey Scorers: LB Hewes & A West
** SKW Wood replaced SR Patel

Stephen Moore

WHATEVER else happens in Stephen Moore's career, it will be a struggle to top the first two weeks of September, 2011. He became a father for the first time when his wife Ruth gave birth to daughter Emilia, he scored a stunning 230-ball 169 not out in the penultimate match of the season against Hampshire and was then crowned a county champion after scoring two crucial half-centuries in the win over Somerset. It capped off what had been an exceptional season for the Johannesburg-born opening batsman, who scored 1,013 runs in the Championship and a total of 1,835 across all three competitions.

Moore's knocks of 124 not out against Nottinghamshire at Trent Bridge, which underpinned a tricky final day chase of 237, and the innings against Hampshire at Liverpool were the stand-out performances of his summer, but it was his absence from the second and final day of Lancashire's defeat against former county Worcestershire at New Road that got tongues wagging.

Moore left the ground before play started to head back to Manchester to be at the birth of Emilia. He's certainly not the first sportsman to make that decision and he definitely won't be the last. He has since admitted that, despite failing to make it back to the Midlands to play any further part in the game that Lancashire eventually lost inside five sessions, there was never any doubt in his or his team-mates' mind about what the right thing to do was.

He explained: "I still can't exactly describe what happened on that day because it was the most emotionally intense day I've ever had. It was a complicated pregnancy, and I actually missed the birth because Ruth had to have an emergency caesarian. I got there pretty relaxed, expecting the hard yards of a long labour, but I was handed Emilia as soon as I walked through the door. I wanted to know where Ruth was and was told 'you can't have Ruth, but here's your baby daughter'. In the space of 30 seconds I'd gone from being pretty calm to being in a completely different world. I didn't see Ruth for over an hour, even though I was told she was ok.

"After I'd seen Ruth, I got back in the car and kept getting messages on the hands free that we were two down, four down, seven down. I realised I wasn't going to make it when I was just before Birmingham and we were eight down. It was about Birmingham when I turned around. Everyone in the team was incredibly supportive. To me, that's another sign of a quality team, that they can put the happiness of one of their players before cricket, realising that there are more important things in life."

With his new and hectic circumstances in mind, Moore admitted that winning the Championship had still not sunk in, even when he visited Buckingham Palace in October. Even so, he said: "Winning it with Lancashire is such a special achievement. No matter what happens in the rest of my life, nobody can take that away from me."

Just 12 months earlier, Moore was left fearing for his career after badly dislocating his right shoulder in a nasty fielding accident during the Twenty20 quarter-final against Essex at Chelmsford. As late as February, he was still wondering whether he would make it back onto the field.

"Around that time, when I was chatting to our physio Sam Byrne, I was really worried about my throwing," he said. "My batting was coming on fine, but I just felt that my throwing wasn't progressing quick enough for me to get into the team. To be fair to Sam and the rest of the back-room team, their support was brilliant. They showed a lot of faith in me and built my confidence up when I was down."

Part of Moore's recovery saw him go to Abu Dhabi with Gary Keedy as part of the MCC squad to play in the champion county match against Nottinghamshire, in which he scored a useful 61. Having also played in the 2009 match against Durham, it will be third time lucky as he will finally be part of the champions' squad in the build-up to the 2012 campaign.

He added: "I remember me and Keeds were sat in our hotel room before the game and we were talking about what a great honour it was to be part of the fixture and how great it would be if we could be back here again next year with Lancashire. It will be a special feeling when that happens."

CHAMPAGNE MOMENT: *"To get presented with my county cap at the Player of the Year dinner was a special moment. It was a great honour and a surprise. The ovation the team received at the start of that night was something I will remember for a long time."*

Match 9

Lancashire v Durham

(Aigburth, Liverpool) June 27–29

DAY ONE

THERE are some days in the course of a season which just leave you scratching your head – this was one of them. With Durham top and Lancashire second in the table going into the game, most at Aigburth were prepared for a long, gruelling battle. What followed, however, was complete mayhem as wickets tumbled like confetti on a stunning opening day which left everyone breathless.

Lancashire suffered a double injury blow just before the match, with Tom Smith needing a scan on a knee problem and Farveez Maharoof suffering a stiff back and therefore missing his last Championship game before having to return to Sri Lanka to play in a domestic Twenty20 competition.

With Glen Chapple also facing another scan on a troublesome leg muscle injury which had seen him miss the previous match at Nottinghamshire, Junaid Khan was handed his first-class debut for the club. The Pakistan youngster, who was recommended to Lancashire by Red Rose legend Wasim Akram, had impressed all with his performances in the Friends Life t20 group stages.

Durham, on the other hand, had all their big-guns out. Their team was littered with internationals – Paul Collingwood, Graham Onions, Steve Harmison, Dale Benkenstein, Michael Di Venuto, Phil Mustard and Ian Blackwell. So crammed were they with big names that they couldn't find room for another former Test player in Liam Plunkett, who was 12th man. No wonder they were tipped as title favourites. In contrast, in the Lancashire side only Sajid Mahmood and Junaid had played international cricket.

Mark Chilton again captained the side in the absence of Chapple, but it didn't change Lancashire's luck at the toss as they were put in to bat by Durham. It proved to be a crucial toss as the Red Rose were skittled out for just 84 in only 34 overs. It was their lowest score in a first-class match for 14 years – since they were bowled out for 51 by Glamorgan at the same ground.

But that was just the start of the drama. Instead of feeling sorry for themselves, Mahmood hit back with the ball and his three wickets played a key part in Durham slumping to 61-6. Led by Benkenstein, the visitors recovered slightly, but were still all out for 186 as 20 wickets fell in the first 84 overs on the opening day.

It left all in the ground bewildered, including the ECB's pitch inspector, Peter Walker, who ended fears of a points deduction for a below par wicket by saying at the tea interval:

"It is as good a pitch as I have seen. How the best two sides in the country have struggled to put on 200 runs between them is baffling."

Only two batsmen reached double figures for Lancashire, with Stephen Moore's 27 the top-score as Callum Thorp made the most of the swinging conditions by taking 6-20, his best of the season. It could have been even worse for Lancashire if Durham's former

> *"I can't remember being involved in a Championship game where 20 wickets have fallen in a day."*
> **– Peter Moores**

England seamer Harmison hadn't added 16 to the tally through wides, 15 of them coming from three deliveries which all went to the boundary.

The Red Rose nightmare started with the third ball of the game as Paul Horton went lbw to Ashes winner Onions. Karl Brown was given a life when he was dropped on five by Scott Borthwick at third slip in the fourth over, but he didn't take advantage as he went without adding to that score by edging Thorp to wicketkeeper Mustard. Lancashire were soon 11-3 as Mark Chilton repeated the dismissal of Brown for three. Thorp and Mustard completed a hat-trick of dismissals with Steven Croft going for two and Lancashire were in deep trouble at 37-4.

While all around him were losing their heads, Moore was managing to survive and, amazingly in the context of the morning, smashed Harmison for six. Normal service quickly resumed as Luke Procter went lbw for four and Moore himself finally succumbed in the next over, with Harmison gaining his revenge by finding his edge and Mustard taking the catch.

Lancashire trudged in at lunch on 71-6 and in need of some lower-order resistance. They didn't get it. Thorp claimed his fourth wicket when Gareth Cross was caught by Collingwood at slip, and Onions comfortably took a catch off his own bowling after a top-edge from Mahmood. Junaid lasted just two balls before he was caught by Di Venuto and when Kyle Hogg was bowled to become Thorp's sixth victim, Lancashire were all out for 84, the lowest score they have ever made against Durham.

That was that, we all thought. The game was over and the visitors would soon be heading back up the motorway with a big points haul having extended their lead at the top of the table. Having been bowled out for 84, Lancashire had no chance of winning.

However, nobody had told the players that. Durham lost their first wicket to the third ball of their innings too as Hogg continued his impressive form by trapping Will Smith lbw. He struck in his next over too; this time Di Venuto failed to move his feet and was out lbw. Suddenly, the visitors were 8-2 and Lancashire smelt blood.

Mahmood claimed the key scalp of former England one-day captain Collingwood with his second ball, caught by Gary Keedy at mid-on. Junaid then claimed his first Championship wicket for the club as Gordon Muchall feathered the ball to Cross behind the stumps. Mahmood produced a beauty which swung in late to demolish Blackwell's stumps, and then claimed wickets in successive overs when Mustard was lbw for six. It left Mahmood with stunning figures of 3-9 off six overs and Durham on 61-6. At that stage, there was a chance that – astonishingly – Lancashire could even secure a first-innings lead.

Dale Benkenstein, however, had other plans. The Rhodesian-born South African international had hit 137 in the win over Lancashire just four weeks earlier, and he proved to be the thorn in their side again here. He took Durham in front with a 41-run partnership with Borthwick before Procter took two wickets in two balls, with Borthwick caught by Horton at first slip and Thorp by Chilton at gully as the visitors went into tea on 114-8. It ended a breathless afternoon session in which 12 wickets fell.

As the overhead conditions changed, batting became easier and Durham took full advantage, with Benkenstein and Onions putting on what proved to be a crucial stand of 79, which put the Championship leaders firmly in control. Procter finally broke the frustrating stand as Horton pulled off a good catch low down at slip to end Onions' resistance on 21, and Keedy claimed his only wicket of the innings by bowling Harmison.

Durham were all out for 186, a lead of 102, thanks mainly to Benkenstein's unbeaten 83. Horton and Moore then took Lancashire to 4-0 before bad light brought an early end to a remarkable day.

Peter Moores said: "It swung around, but I still haven't worked out why so many wickets fell. I can't remember being involved in a Championship game where 20 wickets have fallen in a day. The pitch was pretty blameless. We were put under pressure, there were a few indifferent shots and some decent deliveries, but when you are bowled out for less than a hundred you are disappointed.

"But we have kept ourselves in the game when half-way through the day it looked like we could be out of it. It takes a lot of hard work to come back from a deficit of a hundred, but it is the type of pitch you can do that on. We have shown we can score big runs, we have scored 450 here already this season. But we have a lot of work to do."

CLOSE OF PLAY DAY ONE:
Lancashire, having lost the toss and been invited to bat, 84 (CD Thorp 6-20) and 4-0 trailed Durham 186 (DM Benkenstein 83no) by 98 runs

DAY TWO

NOT many sides in the history of the LV= County Championship have come back from being bowled out for 84 in their first innings to win, but Lancashire spent the whole of 2011 proving people wrong. At the end of the second day of this table-topping clash with Durham an amazing victory was still possible.

The Red Rose batsmen put their first-innings woes behind them and dug in to give Lancashire a small, but defendable lead of 180. The bowlers then claimed three quick wickets in the final 10 overs of the day to leave the match on a knife-edge.

Stephen Moore, who was the top-scorer for Lancashire first time around, was the first wicket to fall in the second innings, but not before he and Paul Horton had put on 58. At the same total 24 hours earlier, Lancashire had six wickets down! Graham Onions was the bowler as Scott Borthwick took the catch at cover to end Moore's innings on 14. It was to be Durham's only success of the morning as Horton reached his fifth half-century of the campaign and, along with Karl Brown, guided the home side to 104-1 at lunch, a lead of two.

The leaders hit back in the afternoon session, however. Horton's hopes of a first century of the season were ended three overs after the interval when he was given out lbw to first-innings destroyer Thorp. The Lancashire opener was far from happy as he, and much of the crowd, were convinced he had got some bat on it. Brown followed him seven overs later, although he too thought he had hit the ball before being adjudged lbw to Ian Blackwell for 37.

Mark Chilton got a start, but he too was given out leg before, this time to Steve Harmison, for 23, and when Steven Croft was caught low down by Thorp off the former England bowler for 26, Lancashire were 179-5 and in a spot of bother. With a first-innings deficit of 102, it meant Peter Moores's men were effectively 77-5 and staring defeat in the face after just five sessions of the game. Having been 112-1, with two batsmen set and the new ball seen off, Lancashire would have been looking at a score of around 350. Now they were struggling to get 250.

But Luke Procter hadn't given up the fight. The youngster from Royton, playing just his 11th Championship innings for the club, defied his inexperience to put the pre-season title favourites on the back foot. He skilfully mastered the threat of both Onions and Harmison to give Lancashire hope with an impressive half-century, just his second for the club in first-class cricket.

Unfortunately, he couldn't find anyone to stay with him. Gareth Cross played on to an Onions delivery in the second over after tea for eight, and four overs later Sajid Mahmood repeated the trick to the same bowler, again for just eight. Then, with the second new ball due, Kyle Hogg was caught by Will Smith at short leg off a Borthwick delivery to leave Lancashire 243-8.

Procter was still there, however, and brought up his half-century, at last finding an ally in Junaid Khan, who stunned Borthwick by launching him into the pavilion for six. He added a second to his tally – although it came after he ran two and the return throw went for four overthrows, but every run helps in a tight game like this.

Luke Procter's impressive half-century was just his second for the club

> *"After getting bowled out for 84 many people would have expected the game to be over, but it shows if you bowl well you can create pressure."*
>
> **– Kyle Hogg**

Procter's battling innings came to an end in the 84th over when he was bowled by Thorp for 52. Lancashire were all out for 282 in the next over as Junaid's cameo was brought to an end when Onions, who finished with 4-74, sent his stumps flying. It left them with a lead of 180, which didn't really look enough in conditions that were completely different from on day one, but strange things can happen when teams chase low scores to win.

Durham had 10 overs left in the day to negotiate, and if you'd have asked any Lancashire player as they strode out to the field for the final 45 minutes, they would have been happy to sneak one batsman out before close. So they were over the moon when a shell-shocked Durham closed on 27-3.

A fired-up Hogg pounced in the third and fifth overs, trapping both Michael Di Venuto and Gordon Muchall lbw. Croft then enhanced his reputation as one of the best fielders in the country with a stunning catch at third slip off the bowling of Mahmood to send night-watchman Onions back to the pavilion. Amazingly, Lancashire were right back in what was an enthralling game, with Durham needing 154 more to win and the Red Rose seven wickets.

Hogg said: "I would back us to win this now. It is a funny game and we believe we can win from here. After getting bowled out for 84 many people would have expected the game to be over, but it shows if you bowl well you can create pressure. Pressure does weird things to people, makes them play shots they shouldn't.

"Every one of those batsmen know they are only one bad shot away from being out. Durham know now they are going to have to play very well and if they do win they will have worked very hard to do it."

CLOSE OF PLAY DAY TWO:
Lancashire 84 (CD Thorp 6-20) and 282 (PJ Horton 64, LA Procter 52) led Durham 186 (DM Benkenstein 83no) and 27-3 by 153 runs

DAY THREE

OVER recent years, Lancashire have prided themselves in being one of, if not the, best fielding teams in the country. In Paul Horton, Stephen Moore and Tom Smith they have a trio in the slips who you would back to take any catch, and with Mark Chilton and Steven Croft also having hands like buckets, batsmen are usually made to pay for their mistakes. But today of all days, it was Lancashire who were made to pay as two crucial chances went begging.

With the club opening the doors to the crowd for free, fans arrived at Aigburth prepared for another thriller. At 27-3, Durham still needed another 154 for victory to stretch their lead at the top of the table, but Lancashire's bowlers had developed a reputation in the first-half of the season for pulling a little piece of magic out of the hat when they needed to most to turn defeats into victories. Just ask Warwickshire and Yorkshire!

Sajid Mahmood and Kyle Hogg continually beat the bat in the early exchanges and gave Paul Collingwood and Will Smith plenty to think about. So when Collingwood edged a fine delivery from Kyle Hogg towards the slips in the seventh over of the day, it looked like yet another miracle was on the cards. Having been bowled out for 84 in the first innings, Lancashire looked like they were closing in on victory.

Just as Hogg was beginning to celebrate, however, the ball bobbled agonisingly out of Horton's hands and, almost in slow motion, hit the floor. If that catch had been taken, Durham would have been 49-4. Instead, Collingwood escaped and put on 58 for the fourth wicket with Smith before Lancashire finally got their man. This time Croft showed how it should have been done by pulling out a stunning catch at third slip to dismiss Collingwood for 45 as Luke Procter claimed a wicket with just his second ball of the day.

In his last two knocks against Lancashire, Dale Benkenstein had made 137 and an unbeaten 83, so the Red Rose knew what to expect from the former South African international, but they couldn't do anything about it as he slowly began to take the game away from Peter Moores's men.

They kept their hopes up when Gary Keedy struck with his second delivery, trapping Smith lbw for 30 to leave the visitors on 113-5 at lunch, needing 68 more to win. With 12 wickets falling in the afternoon session on the opening day, Lancashire still believed, but conditions had changed and in Benkenstein the Red Rose had an immovable force with which to contend.

In order to pull it off, Lancashire needed to hold on to all their chances, but they didn't. With Durham still 58 runs shy, Ian Blackwell skied an attempted pull-shot off Mahmood to long leg where Hogg was waiting with hands at the ready. However, and the player himself probably couldn't tell you how it happened, once again the ball bounced out and fell to the floor. With it went any hopes Lancashire had of winning the game.

Blackwell went on to finish off the match in sharing a 71-run stand with Benkenstein, who notched up several milestones on his way to his unbeaten 60 off just 89 balls. He passed 1,000 runs for the season just before reaching his half-century, and then as he creamed his seventh boundary of the innings to seal the win, he became Durham's highest run-scorer in first-class cricket. That's what you call an innings to remember.

The five-wicket defeat was Lancashire's second loss of the season, the only other one coming at the hands of Durham as well. It became obvious that if the Red Rose were to win the Championship, somebody had to take points off their rivals from the North East.

> *"We're still well in the hunt, there's no doubt about that. It's not a season-defining moment as far as I'm concerned."*
>
> **– Mark Chilton**

Chilton said: "We're still well in the hunt, there's no doubt about that. It's not a season-defining moment as far as I'm concerned. We've a game in hand and have won six games out of nine, so we're still in pretty good shape.

"The first day hurt us a lot but it allowed us to bowl at them in the same conditions and Durham found it difficult as well. We underperformed with the bat in the second innings. We should have made a more significant score having been 100-1 and having seen off the new ball on quite a flat wicket. All the top-six batsmen got in and reached double figures and other than Paul Horton no-one went on to make a significant score, which in previous games we have done."

Collingwood said: "Lancashire look a very solid side. We're obviously in a very good position, but we haven't won anything yet and they've got Glen Chapple to come back in."

CLOSE OF PLAY DAY THREE:
Lancashire 84 (CD Thorp 6-20) and 282 (PJ Horton 64,
LA Procter 52) lost to Durham 186 (DM Benkenstein 83no)
and 182-5 (DM Benkenstein 60no) by five wickets

Lancashire 3pts (Bowling 3)
Durham 19pts (Bowling 3)

LV= County Championship table June 29

	P	W	L	D	BaP	BoP	Pts
Durham	10	6	1	3	36	28	169
Lancashire**	**9**	**6**	**2**	**1**	**23**	**25**	**146**
Warwickshire*	8	5	3	0	22	21	115
Somerset	8	3	4	1	24	20	95
Nottinghamshire	8	3	4	1	16	22	89
Sussex	7	3	1	3	13	16	86
Worcestershire	8	2	6	0	18	22	72
Yorkshire	9	1	4	4	18	21	67
Hampshire	7	0	4	3	11	16	36

* Warwickshire deducted eight points for poor pitch
** Lancashire deducted one point for slow over rate

SCORECARD

Lancashire first innings		Runs	Balls	Mins	4s	6s
PJ Horton	lbw b Onions	0	3	1	-	-
SC Moore	c Mustard b Harmison	27	60	103	2	1
KR Brown	c Mustard b Thorp	5	20	26	1	-
*MJ Chilton	c Mustard b Thorp	3	22	20	-	-
SJ Croft	c Mustard b Thorp	2	16	23	-	-
LA Procter	lbw b Benkenstein	4	22	22	-	-
+GD Cross	c Collingwood b Thorp	8	29	24	-	-
SI Mahmood	c and b Onions	14	12	24	1	-
KW Hogg	b Thorp	1	7	17	-	-
Junaid Khan	c Di Venuto b Thorp	0	2	4	-	-
G Keedy	not out	1	7	6	-	-
Extras	(2 lb, 17 w)	19				
Total	(all out, 33.2 overs)	84				

Fall of wickets:
1-0 (Horton, 0.3 ov), 2-7 (Brown, 7.1 ov), 3-11 (Chilton, 12 ov), 4-37 (Croft, 17.4 ov), 5-52 (Procter, 23.3 ov), 6-54 (Moore, 24.2 ov), 7-76 (Cross, 29.5 ov), 8-82 (Mahmood, 30.5 ov), 9-83 (Junaid Khan, 31.5 ov), 10-84 (Hogg, 33.2 ov)

Durham bowling	Overs	Mdns	Runs	Wkts	Wides	No-Balls
Onions	10	4	19	2	-	-
Thorp	12.2	5	20	6	-	-
Harmison	7	2	37	1	4	-
Benkenstein	4	1	6	1	1	-

Durham first innings		Runs	Balls	Mins	4s	6s
MJ Di Venuto	lbw b Hogg	1	7	13	-	-
WR Smith	lbw b Hogg	0	2	1	-	-
GJ Muchall	c Cross b Junaid Khan	28	38	72	5	-
PD Collingwood	c Keedy b Mahmood	11	23	32	1	-
DM Benkenstein	not out	83	133	173	10	-
ID Blackwell	b Mahmood	1	4	5	-	-
*+P Mustard	lbw b Mahmood	6	11	10	1	-
SG Borthwick	c Horton b Procter	13	21	25	2	-
CD Thorp	c Chilton b Procter	0	1	1	-	-
G Onions	c Horton b Procter	21	55	89	2	-
SJ Harmison	b Keedy	0	5	6	-	-
Extras	(4 b, 10 lb, 2 nb, 6 w)	22				
Total	(all out, 49.5 overs)	186				

Fall of wickets:
1-1 (Smith, 0.3 ov), 2-8 (Di Venuto, 3 ov), 3-38 (Collingwood, 9.2 ov), 4-52 (Muchall, 16.1 ov), 5-53 (Blackwell, 17.1 ov), 6-61 (Mustard, 19.3 ov), 7-102 (Borthwick, 25.5 ov), 8-102 (Thorp, 26 ov), 9-181 (Onions, 48.2 ov), 10-186 (Harmison, 49.5 ov)

Lancashire bowling	Overs	Mdns	Runs	Wkts	Wides	No-Balls
Hogg	12	2	34	2	1	-
Junaid Khan	13	1	44	1	-	-
Mahmood	12	2	50	3	-	1
Procter	9	1	39	3	1	-
Keedy	3.5	1	5	1	-	-

Lancashire second innings		Runs	Balls	Mins	4s	6s
PJ Horton	lbw b Thorp	64	100	130	9	-
SC Moore	c Borthwick b Onions	14	48	70	2	-
KR Brown	lbw b Blackwell	37	74	85	4	-
*MJ Chilton	lbw b Harmison	23	42	50	3	-
SJ Croft	c Thorp b Harmison	26	39	42	4	1
LA Procter	b Thorp	52	105	133	8	-
+GD Cross	b Onions	8	44	47	-	-
SI Mahmood	b Onions	8	14	17	1	-
KW Hogg	c Smith b Borthwick	15	23	29	3	-
Junaid Khan	b Onions	16	13	22	1	2
G Keedy	not out	0	4	3	-	-
Extras	(14 lb, 5 w)	19				
Total	(all out, 84.2 overs)	282				

Fall of wickets:
1-58 (Moore, 17.2 ov), 2-112 (Horton, 33.2 ov), 3-136 (Brown, 40.3 ov), 4-160 (Chilton, 47.4 ov), 5-179 (Croft, 51.5 ov), 6-206 (Cross, 66.2 ov), 7-220 (Mahmood, 70.4 ov), 8-243 (Hogg, 79.2 ov), 9-278 (Procter, 83.2 ov), 10-282 (Junaid Khan, 84.2 ov)

Durham bowling	Overs	Mdns	Runs	Wkts	Wides	No-Balls
Onions	15.2	1	74	4	-	-
Thorp	15	4	53	2	-	-
Harmison	15	4	39	2	3	-
Blackwell	24	7	55	1	-	-
Borthwick	12	3	44	1	-	-
Benkenstein	3	2	3	0	-	-

Durham second innings		Runs	Balls	Mins	4s	6s
WR Smith	lbw b Keedy	30	96	143	4	-
MJ Di Venuto	lbw b Hogg	7	9	12	1	-
GJ Muchall	lbw b Hogg	8	9	14	2	-
G Onions	c Croft b Mahmood	1	5	6	-	-
PD Collingwood	c Croft b Procter	45	69	84	5	-
DM Benkenstein	not out	60	89	99	7	-
ID Blackwell	not out	26	46	75	2	-
*+P Mustard	did not bat					
SG Borthwick	did not bat					
CD Thorp	did not bat					
SJ Harmison	did not bat					
Extras	(3 lb, 2 nb)	5				
Total	(5 wickets, 53.4 overs)	182				

Fall of wickets:
1-11 (Di Venuto, 2.4 ov), 2-23 (Muchall, 6.1 ov), 3-24 (Onions, 7.1 ov), 4-82 (Collingwood, 27.2 ov), 5-101 (Smith, 33.2 ov)

Lancashire bowling	Overs	Mdns	Runs	Wkts	Wides	No-Balls
Hogg	15	2	51	2	-	-
Junaid Khan	14	3	46	0	-	-
Mahmood	15	4	40	1	-	1
Procter	4	0	11	1	-	-
Keedy	5.4	0	31	1	-	-

Umpires: MR Benson & SA Garratt Scorers: A West & B Hunt

Junaid Khan

JUNAID Khan may have only played one County Championship match – against Durham at Liverpool – but the left-arm fast bowler from Pakistan left the North West with his stock having risen through the roof.

At 21 years old and with a basic grasp of English, it was quite a surprise to see him take to Red Rose life like a duck to water, doing so well in the Twenty20 format that he drew a number of comparisons to club legend Wasim Akram. Wasim actually recommended him to Mike Watkinson, and the international went on to claim 12 wickets from eight T20 matches, including a best of 3-12 against Derbyshire and other match-winning performances against Northamptonshire and Warwickshire, which will live long in the memory.

"In his first game against Nottinghamshire at Trent Bridge, nobody really knew what he could do," said wicketkeeper Gareth Cross, who had the best view of his team-mate's trademark spearing yorkers. "We knew he could bowl a few slower balls and yorkers, but we didn't know how good he was.

"His performance was a bit mixed. He went for a few runs, but got a couple of wickets. We'd seen enough to know he was a good bowler, and that he would be important for us. He ended up being unbelievable, winning us four or five games. Even when he didn't get too many wickets, he could win a game for us on his economy rate alone."

Cross described keeping to the new Wasim as "an enjoyable challenge", saying the comparisons between the two are not wide of the mark. "I've obviously never played with Wasim, but the games you see on TV where he's going over and around the wicket to change the angle, it's something that Junaid does really well too," he added. "Give him a couple of years, and he'll be a more rounded player, someone who can play four-day cricket as well."

He only took one wicket against Durham, but there was far more evidence to suggest that the club's hierarchy should look to bring him back to Old Trafford in the future. Even Wasim has promised to do his bit: "This is the best county he could play for," he said.

Oliver Newby

OLIVER Newby is the answer to a quiz question that had Red Rose fans scratching their heads this season on the Manchester Evening News's Twitter feed. The question was: Who is the only member of Lancashire's current squad to have experience of a Championship-winning campaign? Answers were wide ranging, and even Newby's team-mate Steven Cheetham thought it was ex-Worcestershire batsman Stephen Moore.

Newby played two matches on loan at Nottinghamshire early in 2005. Now it is with great delight that we can rephrase that question: Who is the only member of the current Lancashire squad to have experienced TWO Championship-winning campaigns?

"I only played two games for Notts, but was there long enough to see what it's like when you're going for the title," said the fast bowler, 27. "Once you build confidence and wins come, little things start to go for you. It's infectious. At Notts, the lads were getting a lot of runs and the wickets were quite tough to come by. Here, the wickets have certainly come easier than runs."

Newby went one better this season, playing three matches. He played the first two against Sussex and Somerset at Liverpool before returning earlier than he thought from a hamstring tear to line up against Hampshire at the Rose Bowl in late May, taking eight wickets in total. Despite his involvement being minimal, the former Read man was highlighted by Peter Moores as a key factor in the opening week win over Sussex at Liverpool.

"I remember that game," said Newby. "Chappie was going for a few early runs, which is very unusual, but I managed to keep it tight and build pressure. I got Ben Brown, and there were wickets for the other lads. Chappie got five in the first innings and Keeds in the second. Although it's been a bit of a frustrating one personally, I've played a part in what has been a great season for the club. As I said to Mooresy, there's not a lot you can do if other lads are bowling well."

CHAMPAGNE MOMENT: *"You'll have to speak to Tom Smith. He's full of sayings that he's come up with. I believe he was asked how his hamstring was feeling and he said 'I'm on top of the moon'."*

Match 10

Yorkshire v Lancashire

(Headingley, Leeds) July 20-23

DAY ONE

WHAT do Toy Story 2 and Lancashire's LV= County Championship match against Yorkshire at Headingley have in common? The answer: they were both amazing sequels. At a guess, that wasn't the start to this chapter of the book you were expecting. Mind you, very little about the four days over the other side of the Pennines was predictable.

The fourth day of the Roses clash at Liverpool has been compared to an Oscar-winning Hollywood movie script and the return at Headingley, as sequels go, was just as good. Terminator 2, The Bourne Supremacy, Superman 2, even Shreck 2 get honourable mentions, as do the two Twenty20 encounters between the Lightning and Carnegie. Yorkshire may have come out on top of both of those mid-June North Division clashes, but they were memorable nonetheless, especially the low-scoring encounter at a packed Old Trafford. They both added to the buzz and drama as the plot thickened ahead of this crucial four-day meeting for both sides, who were now chasing completely different goals. While Lancashire were trying to rein in leaders Durham, Yorkshire were attempting to halt a surprise slide down the table.

There was also plenty of underlying tension between the two camps after the verbals between Jimmy Anderson, Joe Sayers and Andrew Gale, the Yorkshire captain, who even said in the lead-up to the Headingley clash that he felt Lancashire tried to "bully us" at Liverpool. Incidentally, Gale had cranked up the pressure on Lancashire at the start of the season, tipping them as relegation favourites in a TV interview.

Gary Keedy explained: "He was talking about Yorkshire really, saying that coming third the year before was a good platform to try and kick on from. He was obviously asked a question about how the rest of the clubs were going to fare, and he certainly tipped Lancashire to be relegated. I've played in a few Roses games, but these two were as spicy as I've ever been involved in. The history carried over from the first to the second."

Glen Chapple was back after recovering from his Iliacus problem, and having replaced Farveez Maharoof, he lost the toss and was asked to bat first under overcast skies. It was a brave decision from Gale, who was giving a Championship debut to seamer Iain Wardlaw, an unproven 26-year-old recently signed from his own Bradford League club, Cleckheaton. He would later drop out of the match when England chose to release Tim Bresnan from their squad ahead of the first Test against India at Lord's.

> *"It's as well as I've seen Crofty play. He was positive, he batted with the right tempo and put the bad ball away on a pitch where runs could be hard to come by."*
>
> **– Peter Moores**

Yorkshire made the ideal start when Ryan Sidebottom trapped Stephen Moore lbw for a four-ball duck in the third over, but Lancashire recovered to have the better of day one. Nine of their 11 batsmen scored 17 or above, with middle order pair Steven Croft and Tom Smith both scoring fifties. Paul Horton, Mark Chilton, Gareth Cross and Chapple all added useful contributions as the visitors closed on 304-7 from 85.3 overs.

After Moore's departure, Karl Brown was next to fall, slashing Sidebottom to Jacques Rudolph at first slip and leaving the score at 41-2, though the Red Rose reached lunch in reasonable health at 79-2.

However, there was more rebuilding work to be done shortly after the break because Horton edged Ajmal Shahzad behind to Jonny Bairstow six balls into the afternoon with only four more runs added. Chilton followed quickly when Sidebottom struck for a third time by forcing him to edge to Anthony McGrath at second slip, and that left the score on 116-4. It should have been 131-5 because McGrath, a former Lancashire target, spilled a chance with Croft on 25 and Sidebottom on the rampage. It allowed Lancashire's stand-in one-day skipper, who had just steered his side into the FLt20 quarter-finals thanks to a run of seven wins on the bounce, the opportunity to share a crucial 77-run stand with Smith for the fifth wicket inside 23 overs.

Croft was in determined mood, posting 54 off 108 balls. Smith, meanwhile, counterattacked his way to 51 off 81, with the pair hitting 17 boundaries between them. It was just unfortunate for Croft that when he fell to the ball before tea, losing sight of a Shahzad full toss, bad light was becoming an issue. It was clear Croft thought so, and he seemed to suggest as much to umpire Neil Mallender. The pair would reconvene in the umpires' room at close of play!

With Lancashire at 193-5 after 64 overs, the day could still have gone either way. When, in the space of six overs, Smith was caught behind as he cut expansively at Wardlaw and Cross was trapped lbw by Rich Pyrah, it looked as if Yorkshire were grabbing the initiative with their visitors at 251-7. Cue Sajid Mahmood and Chapple, who shared an unbroken 53 inside 10 overs to tip the balance before bad light finished the day's play two overs early. Mahmood even whacked his big mate Adil Rashid, the out of form leg-spinner, over long-on for six twice to end the day on a high.

Peter Moores said: "We played pretty well. The ball did something all day, but we did what we've done all season. We fought really hard and put partnerships together in order to build a score. We played some really positive cricket to get ourselves in a good position. It's as well as I've seen Crofty play. He was positive, he batted with the right tempo and put the bad ball away on a pitch where runs could be hard to come by."

CLOSE OF PLAY DAY ONE:
Lancashire, having lost the toss and been invited to bat, 304-7 (SJ Croft 54, TC Smith 51)

DAY TWO

THERE were plenty of stunning individual performances to reflect on during Lancashire's title-winning season, both for them and against them. Simon Kerrigan appears a couple of times with 5-7 and 9-51 against Warwickshire and Hampshire respectively, Stephen Moore's 124 not out to seal the win against Nottinghamshire at Trent Bridge is up there and Rikki Clarke's world record equalling haul of seven catches for Warwickshire at Liverpool is too. To that list can be added Rich Pyrah's 117 off 126 balls. There is even a very good argument for suggesting this knock would be top of the pops given the way this particular clash was heading.

Pyrah had spent most of his early career in the shadows of England's Ashes winner Tim Bresnan, but was having the season of his life to date, starring with ball and bat on a number of occasions. Having seen his team-mates slip into peril at a staggering 45-8 in reply to 328, he had the opportunity to further enhance his growing reputation.

With the help of team-mate Ryan Sidebottom, Pyrah did exactly that with devastating effect from number nine, smashing 12 fours and three sixes to help post a respectable first innings score of 239. It still may have amounted to a deficit of 89, but it shifted the momentum of the contest dramatically.

It was quite ironic that his knock came 30 years to the day after the 1981 Headingley Test match when Ian Botham and Bob Willis fashioned their legendary fightback against Australia. Sidebottom played the role of the late Graham Dilley, compiling 52 to share in a partnership of 100 or more for the second week in a row.

In all, Pyrah and Sidebottom added 154 in 30 overs for the ninth wicket, which preceded a last-wicket stand of 40 between Pyrah and Bresnan, who had made it back from Lord's just in the nick of time. Bresnan was at the crease when Pyrah reached a maiden Championship ton off 92 balls, including sixes off Tom Smith, Kyle Hogg and Glen Chapple.

On any other normal day, the headlines would have all been about Kyle Hogg, who claimed five wickets in his first seven overs with the new ball to demolish Yorkshire's top order in the blink of an eye. After Lancashire had added 24 more runs to their overnight total of 304-7, of which Hogg scored 17, he put his side bang on course for win number seven.

His first victim was Joe Root caught behind by Gareth Cross with the seventh delivery of his first over, the sixth having been a no-ball, leaving the score at 3-1. Next came the massive wicket of Jacques Rudolph, caught in the gully by Mark Chilton seven and a half overs later. It was the first of two in two balls because Andrew Gale was trapped lbw for a golden duck. 22-3 in the 10th over soon became 32-5 in the 14th when Jonny Bairstow and Gary Ballance also fell in successive balls, both rapped on their pads, the latter playing no stroke.

> *"To bowl them out for 230-odd, we'd have taken that. It was just disappointing after having them in trouble. Sometimes though, you've just got to say 'well played'. You've got to give credit to Sidebottom and Pyrah."*
>
> – Kyle Hogg

At that stage, it was threatening to be a two-day massacre. That belief was only strengthened either side of lunch when Adil Rashid departed lbw to Smith, Ajmal Shahzad edged Sajid Mahmood behind and Anthony McGrath loosely drove the same bowler to a diving Smith at second slip, but that wicket brought Sidebottom and Pyrah together to change the course of the day, also perking up their skipper Gale in the process.

One of the images that will remain long in the memory was of Gale slumped in a chair on the balcony of the new Carnegie Pavilion at Headingley for at least an hour with his head in his hands. His mood was about to change thanks to two hours of mayhem. Pyrah and Sidebottom's stand, the highest for the ninth wicket in Championship cricket on this ground, was broken when the latter was adjudged in front off Chapple in the 54th over, leaving the score at 199-9 with the follow-on saved. The innings was wrapped up 40 runs later when Pyrah fell to Smith.

When Lancashire began their second innings, the action continued at pace. Not surprisingly to a degree, the visitors continued to be frustrated, losing three wickets at a cost of just 33 runs. Paul Horton and Stephen Moore were both caught at second slip by McGrath off Bresnan to leave the Red Rose on 3-2 in the fifth over. When Karl Brown was caught behind by Bairstow off Shahzad at the start of the day's last over, Lancashire still held the advantage with a lead of 122, but only just!

Hogg said: "To bowl them out for 230-odd, we'd have taken that. It was just disappointing after having them in trouble. Sometimes though, you've just got to say 'well played'. You've got to give credit to Sidebottom and Pyrah

"We'd have loved to have gone in two down, but these things happen. We'll still come out fighting in the morning. As it showed in our innings, it becomes a lot easier to bat when you get through the new ball. With the new ball, you feel like you're going to get a wicket every over. With the old ball, I don't think we looked like getting Sidebottom and Pyrah out."

CLOSE OF PLAY DAY TWO:
Lancashire 328 (SJ Croft 54, TC Smith 51) and 33-3 led Yorkshire 239 (RM Pyrah 117, RJ Sidebottom 52; KW Hogg 5-62) by 122 runs

DAY THREE

THIS fixture clashed with the opening match of the Test series between England and India at Lord's, which would decide who would be the world's number one ranked side at the end of the summer. It was a hotly anticipated contest from Bombay to Blackburn. For some, there was nothing that could compare. Followers of Lancashire and Yorkshire would disagree wholeheartedly. You couldn't have given some of them a price to swap Headingley for Lord's during this particular week of the summer as stunning performances with both bat and ball contributed to the pendulum swinging this way and that. This was a Roses classic for the second match running!

Lancashire ended day three knowing they were in pole position to win yet again, needing just four more wickets for the concession of less than 147 runs, having reduced the hosts to 136-6 in their pursuit of 284. There were times, however, when their grip on the contest was loose to say the least. Starting the day at 33-3 in their second innings and leading by 122, Lancashire slipped to 87-8 inside another 28 overs as Tim Bresnan, Rich Pyrah and Ryan Sidebottom all struck, with Pyrah the pick of the morning bowlers with two wickets.

Having smashed a special hundred 24 hours earlier, Pyrah trapped Mark Chilton lbw and had Glen Chapple caught behind by Jonny Bairstow. Bresnan bowled Steven Croft and had Gareth Cross lbw, while Tom Smith fell the same way to Sidebottom. Still, there

Sajid Mahmood turns Tim Bresnan to fine-leg. Mahmood's enterprising 80-run stand with Kyle Hogg turned this pulsating contest back Lancashire's way

was a twist. Sajid Mahmood and Kyle Hogg shared numerous crucial partnerships through the season, and this was one of them. Having seen Pyrah and Sidebottom share 154 for the ninth wicket in Yorkshire's first innings, they followed suit.

The pair, taking advantage of a life for Mahmood on 23, dropped by Bresnan at third slip off Sidebottom's bowling, turned the tables with an entertaining stand of 80 in 15 and a half overs to boost a flimsy looking lead of 176 to a healthy one of 256 with two wickets in hand. They hit 16 fours and a six between them. Four of Mahmood's boundaries even came off successive balls during a Sidebottom over that went for 18, while Hogg swatted Ajmal Shahzad over the ropes.

> *"Six down looks good on the scoreboard. They're under a lot of pressure. I wouldn't want to be in their dressing room at the moment."*
>
> **– Sajid Mahmood**

Gary Keedy, who would have his say with the ball later in the day, also contributed following Mahmood's departure, bowled by Adil Rashid for 50 off 51 balls, with three off 30 balls. It may not look much, but it was part of a 27-run last-wicket stand with Hogg, who was run out for 52 off 67 balls to end the innings at 194.

Yorkshire made a solid start to their chase, with Jacques Rudolph looking dangerous as he shared 41 for the first wicket with opening partner Joe Root, the young right-hander who bears more than a passing resemblance to fellow Sheffield resident Michael Vaughan. It was Root who handed Lancashire their first wicket when he edged a Chapple out-swinger to Paul Horton at first slip. Rudolph and Anthony McGrath then added another 39 to boost their side's hopes, reaching 80-1 in the 21st over. However, those hopes were short-lived because the pair fell in the space of four balls, leaving the score at 84-3 in the 22nd. It was no surprise that Hogg and Mahmood were in the thick of the action, the former getting McGrath lbw and the latter getting Rudolph in identical fashion for 35.

Chapple bowled Bairstow with 118 on the board shortly after play had resumed following a short rain delay, and when Keedy had Gary Ballance caught at silly point by Tom Smith 10 balls later, it looked like it was game over for the hosts at 119-5. Bresnan's departure, caught at second slip by Smith off Chapple, stiffened the hosts' task with them at 134-6 in the day's penultimate over and needing another 150 to win only their third match of the season.

We should have known better than to write this contest off. After all, captain Andrew Gale was still in on 28 at the close, while Sidebottom, Rashid, Shahzad and Pyrah, the first innings centurion who had been demoted to number eleven, were either not out or yet to bat. Even so, Lancashire were in charge and sniffing a famous Roses double. If claimed, it would be the first since 1989 when the likes of Mike Atherton, Wasim Akram, Gehan Mendis, Neil Fairbrother, Dexter Fitton and Graeme Fowler all starred in wins at Old Trafford and Scarborough's North Marine Road.

Keedy said: "For Saj and Hoggy to put some runs on, then myself and Hoggy to chip in at the end, was crucial. The difference between chasing 200 and 280 is massive."

Mahmood said: "Six down looks good on the scoreboard. They're under a lot of pressure. I wouldn't want to be in their dressing room at the moment. We need to build pressure and get the ball in the right areas. Hopefully it will keep swinging for us."

CLOSE OF PLAY DAY THREE:
Lancashire 328 (SJ Croft 54, TC Smith 51) and 194 (KW Hogg 52, SI Mahmood 50) led Yorkshire 239 (RM Pyrah 117, RJ Sidebottom 52; KW Hogg 5-62) and 136-6 by 147 runs

DAY FOUR

EXPECT the unexpected is a phrase that goes hand in glove with the Lancashire versus Yorkshire clashes of 2011, and this was no different as the Red Rose sneaked home amidst yet more drama at Headingley to close the gap between themselves and Division One leaders Durham. Glen Chapple's side clinched a seventh win from 10 matches, something which the county had never achieved before at this stage of the season, by the skin of their teeth as Yorkshire's tail fought like tigers to pull this one out of the fire.

Defending a target of 284, which had been reduced to 148 with only four Yorkshire wickets left at the start of the day, the visitors were made to work hard as Adil Rashid and Ajmal Shahzad contributed to a tense and fascinating finale. This may not quite have been as nail-biting as the one at Aigburth earlier in the season, but it wasn't far off as Chapple and company sealed the win by 23 runs in the early stages of the final afternoon, sparking the majority of the Lancashire side to pile on Gary Keedy in the middle of the pitch after he had trapped first innings centurion Rich Pyrah lbw for 14.

Chapple was the Red Rose county's stand-out performer, finishing with 5-71 from 26 overs. Three of his wickets had been claimed on day three, and he added Ryan Sidebottom and Andrew Gale to the list the following morning. Sidebottom fell in the seventh over of the day when he was caught at second slip by Tom Smith, leaving the score at 164-7 in the 48th over. Left-handed Gale (47) then fell exactly four overs later when he became the 13th man in the match to be given out lbw, although he will count himself rather unfortunate as the inside edge of his bat seemed to play a part.

At that stage, Yorkshire were really under the cosh at 177-8, but it was no surprise when the ninth-wicket partnership flourished for a third time in the match to keep home hopes alive. Rashid, who top-scored with 48, and Shahzad (22) shared 53 inside 16 overs to take their side within 54 of a famous come-from-behind victory. Both are noted strikers of the ball and they managed to find the boundary rope 12 times between them. The pressure of the situation was telling, however, as they went through a spell of only scoring two runs in 29 balls against Kyle Hogg and Sajid Mahmood. Shahzad hit four boundaries in total, but perished trying to hook a fifth off a Hogg short ball, gloving behind to Gareth Cross. Yorkshire went into lunch at 244-9, needing another 40 runs from two sessions with just one wicket in hand.

Pyrah, relegated to number eleven following Bresnan's return from England duty and Sidebottom's employment as a night-watchman, hit a couple of fours after the break, but in the sixth over after lunch was struck on the pads by Keedy as he played back, stuck on the crease. Lancashire had pulled off a crucial victory, and their players knew it. They all dived on wicket-taker Keedy, which further angered the home camp.

Hogg takes up the story: "Bresnan tweeted something about our celebrations at the end, 'gracious Lancashire' or

> *"It was an unbelievable game. It took a different path to most games because the tail-enders came up with the goods. It was a struggle to bowl at the tail, especially Yorkshire's. I've never seen a team that bats that deep before."*
>
> **– Glen Chapple**

something (The exact tweet was 'Lancs gracious winners as ever!?'), but we were saying that they'd have done exactly the same. It wasn't as if we were rubbing their faces in it. To get a win the way we did, we had every right to be happy.

"There was a lot of abuse flying around from the stands that week. There were a lot of idiots there abusing us. It was getting worse the more and more they believed their side was going to win. When we got our wickets quickly, it kept a few of them quiet. The thing with Championship cricket is that because there's not thousands of spectators there, you can hear absolutely everything."

Tension or no tension, Lancashire had pulled off yet another incredible win, moving to within just a point of leaders Durham. Incidentally, Lancashire had a CB40 match against the Unicorns at Colwyn Bay to play the following day, so Steven Croft had to drop Mahmood, not involved in the Welsh trip, off at Birch Services on the M62. In getting out of Crofty's car, Saj picked up the wrong kitbag. It left Crofty with only Saj's gear to use the following day. He notched 59 not out off 51 balls, including five fours and three sixes as the Lightning chased down 180 with eight wickets and 12 overs to spare!

On the match itself, Chapple said: "It was an unbelievable game. It took a different path to most games because the tail-enders came up with the goods. It was a struggle to bowl at the tail, especially Yorkshire's. I've never seen a team that bats that deep before.

"On the evidence of the first three days, it was set up for the tail-enders to make hay when the ball got soft, but we knew it was slightly in our favour. You get it down to 26 or 27 or whatever it was, and it could have gone either way. We stuck to our task and kept believing."

CLOSE OF PLAY DAY FOUR:
Lancashire 328 (SJ Croft 54, TC Smith 51) and 194
(KW Hogg 52, SI Mahmood 50) beat Yorkshire 239 (RM Pyrah 117,
RJ Sidebottom 52; KW Hogg 5-62) and 260 (G Chapple 5-71)
by 23 runs

Yorkshire 4pts (Batting 1, Bowling 3)
Lancashire 22pts (Batting 3, Bowling 3)

LV= County Championship table July 23

	P	W	L	D	BaP	BoP	Pts
Durham	10	6	1	3	36	28	169
Lancashire∗∗	**10**	**7**	**2**	**1**	**26**	**28**	**168**
Warwickshire∗	10	7	3	0	29	27	160
Sussex	10	4	3	3	18	23	114
Nottinghamshire	10	3	4	3	21	28	106
Somerset	9	3	4	2	28	22	104
Yorkshire+	11	2	5	4	23	27	92
Worcestershire	9	2	7	0	18	25	75
Hampshire++	9	0	5	4	13	22	39

∗ Warwickshire deducted eight points for poor pitch
∗∗ Lancashire deducted one point for slow over rate
+ Yorkshire deducted two points for slow over rate
++ Hampshire deducted eight points for poor pitch

SCORECARD

Lancashire first innings		Runs	Balls	Mins	4s	6s
PJ Horton	c Bairstow b Shahzad	36	92	126	4	-
SC Moore	lbw b Sidebottom	0	4	11	-	-
KR Brown	c Rudolph b Sidebottom	22	33	40	5	-
MJ Chilton	c McGrath b Sidebottom	33	89	118	5	-
SJ Croft	b Shahzad	54	108	130	8	-
TC Smith	c Bairstow b Wardlaw	51	81	117	9	-
+GD Cross	lbw b Pyrah	30	38	58	6	-
*G Chapple	run out	30	64	74	4	-
SI Mahmood	b Shahzad	27	22	38	2	2
KW Hogg	c Bairstow b Sidebottom	17	15	23	4	-
G Keedy	not out	1	8	11	-	-
Extras	(13 b, 14 lb)	27				
Total	(all out, 92.2 overs)	328				

Fall of wickets:
1-7 (Moore, 2.4 ov), 2-41 (Brown, 13 ov), 3-83 (Horton, 31.2 ov), 4-116 (Chilton, 41.5 ov), 5-193 (Croft, 64 ov), 6-235 (Smith, 72.1 ov), 7-251 (Cross, 77.4 ov), 8-305 (Mahmood, 87.1 ov), 9-314 (Chapple, 89.3 ov), 10-328 (Hogg, 92.2 ov)

Yorkshire bowling	Overs	Mdns	Runs	Wkts	Wides	No-Balls
Sidebottom	22.2	4	68	4	-	-
Wardlaw	13	0	68	1	-	-
Shahzad	24	4	61	3	-	-
Pyrah	22	7	51	1	-	-
Rashid	11	2	53	0	-	-

Lancashire second innings		Runs	Balls	Mins	4s	6s
PJ Horton	c McGrath b Bresnan	2	13	10	-	-
SC Moore	c McGrath b Bresnan	0	10	19	-	-
KR Brown	c Bairstow b Shahzad	27	48	48	4	-
MJ Chilton	lbw b Pyrah	10	49	87	1	-
SJ Croft	b Bresnan	8	37	36	1	-
TC Smith	lbw b Sidebottom	4	32	48	-	-
+GD Cross	lbw b Bresnan	19	48	66	1	-
*G Chapple	c Bairstow b Pyrah	5	5	5	1	-
SI Mahmood	b Rashid	50	51	84	6	-
KW Hogg	run out	52	67	87	8	1
G Keedy	not out	3	30	25	-	-
Extras	(5 b, 9 lb)	14				
Total	(all out, 65 overs)	194				

Fall of wickets:
1-2 (Horton, 2.4 ov), 2-3 (Moore, 4.4 ov), 3-33 (Brown, 15.1 ov), 4-50 (Croft, 24.5 ov), 5-50 (Chilton, 27.2 ov), 6-66 (Smith, 36.1 ov), 7-71 (Chapple, 37.3 ov), 8-87 (Cross, 42.3 ov), 9-167 (Mahmood, 57.5 ov), 10-194 (Hogg, 65 ov)

Yorkshire bowling	Overs	Mdns	Runs	Wkts	Wides	No-Balls
Bresnan	24	8	50	4	-	-
Sidebottom	12	2	54	1	-	-
Shahzad	13	4	47	1	-	-
Pyrah	11	4	26	2	-	-
Rashid	4	3	2	1	-	-
Root	1	0	1	0	-	-

Yorkshire first innings		Runs	Balls	Mins	4s	6s
JE Root	c Cross b Hogg	0	11	9	-	-
JA Rudolph	c Chilton b Hogg	12	26	39	2	-
A McGrath	c Smith b Mahmood	15	56	93	2	-
*AW Gale	lbw b Hogg	0	1	1	-	-
+JM Bairstow	lbw b Hogg	7	14	18	1	-
GS Ballance	lbw b Hogg	0	1	1	-	-
AU Rashid	lbw b Smith	3	12	10	-	-
A Shahzad	c Cross b Mahmood	4	10	15	1	-
RM Pyrah	c Chilton b Smith	117	126	179	12	3
RJ Sidebottom	lbw b Chapple	52	103	115	7	-
**TT Bresnan	not out	19	53	52	3	-
Extras	(8 lb, 2 nb)	10				
Total	(all out, 68.4 overs)	239				

Fall of wickets:
1-3 (Root, 2 ov), 2-22 (Rudolph, 9.2 ov), 3-22 (Gale, 9.3 ov), 4-32 (Bairstow, 13.5 ov), 5-32 (Ballance, 14 ov), 6-35 (Rashid, 17 ov), 7-44 (Shahzad, 21.1 ov), 8-45 (McGrath, 23.2 ov), 9-199 (Sidebottom, 53.2 ov), 10-239 (Pyrah, 68.4 ov)

Lancashire bowling	Overs	Mdns	Runs	Wkts	Wides	No-Balls
Chapple	16	4	43	1	-	-
Hogg	15	1	62	5	-	1
Smith	10.4	5	24	2	-	-
Mahmood	14	1	64	2	-	-
Keedy	13	2	38	0	-	-

Yorkshire second innings		Runs	Balls	Mins	4s	6s
JA Rudolph	lbw b Mahmood	35	52	91	5	-
JE Root	c Horton b Chapple	14	38	47	1	-
A McGrath	lbw b Hogg	19	37	38	3	-
*AW Gale	lbw b Chapple	47	83	117	5	-
+JM Bairstow	b Chapple	16	35	40	2	-
GS Ballance	c Smith b Keedy	0	5	7	-	-
**TT Bresnan	c Smith b Chapple	11	18	20	2	-
RJ Sidebottom	c Smith b Chapple	16	28	27	3	-
AU Rashid	not out	48	87	113	8	-
A Shahzad	c Cross b Hogg	22	55	64	4	-
RM Pyrah	lbw b Keedy	14	26	30	2	-
Extras	(1 b, 10 lb, 6 nb, 1 w)	18				
Total	(all out, 76.5 overs)	260				

Fall of wickets:
1-41 (Root, 11.5 ov), 2-80 (McGrath, 20.4 ov), 3-84 (Rudolph, 21.1 ov), 4-118 (Bairstow, 31.2 ov), 5-119 (Ballance, 33 ov), 6-134 (Bresnan, 39.1 ov), 7-164 (Sidebottom, 47.1 ov), 8-177 (Gale, 51.1 ov), 9-230 (Shahzad, 66.5 ov), 10-260 (Pyrah, 76.5 ov)

Lancashire bowling	Overs	Mdns	Runs	Wkts	Wides	No-Balls
Chapple	26	3	71	5	-	-
Hogg	17	1	62	2	-	1
Smith	6	3	12	0	1	-
Mahmood	12	1	53	1	-	2
Keedy	15.5	2	51	2	-	-

**TT Bresnan replaced I Wardlaw

Umpires: NA Mallender & G Sharp   Scorers: JT Potter & A West

Sajid Mahmood

THAT Sajid Mahmood classed Lancashire's County Championship triumph as the greatest moment in his career speaks volumes. Here is a man who has played on the biggest stage there is in terms of an Ashes series Down Under, yet lifting the trophy at Taunton even topped that. On the face of it, the 2006/7 Ashes series was one to forget. England were whitewashed 5-0 by an Australian team including Warne, McGrath, Ponting, Gilchrist, Langer and Hayden. They were the cream of the crop, but just to be involved, whatever the result, must have been an incredible feeling for the likeable Boltonian.

"We won the VB one-day series in Australia with England, I've played in the Ashes, I've played in the World Cup, but nothing compares to this," he said. "I'm at home, playing cricket where I've been brought up with my mates. So, yes, winning the Championship is the best feeling I've ever had during my career. To win it after 77 years is unbelievable."

Not even missing out on selection for the last two matches could take the gloss off it for the 29-year-old fast bowler, who finished the season with 35 wickets and 256 runs to his name.

"Even though I didn't play at Somerset, I almost felt like I was part of the side and in the actual game because it was so tense all the way through. You were living each moment," he continued. "On that last day, I watched every single ball. During that last day, especially in the last session, none of us moved in the dressing room. Cricketers are quite superstitious, so literally no-one moved from the start of the innings.

"I had a pretty bad position to be honest. All of the lads got their balcony seats, and I was stood behind them at the patio doors with my foot on the little ledge at the bottom. My foot was so sore by the end of it, but I didn't want to move it just in case. Every time someone wanted to move or go to the toilet, they'd do it in between overs so they were ready and back in position by the time the next ball was bowled. I'm not a massive watcher of the game, but I knew that game was crucial and that all the hard work we'd put in through the season came down to one match."

Mahmood's stand-out performance was against Nottinghamshire at Trent Bridge in June when he took five wickets in each innings to help clinch a six-wicket win against the defending champions, but that wasn't necessarily his highlight of the season. He said: "I got the five in each innings at Trent Bridge, which was obviously my best haul, but little things like getting Rudolph out in the second dig at Headingley was a massive moment for me. He'd got off to a bit of a flier and was looking strong. To come on and take his wicket was quite crucial for the team.

"Performances like that may not look much on the scorecard, but it was crucial for us to get a player like that out. He was looking good and had a lot of pressure on his shoulders to get a big score for his team. He's one of those players who performs really well under pressure as well."

When asked whether it had sunk in yet that he was a Championship winner, whether there was a specific moment, he stated with some gusto: "Yeah, I was at home the other day, just lying down on the couch, and all of a sudden I thought 'wow, we've won the Championship'. It was a fantastic feeling."

Another question Mahmood gets asked regularly is about his England ambitions. Following eight Tests, 26 one-day and four Twenty20 internationals, he has fallen down the pecking order during the last couple of years, but that doesn't mean he has given up hope of adding to those caps.

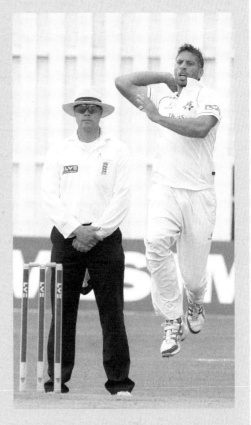

"I still want to play for England," he said. "I know that it's going to be tough to get in there because they've got a lot of young bowlers doing well for them, and I'm 29, but Ryan Sidebottom got back in there when he was 30 or something like that, and did well. I can't see why I can't do it. My ambition is always to get back into the England side. I don't know how you can be in any field or any line of work and not try to do it at the highest level. I'm not just happy at playing county cricket, I want to be successful at international level. That's still my goal. But I know for a fact that I've got to do well for Lancs to even come close to a call-up."

CHAMPAGNE MOMENT: *"For Keeds to get that last wicket of Pyrah at Headingley was amazing. We'd worked so hard during the game, which could have gone either way. I didn't play when we beat them at Liverpool, so to be involved in a Roses win was special."*

MATCH 11

Lancashire v Nottinghamshire

(Trafalgar Road, Southport) July 26-28

DAY ONE

**Glen Chapple and Chris Read toss up before the start of the
game at Trafalgar Road in front of Sky TV's cameras**

THE last time Lancashire played a Championship match on this ground, in June of
1999, new overseas star Muttiah Muralitharan took 14 wickets and still ended up on the
losing side. It was, therefore, no surprise to see Peter Moores and Glen Chapple select
two spinners for only the second time in the season in Simon Kerrigan and Gary Keedy.
If that match against Warwickshire prior to the millennium, and countless other second
XI fixtures played at Trafalgar Road, were anything to go by, the pair would be worked like
Trojans as the hosts looked to build on their stunning win over Yorkshire at Headingley
during the previous week.

Nottinghamshire had also picked two spinners in Graeme White and Samit Patel, their two left-armers, but things didn't quite go to plan as only 32 overs out of the 235.5 in the match were bowled by spinners as seam, swing and uneven bounce played its part throughout the three days. After visiting skipper Chris Read won the toss and elected to bat, Keedy and Kerrigan did strike as the visitors were bundled out for 203, but in-form Kyle Hogg, in particular, and Chapple did the bulk of the damage.

Hogg, having taken five wickets in his first seven overs against Yorkshire, also ripped through the Notts top order, taking four of five wickets as they slumped to 27-5 in 12 overs. He had openers Neil Edwards and Alex Hales caught behind by Gareth Cross for 10 apiece before trapping Australian Adam Voges lbw and bowling former team-mate Steven Mullaney, who had fond memories of this ground having scored a double hundred there for Lancashire seconds. Tom Smith also trapped Riki Wessels lbw for a duck – one of three men in the innings who failed to score.

There was brief respite for the visitors as Read and Patel (37) took the score to 53, but Chapple struck the former on the pads and Patel had a rush of blood and lofted Keedy to Smith at mid-off, leaving the total at 69-7 and the hosts well and truly in the box seat. Even at this early stage, an eighth win was on the cards.

That feeling soon ebbed away, however, as White and Andre Adams, a man who had already scolded Lancashire with some lusty hitting at Trent Bridge, united for a game-changing hour. The pair shared 65 for the eighth wicket inside 17 overs, with White shocking us all and taking the attacking lead. He hit Keedy for two straight sixes towards the Harrod Drive End of the ground, with the balls even nestling in the guttering of an adjacent house.

White also found the fence three times in posting 32 off 68 balls, while Adams was more restrained for his 33 off 54, even though he departed in unsurprising fashion, lofting Kerrigan to Smith at long-on. Not only did Smith do his side a favour, leaving the score at 134-8, he also protected the press lap-tops behind him!

White fell shortly afterwards, handing Hogg his fifth scalp courtesy of the third of Smith's four catches in the innings, this time at second slip. That wasn't the

Lost ball! A six from Gareth White ended up lodged in the guttering of an adjacent house!

> *"We've lost two more wickets than we'd have liked, but we've got a lot of batting left, and we're only one partnership away from getting up to their score."*
>
> **– Kyle Hogg**

end of the resistance from the Trent Bridge outfit. Last-wicket pair Darren Pattinson, who finished 35 not out, and Luke Fletcher added 58 inside 19 overs to take the score beyond 200 for an unlikely batting point before the latter was caught at second slip by that man Smith off Chapple. This may not have been the end to the innings Lancashire would have wanted, but they would no doubt have accepted the outcome at the start of the day. So, with that in mind, Paul Horton and Stephen Moore made a confident start to the reply, sharing 67 for the first wicket.

Moore was first to go in the 23rd over when he was trapped in front by the improving Adams, and the fact that it was an innings top-score of 37 gives you an idea of what happened next. Moore was the first of three wickets to fall to the Kiwi in the space of 15 balls, with Horton and Mark Chilton both edging behind to Read to leave the score at 68-3 in the second half of the evening session. When Karl Brown was bowled by Darren Pattinson (being a roof tiler as he built his cricket career, he should have fetched those balls that White hit earlier in the day), Lancashire were 76-4 with 4.3 overs left in the day. Another 10 runs were added to the total before stumps were drawn for the day, which had been yet another fascinating one and witnessed by a season's high home crowd of 2,606.

Hogg said: "We've lost two more wickets than we'd have liked, but we've got a lot of batting left, and we're only one partnership away from getting up to their score.

"If you get two people in, it's quite hard to get rid of them. Once you get through the new ball, it can be quite hard to get it past the bat. If the batters get in, it's a good wicket. We just bowled well, putting them under a lot of pressure. Credit to them because they bowled better the longer things went on.

"People who do well with the ball just bowl it straight and on a good length. If you don't bowl well, you'll get hit for four. If you do bowl well, you have a chance of getting people out. Mind you, that's the same on any wicket anywhere in the world."

CLOSE OF PLAY DAY ONE:
Nottinghamshire, having won the toss and elected to bat, 203 (KW Hogg 5-28) led Lancashire 86-4 by 117 runs

DAY TWO

DURING this match, Lancashire had announced that they would be moving their final Championship home fixture against Hampshire from Old Trafford to Liverpool in order to give the recently re-orientated square at their Manchester HQ more time to bed in. Yet it was the pitch at Southport that was causing a few question marks. After 14 wickets had fallen on day one, 16 more fell on day two, which amounted to Lancashire being set a stiff victory target of 258 on day three, of which eight had been scored before close.

Distinct signs of uneven bounce meant a number of eyes were on the ECB's pitch inspector, Jack Birkenshaw. With Warwickshire, Hampshire and Kent docked points for producing poor pitches throughout the campaign, there were a few in the media tent suggesting this could be another added to the list. Thankfully, Birkenshaw was happy with a "good cricket wicket", saying that the bowlers had just outperformed the batsmen. That was certainly true, highlighted most on this particularly day by captain fantastic Glen Chapple, who took 6-70 in the Notts second innings, bowling them out for 233. They were his best figures since September, 2009 when he took 6-19 against Warwickshire at Old Trafford.

He did an exceptional job in keeping his side in the contest after they were bowled out for 179 in their first innings, with Andre Adams also claiming an impressive 6-71, reducing Lancashire to 125-7 in the 43rd over. He had removed Stephen Moore, Paul Horton and Mark Chilton late on day one, and added the scalps of Tom Smith, bowled, Gareth Cross, lbw, and Steven Croft, sharply caught at first slip by Alex Hales. Adams also had a hand in the first wicket of the day to fall, catching night-watchman Gary Keedy at third slip off Darren Pattinson's bowling.

Pattinson wrapped up the Lancashire innings when he had Simon Kerrigan caught behind, but not before Luke Fletcher had bowled Chapple for 19, including a six off Adams over wide long-off. Kyle Hogg finished 23 not out as the hosts conceded a first innings lead of 24. Hogg may have been the Red Rose bowler taking all the headlines of late – he had taken 36 in five and a half matches prior to this innings – but any opponents will know to underestimate Chapple at their peril. He proved just why during the final two sessions of the day. There was enough time for him to bowl a solitary over before lunch, but he didn't have to wait long to celebrate.

Hogg was actually the man who got the breakthrough as Neil Edwards loosely drove to Horton at first slip in the third over, but Chapple struck in the seventh over when Riki Wessels edged behind, falling in the same way that Adam Voges, Chris Read and later Pattinson did. Hales and Samit Patel shared 56 for the third wicket to take the score from 25-2 to 81-2, with the former demonstrating the kind of clean striking that would see him picked for England's Twenty20 side for matches against India and the West Indies later in the summer as he posted 50 off 60 balls.

Thankfully for Lancs, the tall right-hander fell just two balls later when he skewed Smith to Croft at backward point without adding to his score. He was followed back to the pavilion shortly afterwards by Patel, who opted not to play a shot at Chapple and saw his off-stump cartwheel, leaving the score at 97-4. Voges was on his way 11 runs later before Read departed in identical fashion, the sixth man to go with the score at 138 early in the evening session. Hogg added his second wicket to make it 139-7 as Adams was bowled first ball attempting a horrid heave across the line. At that stage, Lancs were back on top as Notts were seven down with a lead of just 163.

Unfortunately the Red Rose were frustrated by Graeme White, the left-arm spinner who had not yet bowled an over in the match, and former player Steven Mullaney. Mullaney

> *"We're definitely due an easy victory, but they don't seem to be coming. We'll just have to grin and bear it. We'll definitely be up for it, and it should be a great game."*
>
> ## – Glen Chapple

had decided to leave Old Trafford at the end of the 2009 season due to a lack of opportunities. He had only played one Championship match in four campaigns as a Lancashire player, ironically against Notts at Trent Bridge, so it was understandable that he made the move to the East Midlands. He and White, who shared a house in Nottingham, put on what turned out to be the most productive stand of the match, 71 in 16 overs, for the eighth wicket to tip the balance yet again. Mullaney scored 42, while White added 54 not out off 75 balls, including eight fours and a half-century recording six off Smith over straight mid-wicket.

Chapple was key in limiting the damage, even allowing his opening batsmen time to start the chase before stumps. Mullaney was trapped lbw as he tried to whip Smith across the line before Pattinson's departure secured Chapple's third five-wicket haul of the campaign and Fletcher was caught at mid-on by Stephen Moore.

Chapple said: "We're definitely due an easy victory, but they don't seem to be coming. We'll just have to grin and bear it. We'll definitely be up for it, and it should be a great game. We've done pretty well and set up a good game. We're only into day two, and there's no help for the spinners yet, it means the seamers have had to be greedy and do a lot of the work."

CLOSE OF PLAY DAY TWO:
Nottinghamshire 203 (KW Hogg 5-28) and 233 (GG White 54, AD Hales 50; G Chapple 6-70) led Lancashire 179 (AR Adams 6-71) and 8-0 by 249 runs

DAY THREE

LANCASHIRE'S title challenge hit a road block thanks to the reigning champions, who consigned them to a third defeat of the campaign to add to the two previous losses against Durham. The Red Rose county would have gone top of the Division One table had they chased down 258 on day three, but they were skittled for 128 as Darren Pattinson and Andre Adams shared nine wickets to claim the 20 points in the latter stages of the afternoon session, also securing their side's first win since April.

Having been bowled out for 179 in the first innings, Lancashire succumbed inside 51 overs to raise further question marks about their batting, with nobody managing to top Karl Brown's 23 off 67 balls. Only five other men could get into double figures. This was definitely an opportunity missed, especially as Notts had been on the ropes at 27-5 and 69-7 before lunch on the opening day. Amazingly, Pattinson took five wickets in county cricket for only the third time since he made his solitary Test appearance for England against South Africa at Headingley in July 2008, while Adams finished with four to add to his six in the first innings, thus collecting 10 in the match.

The Red Rose, who only claimed three points, actually made an encouraging start to the day, which was overcast, as Paul Horton and Stephen Moore shared 37 for the first wicket in 11 and a half overs. Moore even hit the first ball of the day, bowled by Pattinson, wide of gully for four. The former Worcester man also emphatically pulled the same bowler for six, but both fell for the addition of four more runs in the space of five overs to put a different complexion on the chase. Moore will have been disappointed with the manner of his dismissal, chasing a wide one from Pattinson and edging to first slip Alex Hales, who had already proved in this contest that he had a safe pair of hands.

Horton was another who would, no doubt, look back on his departure with regret because he fell the same way that Samit Patel had on day two, bowled as he opted not to play a shot. And the wickets kept tumbling. The very next ball, Mark Chilton edged Adams behind to make it a pair in the match before Steven Croft fell the same way a little over four overs later, leaving the score at 51-4.

By now it was Nottinghamshire's to lose, something which they never looked like doing. Brown went three balls after lunch, bowled by one that jagged back through the gate from Pattinson and Tom Smith was next out when he edged Adams to Adam Voges at second slip. With only 103 on the board, the fat lady was certainly gargling, if not singing already.

Smith was the first of three wickets to fall in the space of nine balls, taking the score from 103-5 to 103-8 as Gareth Cross dragged a Pattinson ball onto his stumps, Kyle Hogg edged the same bowler to Voges for a rare duck, and Glen Chapple was bowled off his pads by Pattinson to confirm his five-for. Luke Fletcher wrapped up an away win when number eleven Simon Kerrigan miscued him to Graeme White at mid-off.

Notts might not have been able to have a direct say in the title race, but they would certainly have an indirect say with matches against Durham twice, Somerset and Warwickshire to come. As for Lancashire, they would need to re-group ahead of their crunch clash with Warwickshire at Liverpool just four days later.

Peter Moores said: "We never really got that close in the end. We got off to a flier in the first three overs, but they bowled very well after that. They deserved it. We've been beaten in a tight game, and you have to be able to take a loss.

"At 27-5 on the first morning, the game was obviously with us. But credit to them because their lower order got some valuable runs. I also thought Adams and Pattinson, as a combination, were hard work for us. They just played a little bit better. There were a couple of periods where our bowlers leaked a few runs and we did not get any substantial partnerships with the bat.

"We are still very much in the mix. With five games to go, it will come down to who can maybe win three of those. We know we are playing some really good cricket, and we have some big challenges ahead."

> *"We never really got that close in the end. We got off to a flier in the first three overs, but they bowled very well after that. They deserved it. We've been beaten in a tight game, and you have to be able to take a loss."*
>
> – Peter Moores

CLOSE OF PLAY DAY THREE:
Nottinghamshire 203 (KW Hogg 5-28) and 233
(GG White 54, AD Hales 50; G Chapple 6-70) beat Lancashire 179
(AR Adams 6-71) and 128 (DJ Pattinson 5-44) by 129 runs

Nottinghamshire 20pts (Batting 1, Bowling 3)
Lancashire 3pts (Bowling 3)

LV= County Championship table July 28

	P	W	L	D	BaP	BoP	Pts
Durham	11	6	2	3	37	31	173
Lancashire**	**11**	**7**	**3**	**1**	**26**	**31**	**171**
Warwickshire*	10	7	3	0	29	27	160
Somerset	10	4	4	2	33	25	128
Nottinghamshire	11	4	4	3	22	31	126
Sussex	10	4	3	3	18	23	114
Yorkshire+	11	2	5	4	23	27	92
Worcestershire	9	2	7	0	18	25	75
Hampshire++	9	0	5	4	13	22	39

* Warwickshire deducted eight points for poor pitch
** Lancashire deducted one point for slow over rate
+ Yorkshire deducted two points for slow over rate
++ Hampshire deducted eight points for poor pitch

SCORECARD

Nottinghamshire first innings		Runs	Balls	Mins	4s	6s
AD Hales	c Cross b Hogg	10	36	48	2	-
NJ Edwards	c Cross b Hogg	10	19	28	2	-
MH Wessels	lbw b Smith	0	10	16	-	-
SR Patel	c Smith b Keedy	37	35	41	8	-
AC Voges	lbw b Hogg	0	3	2	-	-
SJ Mullaney	b Hogg	0	2	2	-	-
*+CMW Read	lbw b Chapple	4	15	22	1	-
AR Adams	c Smith b Kerrigan	33	54	64	6	-
GG White	c Smith b Hogg	32	68	83	3	2
DJ Pattinson	not out	35	83	90	6	-
LJ Fletcher	c Smith b Chapple	25	55	62	2	1
Extras	(9 b, 8 lb)	17				
Total	(all out, 63.2 overs)	203				

Fall of wickets:
1-18 (Edwards, 7.2 ov), 2-27 (Wessels, 10.4 ov), 3-27 (Hales, 11.1 ov), 4-27 (Voges, 11.4 ov), 5-27 (Mullaney, 12 ov), 6-53 (Read, 17.5 ov), 7-69 (Patel, 20.3 ov), 8-134 (Adams, 37.2 ov), 9-145 (White, 45.1 ov), 10-203 (Fletcher, 63.2 ov)

Nottinghamshire second innings		Runs	Balls	Mins	4s	6s
AD Hales	c Croft b Smith	50	62	77	9	-
NJ Edwards	c Horton b Hogg	2	7	13	-	-
MH Wessels	c Cross b Chapple	4	11	18	-	-
SR Patel	b Chapple	22	50	71	2	-
AC Voges	c Cross b Chapple	16	37	40	3	-
SJ Mullaney	lbw b Smith	42	90	145	7	-
*+CMW Read	c Cross b Chapple	22	26	49	5	-
AR Adams	b Hogg	0	1	2	-	-
GG White	not out	54	75	114	8	1
DJ Pattinson	c Cross b Chapple	6	21	22	1	-
LJ Fletcher	c Moore b Chapple	4	9	15	-	-
Extras	(2 b, 5 lb, 4 nb)	11				
Total	(all out, 64.3 overs)	233				

Fall of wickets:
1-12 (Edwards, 3.3 ov), 2-25 (Wessels, 6.5 ov), 3-81 (Hales, 19.2 ov), 4-97 (Patel, 24.3 ov), 5-108 (Voges, 29 ov), 6-138 (Read, 37 ov), 7-139 (Adams, 37.4 ov), 8-210 (Mullaney, 55.3 ov), 9-219 (Pattinson, 61 ov), 10-233 (Fletcher, 64.3 ov)

Lancashire bowling	Overs	Mdns	Runs	Wkts	Wides	No-Balls
Chapple	17.2	5	40	2	-	-
Hogg	13	4	28	5	-	-
Smith	7	2	40	1	-	-
Keedy	14	2	50	1	-	-
Kerrigan	12	5	28	1	-	-

Lancashire bowling	Overs	Mdns	Runs	Wkts	Wides	No-Balls
Chapple	25.3	7	70	6	-	-
Hogg	14	1	56	2	-	-
Smith	21	3	81	2	-	2
Kerrigan	2	0	6	0	-	-
Keedy	2	0	13	0	-	-

Lancashire first innings		Runs	Balls	Mins	4s	6s
PJ Horton	c Read b Adams	26	79	95	4	-
SC Moore	lbw b Adams	37	58	88	8	-
KR Brown	b Pattinson	7	20	21	1	-
MJ Chilton	c Read b Adams	0	5	3	-	-
SJ Croft	c Hales b Adams	27	68	94	3	-
G Keedy	c Adams b Pattinson	20	29	42	4	-
TC Smith	b Adams	7	17	19	1	-
+GD Cross	lbw b Adams	0	2	1	-	-
*G Chapple	b Fletcher	19	13	34	3	1
KW Hogg	not out	23	27	46	2	-
SC Kerrigan	c Read b Pattinson	3	29	28	-	-
Extras	(4 b, 5 lb, 1 w)	10				
Total	(all out, 57.5 overs)	179				

Fall of wickets:
1-67 (Moore, 22.4 ov), 2-68 (Horton, 24.1 ov), 3-68 (Chilton, 25 ov), 4-76 (Brown, 27.3 ov), 5-112 (Keedy, 37.3 ov), 6-125 (Smith, 42.4 ov), 7-125 (Cross, 43 ov), 8-137 (Croft, 46.5 ov), 9-167 (Chapple, 51.1 ov), 10-179 (Kerrigan, 57.5 ov)

Lancashire second innings		Runs	Balls	Mins	4s	6s
PJ Horton	b Adams	15	46	65	3	-
SC Moore	c Hales b Pattinson	14	33	46	1	1
KR Brown	b Pattinson	23	67	75	5	-
MJ Chilton	c Read b Adams	0	1	1	-	-
SJ Croft	c Read b Adams	6	14	16	1	-
TC Smith	c Voges b Adams	19	55	78	4	-
+GD Cross	b Pattinson	15	29	42	3	-
*G Chapple	b Pattinson	7	18	23	1	-
KW Hogg	c Voges b Pattinson	0	3	3	-	-
SC Kerrigan	c White b Fletcher	4	15	34	1	-
G Keedy	not out	10	20	18	2	-
Extras	(4 b, 6 lb, 5 w)	15				
Total	(all out, 50.1 overs)	128				

Fall of wickets:
1-37 (Moore, 11.3 ov), 2-41 (Horton, 16.3 ov), 3-41 (Chilton, 16.4 ov), 4-51 (Croft, 21 ov), 5-79 (Brown, 31.3 ov), 6-103 (Smith, 40.3 ov), 7-103 (Cross, 41.2 ov), 8-103 (Hogg, 41.5 ov), 9-114 (Chapple, 45.2 ov), 10-128 (Kerrigan, 50.1 ov)

Notts bowling	Overs	Mdns	Runs	Wkts	Wides	No-Balls
Pattinson	19.5	8	46	3	-	-
Fletcher	14	1	53	1	1	-
Adams	24	9	71	6	-	-

Notts bowling	Overs	Mdns	Runs	Wkts	Wides	No-Balls
Fletcher	11.1	5	19	1	-	-
Pattinson	19	7	44	5	1	-
Adams	18	6	51	4	-	-
Patel	2	1	4	0	-	-

Umpires: SA Garratt & TE Jesty   Scorers: A West & A Cusworth

Paul Horton

IF Paul Horton had scored just 26 more runs this season, he could well have been on the verge of an England call-up, because those runs, at the right time, would have seen him end the campaign with six centuries. Instead, he finished the season without reaching three figures as, remarkably, he was out in the nineties four times in the Championship and left stranded unbeaten on 97 and 95 in successive CB40 knocks. Only Marcus Trescothick, Ian Bell and Alastair Cook would have had more first-class centuries this summer than Horton if he had converted all four.

The opener, however, still ended top of the Red Rose batting charts in the County Championship with 1,040 runs, passing the magical thousand mark for the third time in five seasons. He did it having to play half the matches on what are effectively club grounds, with Lancashire playing all their home games at out-grounds. It is a contribution Horton, who was born in Sydney but moved to England at 15 when he became part of the Lancashire system, is rightly proud of.

"To be leading run-scorer in the year we win the Championship is fantastic," said Horton, who still has an Aussie twang. "If you said at the start of the year I would score over 1,000 runs, be the highest run-scorer for the club in first-class cricket and we would win the Championship, I think I would have taken it! There aren't that many players in the country who scored 1,000 runs this season. I was eighth in the Division One batting rankings and as an opener I feel that is quite an achievement, especially considering I played half of my games on league wickets. If I had scored six centuries people would have been looking at me rather differently. There are only a couple of players who scored more than four hundreds in the country, so if I had done six it would have been miraculous."

Horton played most of the season on his home patch, Liverpool. He first played for Winstanley Park when he and his family moved from Australia, then switched to Sefton Park at the age of 16. "When we play at Liverpool I don't have enough complimentary tickets to go round," said Horton, who celebrated his 29th birthday just five days after helping Lancashire to the title. "Liverpool is my adopted home and my school is just down the road from where we play at Aigburth. It's always been a special place to me. It's where my parents are from and it's where my grandparents are from. I lived there for many years, I schooled there and I became a man in Liverpool. Even though I didn't move to England until I was 15, I'm a product of the Lancashire system. I learnt my cricket in Australia, but was made a cricketer by Lancashire."

Horton won Lancashire's Player of the Year award in 2007 after scoring 1,116 runs, and he broke the thousand mark again the following year. However, he failed to live up to his high standards in 2009 and 2010 as he struggled to combine playing Championship cricket and the one-day form of the game. He spent the winter out of his comfort zone playing for the Matabeleland Tuskers in Zimbabwe, working with their coach Dave Houghton. While there, he scored his first double century in first-class cricket and helped the club to their first title in over 20 years.

He returned re-energised and, after two years in which he had several opening partners – including Tom Smith, Luke Sutton and Stephen Parry – this season he relished batting at the top of the order with Stephen Moore. The duo made four century partnerships, three of which came in their final three innings against Hampshire and Somerset at crucial times in the title race.

"It's been nice to develop a partnership with Stephen," said Horton, who also finished the season third in the country with 32 catches, most of them at slip. "We're of a similar age and we get on well together. It's been nice to have a proper opening partner. In the past couple of years I've had a number of people opening with me, so it's been nice to be given the chance to develop a partnership which has flourished like it has.

"You set out in your career to play for England, if you can't play for England then you want to win trophies. When you do that, it makes you realise all the hard work and dedication has been worth it."

CHAMPAGNE MOMENT: *"For me there were thousands of champagne moments during this season, but the best was seeing Karl Brown score his maiden first-class century for the club. As a senior batsman in the squad, to see a young player come in and score his first hundred was a special moment, knowing how much work he had put in just to get the chance."*

MATCH 12

Lancashire v Warwickshire

(Aigburth, Liverpool) August 1-4

DAY ONE

NOT for the first time in recent seasons, Lancashire's batting was beginning to cause some concern. After starting the season by posting three successive scores of over 450, the Red Rose were all of a sudden struggling with the bat. Following the 84 all out at home to Durham at the end of June, they had gone five innings without passing 350. It meant that in the three matches leading up to the clash with Warwickshire they had picked up just three batting bonus points, and with the title race turning into a tight four-way battle involving Lancashire, Warwickshire, Durham and Somerset, Peter Moores's men couldn't really afford to throw away too many points.

It was ironic that, at a time when the batsmen were beginning to struggle, Shivnarine Chanderpaul arrived at Aigburth, but instead of wearing the Red Rose as he did 12 months earlier to great effect – averaging 53 in eight matches for Lancashire – he sported the colours of Warwickshire as their new overseas signing. To the great relief of the home crowd, however, he was left out of the Bears' line-up, having arrived in the country just 24 hours earlier. Instead, he went to play for Warwickshire's second team against Lancashire's seconds at Rugby School. The West Indies Test star played his part for Warwickshire later in the season, scoring an amazing three centuries in the five games he played to boost their title hopes.

Lancashire were left mulling over their batting woes once again at Aigburth. After losing the toss, they failed to pick up a single batting point as they were rolled over for 189 within two sessions in their first innings. You couldn't see it coming, however, with the start they made. After a 15-minute delay because of rain, Stephen Moore and Paul Horton set off like a pair of steam trains. They raced to 38-0 in the opening six overs before another shower took them off for an hour. The trouble started when they returned.

Horton was first to go as, in the second over after the rain break, he edged Chris Woakes to Rikki Clarke at second slip for 14 and Lancashire went in at lunch on 63-1. The manner of the dismissal set a bit of a trend for the game: Karl Brown fell exactly the same way for nine, this time with Clarke pulling off a good low catch at slip, and the former England Test all-rounder could have made it a hat-trick of catches, but he dropped a tough chance at slip off Moore.

The Lancashire opener made him pay, reaching his half-century off just 66 balls before yet another shower took the players off for 10 minutes with Lancashire on 99-2.

The Red Rose, in hindsight, would have been better off if the rain had washed out the rest of the day! Mark Chilton went for six, caught at first slip by Varun Chopra off Woakes, quickly followed by Steven Croft, who was trapped lbw by Keith Barker. The Warwickshire bowler had started his career at Lancashire League side Enfield, and you can be sure his godfather – a certain Clive Lloyd – wouldn't have been happy with him playing a role in Lancashire's woes!

It then became the Neil Carter show. The all-rounder hadn't bowled a ball all season, having been struck down by a serious pelvic problem in pre-season, but he made Lancashire pay for his frustrations. He brought to an end Moore's fine innings with his first ball in Championship cricket in 2011, the Red Rose opener being caught behind by Tim Ambrose for 76, a knock which included 14 boundaries and took just 94 balls.

> *"Our guys are in nick, they know how to play cricket, they are talented. We are confident we can get ourselves back into the game and push for another win."*
>
> **– Stephen Moore**

Gareth Cross lasted only three deliveries before Carter pulled off a wonderful caught and bowled, clinging on to the ball with his left hand as he completed his follow-through. Three overs later, he was at it again. This time Glen Chapple was the victim as the Lancashire captain slashed him to Will Porterfield at gully for nine. Sajid Mahmood became Carter's fourth wicket in four overs as he was lbw first ball. Having been 101-2, Lancashire were now 155-8 and in desperate trouble.

But Carter wasn't finished. Tom Smith and Kyle Hogg had put on 31 much-needed runs for the ninth wicket when Hogg edged Carter to Porterfield at third slip for 15. Then Carter completed the rout when Smith was caught by Jim Troughton for 35 in his next over. It left him with career-best figures of 6-30 from his first spell of the season.

Lancashire had lost nine wickets in a calamitous afternoon session as they were bowled out for less than 200 for the fourth successive innings. It was the last thing they wanted coming straight after the defeat by Nottinghamshire at Southport.

Skipper Chapple did strike a blow for the Red Rose in a rain-affected final session, claiming the wicket of the in-form Chopra thanks to a great diving catch by Moore at third slip as Warwickshire ended day one 30-1.

Moore said: "We didn't have a great day with the bat. The batsmen haven't been scoring big hundreds recently, but neither have our opponents. We haven't been playing on wickets where 500 plays 500.

"All we have to do is score one more run than the opposition. We also have the benefit of a serious bowling attack which will make life just as difficult – if not more so – for the opposition when they bat.

"Our guys are in nick, they know how to play cricket, they are talented. We are confident we can get ourselves back into the game and push for another win."

CLOSE OF PLAY DAY ONE:
Lancashire, having lost the toss and been invited to bat, 189 (SC Moore 76; NM Carter 6-30) led Warwickshire 30-1 by 117 runs

DAY TWO

AS Lancashire were battling to get back into the game, off the field the club were fighting to get the Ashes back. In 2006, chief executive Jim Cumbes took a crushing phone call from the ECB telling him that they had missed out on hosting a 2009 Test against Australia to Glamorgan's Swalec Stadium. Since that day, Lancashire had done all they could to get the Ashes back. It was a battle which made them think about moving away from Old Trafford, saw them in and out of court, and almost left them bankrupt.

Having finally won their crippling 18-month legal battle with rival developers Derwent Holdings – which cost them around £4m – they were given the green light to start work on the £32m redevelopment of the world-famous ground. Then on August 2, Cumbes led a delegation to Lord's where they put their case forward for hosting a 2013 Ashes Test. If they failed – and they wouldn't find out for another six nail-biting weeks – the financial ramifications weren't even worth thinking about.

While the club's officials were fighting for the very future of the club, on the field the players were fighting to try and stay in the title race, and just as Lancashire weren't willing to give up the battle to take the Ashes back to the North West, on the field the team weren't prepared to let their chances of glory slip through their fingers.

Having been bowled out for 189 on day one, Lancashire knew they had to keep Warwickshire below 300 in their first innings if they were to have any chance of victory, but on a wicket and in conditions which made it much easier to bat than on day one, it wasn't going to be easy. Moreover, they could have done without giving easy runs away.

Sajid Mahmood can be as destructive as any fast bowler in county cricket when he gets it right, just ask Jim Troughton, who saw his stumps sent flying by the former England Test player's opening ball of the day. However, Mahmood had over-stepped with his front foot and turned around to see the umpire's arm out-stretched to signal a no-ball. It became a regular sight for him on day two as he sent down an incredible 12 no-balls from the River End, giving Warwickshire 24 extra runs. It wasn't all bad from Saj, though, as he claimed two wickets on a day of hard slog by Lancashire.

Kyle Hogg – enjoying the best season of his career – claimed the first wicket of the day as Will Porterfield went lbw for 13 in the third over of the morning, and having suffered the Troughton disappointment, Mahmood quickly made amends as Laurie Evans was lbw for 12. He was still finding life tough, however, as his first three overs went for 30 runs. It was in stark contrast to Glen Chapple, who conceded just 18 runs from his first 13 overs in the innings, whilst Hogg struck again in the 29th over as Tim Ambrose was caught behind by Gareth Cross for 11, with Warwickshire heading in at lunch on 112-4, just 77 runs behind.

After a small rain delay, Mahmood found his radar again as Rikki Clarke went lbw for 18, and with Warwickshire 133-5, Lancashire were remarkably eyeing up an unlikely first-innings lead. But Troughton's escape came back to haunt them as he made 49 before Mark Chilton took a stinging catch at cover off Tom Smith's bowling to finally get rid of the Warwickshire captain, but not before he had played a part in the first 50-partnership of the game with Keith Barker.

> *"We just have to scrap for every run, whatever it takes, that's what we will carry on doing."*
>
> **– Gary Keedy**

Barker then put on 55 with Chris Woakes to frustrate Lancashire further before he went, caught by Steven Croft at short leg off Gary Keedy, for 27, from the last delivery before tea. By that stage Warwickshire were 228-7 and leading by 39. Woakes went on to make 60 before he became Keedy's second wicket thanks to a good catch at short extra cover by Smith. Chapple bowled Neil Carter for one in the next over, but Jeetan Patel and Boyd Rankin put on 28 for the final wicket before Keedy finished off Warwickshire when Patel was caught by Croft for 28.

The Bears were all out for 280 – a lead of 91 – and even though as far as Lancashire were concerned it was job done, with Warwickshire being restricted to less than 300, it could have been even better for them but for a late-order rally. Paul Horton and Stephen Moore made in-roads into that lead as they saw off a tricky 16-over spell at the end of the day with Lancashire finishing on 32-0.

Keedy, who finished with 3-48, said: "We thought if we could restrict them to anything under 300 it would give us a chance to win this, to do that was crucial. Now if we can match their first innings total in our second innings, they are going to have to get close to 200 on the last day, which, if we bowl well, will be a challenge. We just have to scrap for every run. Whatever it takes, that's what we will carry on doing."

CLOSE OF PLAY DAY TWO:
Lancashire 189 (SC Moore 76; NM Carter 6-30) and 32-0 trailed Warwickshire 280 (CR Woakes 60) by 59 runs

DAY THREE

IT isn't often you can say you saw history being made, but anybody at Aigburth on August 3, 2011, can do just that. For in the midst of a red-hot title battle, Warwickshire's Rikki Clarke entered the record books. The 29-year-old claimed seven catches to equal the world record for the number of catches made by a non-wicketkeeper in a first-class innings, set by both Mickey Stewart in 1957 and Tony Brown in 1966. If he hadn't dropped Stephen Moore in the first innings, he would have made it 10 for the match to equal Wally Hammond's world record for a game, set in 1928!

He wasn't the only one to set a milestone. Steven Croft was one of Clarke's victims, but not before he had scored only his second first-class century as Lancashire took control of the game. His 122, coincidentally, equalled the score he made in his only other century, which was against Nottinghamshire at Old Trafford in 2008. In doing so he passed 3,000 first-class runs for the club and shared a brilliant 208-run stand with Karl Brown – the biggest partnership of Lancashire's season. Despite Clarke's heroics in the field, Lancashire ended day three on 374-9, a more than useful lead of 283. It also helped to banish their recent batting woes as Croft became the first Red Rose player in four games to reach three figures.

Clarke began his record-equalling day in the eighth over as Paul Horton edged Neil Carter to slip for 32 after moving Lancashire on to 57-1 from their overnight 32-0. Moore joined in with the milestones by passing 8,000 first-class runs for his career when he moved on to 16. Inevitably, the former England Lions batsman fell to Clarke for 39 as he was surprised by a rising Boyd Rankin delivery and the fielder took a good high catch. Lancashire were still trailing by seven when Mark Chilton edged Chris Woakes to Clarke, who took a good low catch at slip, for just two.

At that stage, fears of another Lancashire batting collapse began to emerge, but Croft and Brown had a different plan. The two home-grown youngsters – Croft from Blackpool and Brown from Bolton – turned the game with a devastating partnership. Croft had spent time before the match chatting to coach Peter Moores about how best to transform his impressive form in the one-day game into big scores in the Championship. Whatever the boss said seemed to work. He showed his intent from the off by launching Jeetan Patel over long-on for six. He and Brown took just 58 balls to reach their 50 partnership and guided Lancashire into the lead and on to 139-3 at lunch.

There was no let-up in the afternoon session either. Croft brought up his half-century in style with a pull off Keith Barker for four and the pair celebrated their 100 partnership in just 26 overs. Brown had a let off while on 46 as he was dropped by wicketkeeper Tim Ambrose, but he more than deserved his half-century when it arrived after 123 balls.

Aigburth hasn't always been a happy hunting ground for Croft. In his previous 16 innings at the ground he had amassed a grand total of just 275 runs, but now he had a new weapon. After a winter of hard work, he started the season with a new technique. Just as the bowler releases the ball, he takes a step forward to get his feet moving early, and it seemed to be paying dividends as he cruised to his century in just 141 balls. Lancashire went through the whole session without losing a wicket, going in at tea on 263-3 with a lead of 172.

Having passed Lancashire's previous highest partnership of the season – 180 between Chilton and Brown in the opening match of the season against Sussex at Aigburth – Croft and Brown's partnership was brought to an end by Clarke. Croft was the man to go as Barker led him into a false shot and he edged the ball to slip where 'bucket hands' Clarke was waiting. The duo had rescued Lancashire from a spot of bother and led them into a commanding 201-run lead on 292-4.

Tom Smith was Clarke's fifth victim as the all-rounder went for one having edged Patel, and Brown's innings came to a premature end when he went for 91 in the next over.

If anyone deserved a century it was the 23-year-old from Atherton for this knock against some testing bowling from Barker and Woakes. His wicket was Clarke's sixth catch and made for an amazing scorecard which saw the Warwickshire man's name next to all top-six batsmen in the Lancashire innings. It also led to plenty of frantic research in the press tent at Aigburth in search of catching records.

Barker spoiled the scorecard, taking the catch to dismiss Gareth Cross for 15 when he skied a Rankin delivery while trying to accelerate the scoring with a declaration in mind – then came the moment of history. Sajid Mahmood top-edged Patel and Clarke pocketed the chance at leg-slip to enter the record books.

A quickfire 22 from skipper Glen Chapple ended a good day for Lancashire as they closed on 374-9, with a lead of 283. It also set up the prospect of a nail-biting final day with both teams still in the hunt for a win.

Croft said: "That century has been a long time coming. I tried to bring my tempo up to the same as when I play one-day cricket. I waited for that bad ball and put it away. I used to have a problem getting out lbw not moving my feet, so I have been working hard on that.

Karl Brown and Steven Croft congratulate each other as they put together Lancashire's highest partnership of the summer – they were to team up again in the final game of the season at Taunton with the Championship at stake

> *"We're a hard team to roll over and we will keep on scrapping."*
>
> – Steven Croft

"Karl was patient, waited for his shots and deserved a century. It was a great knock. We kept each other going, and hopefully we've made a big contribution to the game.

"We're a hard team to roll over and we will keep on scrapping. But there's no beating around the bush, we needed to score more runs. I will take a lot out of this innings."

CLOSE OF PLAY DAY THREE:
Lancashire 189 (SC Moore 76; NM Carter 6-30) and 374-9 (SJ Croft 122, KR Brown 91) led Warwickshire 280 (CR Woakes 60) by 283 runs

DAY FOUR

LANCASHIRE just don't do draws at Aigburth. In the previous 14 games the club had played at the Liverpool venue, only once had there not been a positive result for one side or the other. Even then, back in 2004 when Northamptonshire were the visitors, rain washed out the entire first day. Before then you had to go back to 1995, when a Red Rose side which included Wasim Akram, John Crawley, Mike Watkinson and two youngsters called Glen Chapple and Gary Keedy (whatever became of them?), fought out a draw with Nottinghamshire. So with both Lancashire and Warwickshire desperate for victory to strengthen their Championship hopes, the last thing anyone expected was a draw when they arrived for the start of the final day.

The home side, knowing they had been able to put on 342 the previous day, wanted to set Warwickshire a target of at least 300 to chase and so batted on despite being nine wickets down, adding just six to their overnight score before being bowled out for 380 as Kyle Hogg was caught by Jim Troughton off Boyd Rankin for 15. The fact it was Troughton who took the catch denied Rikki Clarke the chance of securing a world record for himself.

It left Warwickshire needing 290 to win in a minimum of 75 overs, and they signalled their intent by promoting big-hitting Neil Carter to open the batting. He and Varun Chopra gave the visitors the perfect start as they raced to 50 in just the 11th over with a blitz of boundaries. However, with rain having delayed the start, further showers forced an early lunch and then bad light reduced the playing time even more to leave Warwickshire needing 231 to win in a minimum of 54 overs. That, the visitors decided, was too many runs in too few overs and they began to shut up shop.

Lancashire continued to smell the scent of victory, scent which grew more pungent as wickets began to tumble. Sajid Mahmood, who was still having no-ball problems from the River End, got one to move away from Carter and Tom Smith took a good low catch at slip. It gave Mahmood his 300th first-class wicket. Three overs later Keedy – who was getting plenty of turn – pulled off a brilliant diving caught and bowled to end Will Porterfield's day. Hogg got in on the act in the next over as Chopra went for 46 edging to Paul Horton at slip, and when Keedy struck again minutes later as Smith claimed Jim Troughton at leg slip, Warwickshire had crumbled from 72-0 to 92-4 in the space of seven overs. Lancashire, having been bowled out for 189 in the first innings, were now well and truly in the box seat heading into the final session.

Former England wicketkeeper Tim Ambrose and Laurie Evans looked to have made the game safe for Warwickshire with a 68-run partnership, which, more importantly, used up 27 valuable overs. Lancashire finally made the breakthrough with just 19 overs remaining in the day when Smith again took the catch, this time at second slip, to send Evans packing for 30 off Hogg's bowling.

Ambrose reached a deserved half-century, and with just eight overs left and Warwickshire 210-5, a draw looked inevitable. But, as was Lancashire's wont this season, there was late drama to come. Clarke went with just six overs left, caught by Horton off Keedy's bowling and all of a sudden the crowd sensed a win was possible.

The excitement even got to the Aigburth PA announcer, Matt Proctor. When Steven Croft came on to bowl, he took off his jumper to reveal a shirt with Gareth Cross's name and number on the back. Matt, without thinking about it, announced to the ground that the wicketkeeper was coming on to bowl. Minutes later, after Croft had bowled Woakes to leave Warwickshire 217-7 and the crowd in a frenzy, Matt then announced Samit Patel as the next Warwickshire batsman – much to the puzzlement of Jeetan Patel as he strode to the middle!

The mad few minutes then got even more chaotic. Croft claimed his second wicket in four balls by bowling Patel to leave Warwickshire on 217-8, but with the scoreboard showing one over remaining and Croft having just one delivery left, all around the ground thought any chance of a Lancashire victory had gone.

However, on the final day of County Championship matches, a minimum of 16 overs are bowled in the last hour, and with Keedy and Croft operating from both ends, the hour wasn't yet up, even though they had bowled the 16 overs. There was still time for six more deliveries.

With nine men around the bat, Ambrose played out the final over from Keedy to salvage the first draw at Aigburth in seven years. Lancashire were handed a bonus the following day when Nottinghamshire held out for what at one stage looked like an unlikely draw with Durham to peg back the league leaders.

Coach Peter Moores said: "The title will depend on who holds their nerve. I don't think we need to win all four of our remaining games. If we win two we will be in with a shout, three and we will be in with a very big chance and if we do win all four we will definitely finish top.

"We've been up there all the way through, we have shown a lot of fight and character. We've already won seven games this season, normally if you win 10 it would be enough to take the title and often it would be less than that. This year it's unique because there are so many teams involved in the title race. We will go very hard in these last four games."

"We've been up there all the way through, we have shown a lot of fight and character."

– Peter Moores

CLOSE OF PLAY DAY FOUR:
Lancashire 189 (SC Moore 76; NM Carter 6-30) and 380
(SJ Croft 122, KR Brown 91) drew with Warwickshire 280
(CR Woakes 60) and 217-8 (TR Ambrose 66no)

Lancashire 6pts (Bowling 3)
Warwickshire 8pts (Batting 2, Bowling 3)

LV= County Championship table August 5

	P	W	L	D	BaP	BoP	Pts
Durham	12	6	2	4	41	34	183
Lancashire**	**12**	**7**	**3**	**2**	**26**	**34**	**177**
Somerset	12	6	4	2	39	30	171
Warwickshire*	11	7	3	1	31	30	168
Nottinghamshire	12	4	4	4	24	34	134
Sussex	11	4	4	3	19	26	118
Yorkshire+	12	2	5	5	26	27	98
Worcestershire	10	2	8	0	23	26	81
Hampshire++	10	0	5	5	18	23	48

* Warwickshire deducted eight points for poor pitch
** Lancashire deducted one point for slow over rate
+ Yorkshire deducted two points for slow over rate
++ Hampshire deducted eight points for poor pitch

SCORECARD

Lancashire first innings		Runs	Balls	Mins	4s	6s
PJ Horton	c Clarke b Woakes	14	19	34	1	-
SC Moore	c Ambrose b Carter	76	94	128	14	-
KR Brown	c Clarke b Woakes	9	19	23	1	-
MJ Chilton	c Chopra b Woakes	6	31	37	1	-
SJ Croft	lbw b Barker	7	6	5	1	-
TC Smith	c Troughton b Carter	31	63	97	5	-
+GD Cross	c and b Carter	0	3	2	-	-
*G Chapple	c Porterfield b Carter	9	22	26	-	-
SI Mahmood	lbw b Carter	0	1	1	-	-
KW Hogg	c Porterfield b Carter	15	24	32	2	-
G Keedy	not out	1	3	8	-	-
Extras	(4 b, 5 lb, 8 nb, 4 w)	21				
Total	(all out, 46.5 overs)	189				

Fall of wickets:
1-45 (Horton, 7.5 ov), 2-69 (Brown, 13.2 ov), 3-101 (Chilton, 23.4 ov), 4-108 (Croft, 24.5 ov), 5-131 (Moore, 30.1 ov), 6-131 (Cross, 30.4 ov), 7-155 (Chapple, 36.5 ov), 8-155 (Mahmood, 37 ov), 9-186 (Hogg, 44.3 ov), 10-189 (Smith, 46.5 ov)

Warwickshire bowling	Overs	Mdns	Runs	Wkts	Wides	No-Balls
Woakes	16	3	54	3	1	-
Rankin	4	0	22	0	1	-
Barker	12	1	52	1	1	1
Patel	1	0	7	0	-	-
Clarke	5	1	15	0	-	-
Carter	8.5	1	30	6	-	3

Lancashire second innings		Runs	Balls	Mins	4s	6s
PJ Horton	c Clarke b Carter	32	74	90	5	-
SC Moore	c Clarke b Rankin	39	85	116	6	-
KR Brown	c Clarke b Rankin	91	210	293	13	-
MJ Chilton	c Clarke b Woakes	2	6	12	-	-
SJ Croft	c Clarke b Barker	122	182	227	11	1
TC Smith	c Clarke b Patel	1	17	18	-	-
+GD Cross	c Barker b Rankin	15	22	27	2	-
*G Chapple	c Patel b Carter	22	46	54	1	-
SI Mahmood	c Clarke b Patel	8	7	13	2	-
KW Hogg	c Troughton b Rankin	15	30	31	2	-
G Keedy	not out	5	9	11	1	-
Extras	(8 b, 6 lb, 10 nb, 4 w)	28				
Total	(all out, 113.5 overs)	380				

Fall of wickets:
1-57 (Horton, 23.3 ov), 2-80 (Moore, 29.3 ov), 3-84 (Chilton, 32.1 ov), 4-292 (Croft, 89.5 ov), 5-305 (Smith, 94.4 ov), 6-305 (Brown, 95.2 ov), 7-334 (Cross, 101.2 ov), 8-350 (Mahmood, 105 ov), 9-365 (Chapple, 110 ov), 10-380 (Hogg, 113.5 ov)

Warwickshire bowling	Overs	Mdns	Runs	Wkts	Wides	No-Balls
Woakes	26	14	43	1	-	-
Barker	21	3	78	1	1	1
Carter	17	2	73	2	1	2
Patel	21	4	63	2	-	-
Rankin	20.5	2	77	4	2	2
Clarke	8	1	32	0	-	-

Warwickshire first innings		Runs	Balls	Mins	4s	6s
V Chopra	c Moore b Chapple	14	30	43	1	-
WTS Porterfield	lbw b Hogg	13	48	58	1	-
LJ Evans	lbw b Mahmood	12	24	49	2	-
*JO Troughton	c Chilton b Smith	49	121	170	2	-
+TR Ambrose	c Cross b Hogg	11	19	35	2	-
R Clarke	lbw b Mahmood	18	43	48	3	-
CR Woakes	c Smith b Keedy	60	112	130	7	-
KHD Barker	c Croft b Keedy	27	58	55	4	-
JS Patel	c Croft b Keedy	28	31	55	3	-
NM Carter	b Chapple	1	4	2	-	-
WB Rankin	not out	7	17	23	1	-
Extras	(5 b, 7 lb, 28 nb)	40				
Total	(all out, 82.1 overs)	280				

Fall of wickets:
1-30 (Chopra, 10.2 ov), 2-36 (Porterfield, 13.5 ov), 3-59 (Evans, 21.2 ov), 4-96 (Ambrose, 29 ov), 5-133 (Clarke, 41.3 ov), 6-173 (Troughton, 53.1 ov), 7-228 (Barker, 68.5 ov), 8-251 (Woakes, 76.2 ov), 9-252 (Carter, 77.1 ov), 10-280 (Patel, 82.1 ov)

Lancashire bowling	Overs	Mdns	Runs	Wkts	Wides	No-Balls
Chapple	25	7	60	2	-	1
Hogg	16	3	43	2	-	1
Mahmood	12	1	86	2	-	12
Smith	12	2	31	1	-	-
Keedy	17.1	3	48	3	-	-

Warwickshire second innings		Runs	Balls	Mins	4s	6s
V Chopra	c Horton b Hogg	46	68	89	7	-
NM Carter	c Smith b Mahmood	25	43	66	4	-
WTS Porterfield	c and b Keedy	2	11	13	-	-
LJ Evans	c Smith b Hogg	30	92	113	2	-
*JO Troughton	c Smith b Keedy	0	10	10	-	-
+TR Ambrose	not out	66	137	162	5	-
R Clarke	c Horton b Keedy	12	38	43	1	-
CR Woakes	b Croft	2	13	11	-	-
JS Patel	b Croft	0	4	2	-	-
KHD Barker	not out	0	1	2	-	-
WB Rankin	did not bat					
Extras	(12 lb, 22 nb)	34				
Total	(8 wickets, 68 overs)	217				

Fall of wickets:
1-72 (Carter, 15.4 ov), 2-87 (Porterfield, 18.4 ov), 3-91 (Chopra, 19.5 ov), 4-92 (Troughton, 22.5 ov), 5-160 (Evans, 50 ov), 6-210 (Clarke, 61.2 ov), 7-217 (Woakes, 66.1 ov), 8-217 (Patel, 66.5 ov)

Lancashire bowling	Overs	Mdns	Runs	Wkts	Wides	No-Balls
Chapple	15	2	40	0	-	-
Hogg	14	4	43	2	-	1
Mahmood	9	0	59	1	-	8
Keedy	23	6	53	3	-	-
Croft	7	3	10	2	-	-

Umpires: SJ O'Shaughnessy & MJ Saggers Scorers: A West & DE Wainwright

Steven Croft

STEVEN Croft proved that there is definitely merit in the London bus theory, in that you wait ages for one to come around and then two come at once. In Croft's case, it was regarding County Championship hundreds. The 27-year-old's first four-day ton came against Nottinghamshire at Old Trafford in 2008, but he failed to convert a further 14 scores above 50 until August 1, 2011. He scored 122 against Warwickshire at Liverpool, and then, would you believe it, another one followed in his very next innings against Worcestershire at Blackpool, a fine 107 on his home ground.

The two knocks contributed to what was a personally memorable season for the all-rounder, who also captained the county with success in one-day cricket, caught more stunning catches than you could shake a stick at and finished it all off by hitting the winning runs at Taunton!

"I feel like, especially batting this year, that it has been quite tough," he said. "The batsmen who did get scores over 50 generally played a part in us winning games. Maybe on paper, some of the scores don't look like that much, but they contributed towards crucial partnerships that helped us in the end."

Croft had actually scored a maiden one-day ton in a Clydesdale Bank 40 match against Somerset at Taunton in May whilst captaining the side in the absence of regular skipper Glen Chapple, and later in the season he led Lancashire on a run of 10 limited overs wins out of 11 matches, only handing back the captaincy reins to Chapple for one of those Twenty20 matches.

"It was a bit unexpected, and it was something that I thought I would slowly work my way into," he continued, "but I'm obviously pleased it worked out the way it did. I learnt quite a lot this year around the games. As a cricketer and a person, it's calmed me down and helped me mature a bit more. I had to lead by example and get out of old habits, sort of grow up. During the last few games that I captained, everything came in my stride. You almost forget that you're captain in a sense, and the lads made it so easy for me. They're a great bunch.

"I had old habits of sulking a bit when I got out, but I had to make sure that I kept my body language positive because nobody wants to see you moping around when you're the captain. You've always got to look on the positive side of things. Even when you lose, you've got to try and give people good feedback."

Now, despite Mark Chilton stepping into the breach in the Championship, it would seem that Croft is the next in line to be named the Lancashire captain on a full-time basis when veteran Chapple decides to call time on his special career.

"The only thing that's been said to me was a brief thing that it might be the same situation again next year if Chappie can't play," Croft admitted. "It's something I'd like to do on a more permanent basis, and hopefully that will come in time. If it doesn't, I'll support anyone else who does it. I didn't set out to be captain, and I don't think anybody plays cricket just to be a captain. You play to win as many games as you can. I'm really pleased for Chappie because he's been at the club for such a long time, and he thoroughly deserves all the success that he gets. He's a fantastic role-model."

Talking of role-models, Croft is definitely one himself, both to youngsters making their way in the game and to current team-mates as well. Widely regarded as one of the best fielders in the country – even the very best by Gary Keedy – Croft took some remarkable catches. There was the Steve Patterson one against Yorkshire at Liverpool, the Alex Hales one against Nottinghamshire at Trent Bridge, and even the one to get Paul Collingwood, a fielder of some repute himself, against Durham at Liverpool. The list goes on.

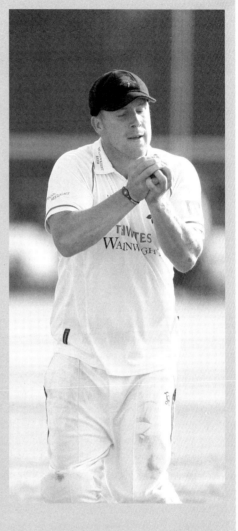

Croft added: "I've always been quite strong and active in the field, but when Francois du Plessis and Lou Vincent were around, I took a lot from them. To see other people do that on the field, and what sort of standard it sets, it's inspiring.

"Since they left the club, I've tried to step it up and have worked on my fielding a bit more. It's sort of trending in the squad now. You've seen for yourself that we're a really good fielding unit. It's made a massive difference to us at the end of the day."

CHAMPAGNE MOMENT: *"To see two of my big mates, Karl Brown and Gareth Cross, both score hundreds early on in the season was special. They were two innings that stood us in good stead for the rest of the summer."*

MATCH 13

Lancashire v Worcestershire

(Stanley Park, Blackpool) August 17-20

DAY ONE

WHEN you go to Blackpool, you would expect to experience a rollercoaster ride, and in the end, it took a towering performance from a local lad to illuminate Lancashire's title challenge. Well, that's all the puns out of the way! To be fair, the Red Rose rarely go to the seaside resort now following the farce of 2008 when there wasn't a ball bowled in the match against Surrey because of a damp outfield – even though it didn't rain during the four days of the game. So the puns are worth getting in when you have the chance.

The opening day of the clash with Worcestershire belonged to local boy Steven Croft. A mad Blackpool football fan, Croft learnt his cricket at the Stanley Park club after joining them as a 10-year-old. Now, 16 years later, he was in the middle leading Lancashire's fightback after another dodgy start with the bat and he relished every minute of it.

Full of confidence following his career-best equalling 122 in the previous match against Warwickshire, muscular Croft – who is probably the most powerful batsman in the Red Rose ranks – fired the Worcestershire attack all over Blackpool. He smashed four huge sixes and 11 fours on the way to 107 off just 111 balls to rescue Lancashire from a spot of bother at 79-4. He was joined in the onslaught by Farveez Maharoof and Gareth Cross, who both shared in crucial partnerships.

Coach Peter Moores and skipper Glen Chapple took the decision to drop one of their most experienced players for the game in Mark Chilton. After a good start to the campaign, the former skipper had struggled for runs in recent matches, so Maharoof returned for his first County Championship outing in two months following his trip back to Sri Lanka to play Twenty20 cricket.

Having been put in to bat, Lancashire were on the back foot from the off against a Worcestershire side who had started to show some form after a dismal start to the season. Stephen Moore, Karl Brown and Tom Smith – who had been promoted up the order following Chilton's omission – all fell cheaply as Lancashire were reduced to 62-3, with Richard Jones claiming two of the three wickets.

When Paul Horton fell 10 minutes before lunch on 47, becoming Moeen Ali's only wicket of the day, the Red Rose innings was in the balance, but Croft, who lives so close to Stanley Park he walked to the ground each morning, ensured it tipped the right way with a stunning innings. His powerful strokeplay helped add 87 for the fifth wicket with Maharoof. After the Sri Lankan was caught behind off Jones for 29,

Steven Croft, playing at his home ground, celebrates his second consecutive ton

Croft embarked on an even more impressive 90-run partnership in under 14 overs with Cross.

Poor weather has ruined Lancashire's title hopes more times than the average Red Rose fan would care to mention down the years, but the sun was definitely shining on them this season. No more so than at Blackpool when Croft was given a life. His big-hitting innings looked to be over on 33 when he launched the ball straight towards long leg. However, substitute fielder Nick Harrison was blinded by the sun's reflection off a window and failed to get even a hand on what looked like a straightforward chance.

Croft, in the shadow of Blackpool Tower, made him pay. He reached his half-century in 60 balls and then punished the Worcestershire attack as he reached his century off only 38 further deliveries. The Worcestershire spinners bore the brunt of his assault as Ali was dispatched for two leg-side sixes and Shaaiq Choudhry conceded 25 runs off two overs as Croft, fittingly, reached his hundred with a six over long-on.

The home-town hero was eventually dismissed when he fended a vicious rising delivery from Aneesh Kapil straight to Worcestershire captain Daryl Mitchell at slip. His departure

> *"It felt a bit weird to score a hundred for Lancashire at Blackpool because I know the place so well. It's something I'll remember for a very long time."*
>
> – Steven Croft

marked the start of a collapse which saw five Lancashire wickets fall for just 26 runs in 8.5 overs, as the Red Rose only picked up two batting points. Skipper Chapple, Sajid Mahmood, and Kyle Hogg all fell in successive overs for single figures while Cross went for 39 as Gareth Andrew got his reward for accurate bowling. Lancashire, who at one stage were 256-5 and looking towards 400, were all out for 282.

After 12 overs of Worcestershire's reply, however, that looked more than enough as the visitors were left in tatters at 21-5. Hogg and Chapple ripped through the top order as they swung the ball late, sharing the first five wickets. Hogg struck first, with Matt Pardoe nudging him to Smith at slip in the fourth over. The skipper then claimed two wickets in two balls as Vikram Solanki and then Ali were sent back to the pavilion in double-quick time, and added Alexei Kervezee to his list of victims in his next over. Hogg then finished off an amazing spell which saw him with figures of 2-9 by bowling Mitchell, leaving the visitors shell-shocked before Andrew and Kapil steadied the rocking ship with a crucial partnership for Worcestershire, who ended what had been a dramatic day on 77-5.

Croft said: "I'm very pleased to get a hundred, especially on my home ground. I got low scores in a couple of games recently, so I was due some runs here, but it feels a bit surreal. It almost felt like I was playing in a club game in a way, I felt really comfortable. I walked to the ground, and I was totally chilled out and relaxed when I went out there, I just played my own game.

"It was a bit tricky because we were three down for not many and it was a bit disappointing how we finished because we were looking to get a target of 300-plus, but we still got a good score and that's given us something to build on.

Chapple said: "Crofty has been playing well in one-day cricket especially and we always felt a big score was around the corner for him. In the last couple of games he has come right into form. He is a really competitive cricketer, his all-round game has been great all year.

"It was a really difficult decision to leave out Mark Chilton but we were picking a team to try and win this game. There is nothing to say Chilly can't play again. We will keep looking at it and pick sides to get results."

CLOSE OF PLAY DAY ONE:
Lancashire, having lost the toss and been invited to bat, 282 (SJ Croft 107) led Worcestershire 77-5 by 205 runs

DAY TWO

CAPTAIN Glen Chapple issued a note of caution at the end of day two that the game was far from over, but however you looked at it, Lancashire were in a commanding position. An unbeaten fourth-wicket stand of 90 from Karl Brown and first innings hero Steven Croft meant the Red Rose were 247 runs ahead with seven wickets still remaining in their second innings as the match moved on at a pace.

There were, however, two issues looming large for Lancashire. One was the skipper himself. He only bowled six overs in the day as he struggled with a groin injury and there was a real chance that he would be unable to bowl in Worcestershire's second innings. The other was – surprise, surprise – the weather. Rain was forecast for both days three and four and it left Lancashire with a quandary about whether to carry on regardless of the forecasters, who, let's face it, are not always right, or to play for a declaration and get Worcestershire in as soon as possible.

Day two started with the visitors still needing 133 to avoid the follow-on. That looked doubtful after the fifth ball of the day when Chapple – at that stage still injury-free – found some swing to break the frustrating sixth-wicket partnership as Aneesh Kapil went for 24 without adding to Worcestershire's overnight score. It could have been even better for Lancashire in the following over. Croft did brilliantly at third slip to get a hand to an edge from Gareth Andrew, but agonisingly he was unable to hold onto the ball. Andrew took advantage of the life, reaching his fourth Championship half-century of the season in the 13th over of the day.

Normally one of the best in the country in terms of fielding, Lancashire put down their second catch of the morning when Stephen Moore, running back from mid-on, spilled a chance from Ben Scott on 26. It proved to be expensive as Scott and Andrew put on 67 for the seventh wicket. Normal service was resumed as Croft pulled off a brilliant one-handed catch at gully to end the partnership as Andrew went for 61 looking to chop Farveez Maharoof away.

Andrew and Scott had done enough to save the follow-on, but Lancashire ended what was a largely frustrating session on a high when Shaaiq Choudhry became Sajid Mahmood's first wicket of the innings when he was caught at slip by Paul Horton as Worcestershire went in at lunch on 164-8.

It took Lancashire another 14 overs to wrap up the tail as Scott continued his resistance. Mahmood claimed the final two wickets to finish with 3-39 as Richard Jones was clean bowled and Alan Richardson caught by Brown at gully, leaving Scott stranded on 65 not out and Worcestershire 202 all out, still 80 behind Lancashire.

Moore and Horton then had to endure a tough 16 overs before tea, with the Worcestershire bowlers putting on the squeeze on a pitch where the new ball was causing problems. Horton took 35 deliveries to get off the mark as Richardson in particular made life tough for the Red Rose openers. Then, with the hard work done, Moore was fuming when he went for 26 off the final ball before tea, caught at backward point.

Horton followed for 35 just after the break, caught at slip off Andrew, and when Tom Smith went four overs later, trapped lbw by Andrew again, Lancashire were wobbling on 77-3. If Moeen Ali had held on to a catch at slip with Croft on one, a repeat of Lancashire's

> *"The last hour of the day was an exceptional period of play for us. It was crucial to see off the new ball."*
>
> **– Glen Chapple**

first innings late-order collapse could have been on the cards. However, Croft, who ended the day on 39, and the in-form Brown, who was unbeaten on 55 having brought up his half-century in 71 balls, went on the attack in an impressive last hour as Lancashire closed on 167-3.

Chapple said: "We are happy where we are so far. But we are not there yet, there is plenty of work still to do. The work done by Moore and Horton to see off the new ball was vital today. The last hour of the day was an exceptional period of play for us. It was crucial to see off the new ball.

"We saw 10 wickets fall for 37 runs on day one, so we had to bat well at the start of the innings. The new ball digs into the pitch and you have to be wary. We were just looking to see that off and get in a good position and we did that really well. When the ball gets softer it can sit up and is easier to hit."

CLOSE OF PLAY DAY TWO:
Lancashire 282 (SJ Croft 107) and 167-3 (KR Brown 55no) led Worcestershire 202 (BJM Scott 65no, GM Andrew 61) by 247 runs

DAY THREE

AT times, cricket can be a mad game. For almost the whole of the opening three days Lancashire out-played Worcestershire and held a lead of 80 from the first innings. Having ended day two well on top, by the end of the third day the outcome of the match was still in the balance thanks to one piece of individual brilliance.

Vikram Solanki, once a regular in the England one-day side, almost single-handedly dragged his side kicking and screaming back into the game with an impressive century as Worcestershire ended the penultimate day on 203-5. The 35-year-old Solanki showed his class with a 175-ball innings of 107 which saw the visitors to within striking distance of their victory target of 329, with their top-scorers from the first innings, Gareth Andrew and Ben Scott, still to come. Gary Keedy, however, eased Red Rose fears by claiming the crucial wicket of Solanki just five overs before the close of play to help keep the game in Lancashire's favour – just.

The home side had a poor morning session as they lost their last seven first-innings wickets for just 81 as they were dismissed for 248. All of Worcestershire's seamers enjoyed the helpful Stanley Park pitch, Andrew bagging three more wickets to finish with 5-59 and Richard Jones removing Gareth Cross, Kyle Hogg and Karl Brown to take 3-70.

Brown was the only highlight of the morning. While no-one in the bottom six of Lancashire's batting order reached double figures, he kept his head to make a battling 85 off 147 balls. Steven Croft backed up his first-innings century by notching his half-century before he became one of Andrew's victims.

Worcestershire's pursuit of what looked like an impossible target – considering no side had passed 300 in the match – got off to a poor start when Matt Pardoe's loose drive off Glen Chapple, who had shrugged off his groin injury, flew to Tom Smith in the third over, but that only saw the arrival of Solanki at the crease to join skipper Daryl Mitchell. The

Karl Brown on his way to 85 and Lancashire on their way to a commanding lead

pair put on 62 runs for the second wicket in just over 20 overs, crucially seeing off the new ball. Mitchell was plumb lbw to Chapple for 22, but Solanki – who reached his half-century in 69 balls – and Moeen Ali added 91 either side of tea before Ali was caught by Croft off Keedy for 47.

Alexei Kervezee will still probably be wondering if he had broken a mirror somewhere in Blackpool as he was out in the most bizarre fashion. His bottom edge flew up to Croft off Gareth Cross's boot. The umpires conferred, agreed it was a fair catch and gave Kervezee the bad news before Lancashire nudged the game back their way with the crucial wicket of Solanki.

Keedy said: "It was an extremely tough day. Worcestershire are a decent side and they've come out and scrapped like mad in this game. All of a sudden, after being in quite a comfortable position, we've found ourselves in a proper fight.

"The pitch was doing a little bit more and Andrew has bowled well all game. They put us under pressure but Browny batted really well and we'd have taken setting a target of 329 in the final innings, but Vikram's a class player and he has been for a long time. This season's been all about scrapping right down to the wire and the simple situation is that if we bowl well and stick to our disciplines, we'll win."

> *"All of a sudden, after being in quite a comfortable position, we've found ourselves in a proper fight."*
>
> – **Gary Keedy**

CLOSE OF PLAY DAY THREE:
Lancashire 282 (SJ Croft 107) and 248 (KR Brown 85, SJ Croft 50; GM Andrew 5-59) led Worcestershire 202 (BJM Scott 65no, GM Andrew 61) and 203-5 (VS Solanki 107) by 125 runs

DAY FOUR

LANCASHIRE fans turned up at Blackpool on the final day with a hint of trepidation. With Worcestershire needing just 126 more to win, and the Red Rose requiring five wickets to go back to the top of the table, another nail-biter looked to be in store. The home fans need not have worried as Tom Smith wiped away any fears of a title hiccup with a crushing spell to win the match.

It hadn't been the best of seasons in terms of bowling for Smudger. A knee problem had kept him out of the attack for a large part of the season, and with such a strong Lancashire seam attack, the former England Under-19 all-rounder had seen little of the ball. Now, Chapple's continued problem with his groin meant Smith was handed the task of making in-roads on the final day – and boy did he deliver. He stunned the visitors in a seven-over blitz which saw him claim four wickets for just seven runs as Worcestershire were bowled out for 230, handing Lancashire victory by 98 runs.

Gary Keedy started the clatter of wickets in the fifth over of the day as Aneesh Kapil was stumped by Gareth Cross. In the following over Shaaiq Choudhry slapped a Smith delivery straight to Stephen Moore at backward point as the rot set in. Smith struck again two overs later with Ben Scott lbw. He then bowled Richard Jones before wrapping up a 21-point haul for Lancashire when Alan Richardson was caught by Steven Croft.

All in all, the Red Rose had taken Worcestershire's last five wickets for just 27 runs in less than an hour, and the last seven wickets for 42 when taking into account the final session of day three.

Keedy finished with 4-58, having claimed his 50th wicket of the season when Kapil was stumped. It underlined why he was a man in demand. It had leaked out during the match that, being out of contract with Lancashire at the end of the season, the spinner had been offered a three-year deal by title rivals Warwickshire. With the Championship race at a crucial point, the left-armer – who moved to Old Trafford from Yorkshire in 1995 – vowed he wouldn't make a decision until the end of the campaign.

Lancashire were given a further boost later in the day when Warwickshire, who looked certain to beat bottom-of-the-table Hampshire in their match earlier in the day, suffered a shock defeat, while Somerset could only draw with Nottinghamshire.

Peter Moores said: "Two wins out of the last three games will be enough for us to win the Championship. All four sides involved in the battle for the title are good teams. We can't underestimate Durham, their batting has been a real powerhouse this year. Somerset are very good and Warwickshire have got themselves in a very good

Tom Smith is congratulated by his team-mates after his four wickets finished off Worcestershire's challenge on the final morning

position with a game in hand. But we have the points in the bag now. We haven't banned talk of the title in the dressing room. If you don't speak about it, it becomes more of an obsession. If you speak about it, it then becomes the norm.

"It was a really good win and it was nice we didn't end up with another twitchy one, which we have done on more than one occasion this year. Tom was really disappointed to miss out with the bat in this game, and that sparked him up a bit with the ball because he was desperate to contribute to the team. He has made a really significant difference in the second innings and I hope he gets a lot of confidence from it. It is a good time to be coming into form. Karl Brown has had an impressive game. He is always calm and has a fantastic gift of timing. He is playing shots of international quality."

Smith said: "It is a great feeling to be back on top of the table. We have played great cricket this year as a team and as a squad in all competitions. It hasn't been the best season bowling-wise for me, I've been a bit inconsistent, but here I bowled in the right areas for the consistent period of time and the results came for me. It is my best spell of bowling so far this season."

> *"We haven't banned talk of the title in the dressing room.*
> *If you don't speak about it, it becomes more of an obsession.*
> *If you speak about it, it then becomes the norm."*
>
> – Peter Moores

CLOSE OF PLAY DAY FOUR:
Lancashire 282 (SJ Croft 107) and 248 (KR Brown 85, SJ Croft 50;
GM Andrew 5-59) beat Worcestershire 202 (BJM Scott 65no,
GM Andrew 61) and 230 (VS Solanki 107) by 98 runs

Lancashire 21pts (Batting 2, Bowling 3)
Worcestershire 4pts (Batting 1, Bowling 3)

LV= County Championship table August 20

	P	W	L	D	BaP	BoP	Pts
Lancashire∗∗	13	8	3	2	28	37	198
Durham	13	6	3	4	41	36	185
Somerset	13	6	4	3	39	33	177
Warwickshire∗	12	7	4	1	33	33	172
Nottinghamshire	13	4	4	5	29	37	145
Sussex	13	4	5	4	25	31	132
Yorkshire+	13	2	5	6	30	29	107
Worcestershire	12	3	9	0	26	32	106
Hampshire++	12	2	5	5	20	26	85

∗ Warwickshire deducted eight points for poor pitch and one point for slow over rate
∗∗ Lancashire deducted one point for slow over rate
+ Yorkshire deducted two points for slow over rate
++ Hampshire deducted eight points for poor pitch

SCORECARD

Lancashire first innings		Runs	Balls	Mins	4s	6s
PJ Horton	c Mitchell b Ali	47	81	113	7	-
SC Moore	b Jones	4	18	32	-	-
KR Brown	c Mitchell b Richardson	16	29	28	3	-
TC Smith	c Richardson b Jones	9	24	36	-	-
SJ Croft	c Mitchell b Kapil	107	111	159	11	4
MF Maharoof	c Scott b Jones	29	66	87	3	-
+GD Cross	lbw b Kapil	39	60	77	6	-
*G Chapple	c Pardoe b Andrew	7	17	14	1	-
SI Mahmood	b Andrew	3	13	19	-	-
KW Hogg	c Choudhry b Andrew	0	2	4	-	-
G Keedy	not out	0	2	7	-	-
Extras	(6 b, 5 lb, 8 nb, 2 w)	21				
Total	(all out, 69.5 overs)	282				

Fall of wickets:

1-11 (Moore, 7.1 ov), 2-36 (Brown, 14.3 ov), 3-62 (Smith, 22.5 ov), 4-79 (Horton, 26.4 ov), 5-166 (Maharoof, 47.3 ov), 6-256 (Croft, 61.1 ov), 7-270 (Chapple, 66 ov), 8-278 (Cross, 67 ov), 9-279 (Hogg, 68 ov), 10-282 (Mahmood, 69.5 ov)

Worcestershire bowling	Overs	Mdns	Runs	Wkts	Wides	No-Balls
Richardson	17	8	48	1	-	1
Jones	14	1	62	3	1	-
Andrew	16.5	3	47	3	-	-
Ali	12	1	51	1	-	-
Kapil	8	0	38	2	1	3
Choudhry	2	0	25	0	-	-

Lancashire second innings		Runs	Balls	Mins	4s	6s
PJ Horton	c Solanki b Andrew	35	79	96	4	-
SC Moore	c Kapil b Choudhry	26	50	66	3	1
KR Brown	c Solanki b Jones	85	147	224	12	-
TC Smith	lbw b Andrew	4	15	17	1	-
SJ Croft	lbw b Andrew	50	92	97	7	-
MF Maharoof	b Andrew	3	16	13	-	-
+GD Cross	c Ali b Jones	9	12	13	1	-
*G Chapple	lbw b Andrew	5	7	11	1	-
SI Mahmood	b Kapil	3	9	15	-	-
KW Hogg	c Scott b Jones	5	6	8	-	-
G Keedy	not out	0	5	9	-	-
Extras	(12 b, 6 lb, 4 nb, 1 w)	23				
Total	(all out, 72.4 overs)	248				

Fall of wickets:

1-41 (Moore, 17 ov), 2-65 (Horton, 25.2 ov), 3-77 (Smith, 29.5 ov), 4-184 (Croft, 56.1 ov), 5-188 (Maharoof, 60.2 ov), 6-199 (Cross, 63.2 ov), 7-206 (Chapple, 65 ov), 8-223 (Mahmood, 69.1 ov), 9-229 (Hogg, 70.1 ov), 10-248 (Brown, 72.4 ov)

Worcestershire bowling	Overs	Mdns	Runs	Wkts	Wides	No-Balls
Richardson	21	10	32	0	-	-
Jones	15.4	5	70	3	-	-
Choudhry	4	1	14	1	-	-
Andrew	19	5	59	5	-	1
Ali	7	0	29	0	-	-
Kapil	6	0	26	1	1	1

Worcestershire first innings		Runs	Balls	Mins	4s	6s
*DKH Mitchell	b Hogg	5	41	50	-	-
MG Pardoe	c Smith b Hogg	5	8	13	-	-
VS Solanki	c Croft b Chapple	4	11	12	-	-
MM Ali	lbw b Chapple	0	1	1	-	-
AN Kervezee	c Maharoof b Chapple	0	3	6	-	-
A Kapil	c Cross b Chapple	24	50	67	3	-
GM Andrew	c Croft b Maharoof	61	94	122	10	-
+BJM Scott	not out	65	117	174	6	-
SH Choudhry	c Horton b Mahmood	9	46	41	2	-
RA Jones	b Mahmood	7	25	27	-	-
A Richardson	c Brown b Mahmood	8	21	32	2	-
Extras	(6 lb, 8 nb)	14				
Total	(all out, 68.5 overs)	202				

Fall of wickets:

1-8 (Pardoe, 3.2 ov), 2-13 (Solanki, 6.4 ov), 3-13 (Ali, 6.5 ov), 4-15 (Kervezee, 8.2 ov), 5-21 (Mitchell, 12 ov), 6-77 (Kapil, 24.5 ov), 7-144 (Andrew, 42.1 ov), 8-162 (Choudhry, 54.2 ov), 9-178 (Jones, 60.5 ov), 10-202 (Richardson, 68.5 ov)

Lancashire bowling	Overs	Mdns	Runs	Wkts	Wides	No-Balls
Chapple	15	1	47	4	-	-
Hogg	13	5	29	2	-	1
Maharoof	10	2	34	1	-	1
Mahmood	11.5	3	39	3	-	1
Keedy	11	0	29	0	-	-
Smith	8	2	18	0	-	1

Worcestershire second innings		Runs	Balls	Mins	4s	6s
*DKH Mitchell	lbw b Chapple	22	77	92	1	-
MG Pardoe	c Smith b Chapple	0	5	10	-	-
VS Solanki	c Horton b Keedy	107	175	233	15	-
MM Ali	c Croft b Keedy	47	91	100	8	-
AN Kervezee	c Croft b Keedy	14	27	25	3	-
A Kapil	st Cross b Keedy	7	44	56	1	-
SH Choudhry	c Moore b Smith	4	36	39	-	-
GM Andrew	not out	14	28	39	1	-
+BJM Scott	lbw b Smith	2	11	11	-	-
RA Jones	b Smith	3	14	13	-	-
A Richardson	c Croft b Smith	1	7	8	-	-
Extras	(5 lb, 4 nb)	9				
Total	(all out, 85.2 overs)	230				

Fall of wickets:

1-5 (Pardoe, 2.5 ov), 2-67 (Mitchell, 23.3 ov), 3-158 (Ali, 50.3 ov), 4-188 (Kervezee, 58.5 ov), 5-199 (Solanki, 64.1 ov), 6-210 (Kapil, 74.3 ov), 7-210 (Choudhry, 75.5 ov), 8-218 (Scott, 79.2 ov), 9-226 (Jones, 83.3 ov), 10-230 (Richardson, 85.2 ov)

Lancashire bowling	Overs	Mdns	Runs	Wkts	Wides	No-Balls
Chapple	19	3	60	2	-	-
Hogg	15	6	39	0	-	-
Smith	14.2	3	32	4	-	-
Mahmood	3	0	16	0	-	-
Maharoof	6	0	20	0	-	2
Keedy	28	8	58	4	-	-

Umpires: MA Gough & IJ Gould Scorers: A West & ND Smith

Tom Smith

TOM Smith is what's known in the game as a complete all-rounder. He has crafted a gritty century opening the batting against the new ball in the County Championship, but also reached three figures coming in at number six, and destroyed bowlers with punishing big-hitting at the top of the order in one-day cricket. In addition, he has opened the bowling in all forms of the game, but is probably even more effective as first change as the ball gets older in the Championship, yet he has also won matches by bowling the pressure-filled final over in nail-biting Twenty20 thrillers.

In the field he is one of the best catchers at the club, regularly claiming victims in the slips. To underline his all-round talents, he bats left-handed and bowls right-handed! He is the sort of player coaches and captains love because he adds the magic ingredient of balance to a side. Despite his arsenal of talent, you will never hear him shouting from the roof-tops about how good he is because he is one of the humblest men you will ever meet.

"It keeps me busy," said Smith, who graduated through the Lancashire age-group ranks having started his career playing for his home club of Chorley. "But I love the challenge of opening the batting, opening the bowling, batting in the middle order. It means I always seem to be involved in the game."

Smudger made his Red Rose debut in 2005 as a 19-year-old, but has been a Lancashire fan ever since he can remember, making the Championship victory even sweeter. "While watching them as I was growing up, I just wanted to get out there and do well for Lancashire," said the 25-year-old, who celebrates his birthday on Boxing Day. "I can't quite believe it was me out there doing it, helping the club I watched as a kid and supported all my life winning the title.

"It is one of my dreams come true. So many great names have tried before and not done it with Lancashire. I kind of just want to go back to that moment at Taunton when we won it. There was a bit of confusion at one point because we thought we needed an extra run. We were on the balcony and not too sure whether to celebrate or not. Then one of the umpires pulled the stumps out of the ground, so we went wild! It was such an amazing moment, an amazing experience. To get a win at Taunton is never easy, so it was a monumental effort from the lads. There were key pressure points which we handled well, but it was an epic four days of cricket.

"At the start of the season we knew it was going to be a special year because we were playing at outgrounds and on wickets where there would be results. To be honest, we're just a group of mates playing cricket. We play hard and play for each other and the team environment is second to none, which I feel is one of the reasons behind why we won the title."

Smith didn't have the best of years with the ball as hamstring and knee injuries took their toll, although he still took 25 Championship wickets. However, he put all that behind him to produce a stunning spell in which he took four wickets for just seven runs to demolish Worcestershire on the final day of their tense Championship match at Blackpool. However, he will go down in Lancashire folklore as the man who took the catch which dismissed Neil McKenzie to secure the win over Hampshire at Aigburth with just four minutes of the game remaining.

"Mal Loye sent me a message after the Hampshire game saying it had to be our year having won that match with four minutes to go," revealed Smith. "It wouldn't have been right if we hadn't taken it to the last session at Taunton. In hindsight, we won the match at Somerset relatively easily; we half expected it to go down to the last over!"

At the start of that final day, the title looked destined for Warwickshire, but as Lancashire were overcoming Somerset, Hampshire's McKenzie and Michael Carberry both made centuries to deny the Bears. "We finished day three before Hampshire had finished and we saw them lose three wickets on the TV and we thought it wasn't good," said Smith. "The way Carbs and McKenzie batted the next day was amazing. I sent Carbs a text calling him a legend!

"Peter Moores said at the start of the final day we just had to win the game, there was nothing we could do about what was happening to Warwickshire. That's what we did and now we are champions."

CHAMPAGNE MOMENT: *"Just being on the field celebrating at the end of the game at Taunton having won the title. It doesn't really get any better than that."*

MATCH 14

Worcestershire v Lancashire

(New Road, Worcester) Aug 31-Sept 1

DAY ONE

LANCASHIRE could sniff LV= County Championship glory. A win at New Road would see them with one hand on the trophy ahead of their final two matches of the campaign. On the other hand, a loss would severely damage their chances with Warwickshire and Durham closing in. Worcestershire started the season as many people's favourites for relegation, and they only enhanced their reputation as the division's whipping boys with a run of six successive defeats. In the end, they deservedly beat the drop. By the time Lancashire reached the Midlands, the Pears were a rapidly improving force, having beaten champions Notts, Hampshire and Sussex.

They showed their improvement again here as they enjoyed by far the better of the opening day against a side still hurting from a Super Over defeat in the Friends Life t20 semi-final against Leicestershire at Edgbaston just four days earlier. Only five Lancashire batsmen made it to double figures as they were bowled out for 161 in just 35.2 overs, with Steven Croft, Gareth Cross and Glen Chapple all failing to trouble the scorers.

Richard Jones struck with successive balls in the 15th over to get Stephen Moore and Croft, while fellow seamer Gareth Andrew removed Mark Chilton, Cross and Chapple in the 20th over, leaving the score at 67-7 after it had been 51-2 shortly before. Home debutant Kemar Roach, the West Indian with express pace and a recent World Cup hat-trick under his belt, then reduced the visitors to tatters at 113-9, despite being flayed over cover point for six by Sajid Mahmood before lunch. Kyle Hogg counter-attacked with 46 off 43 balls, sharing 48 for the last wicket with Gary Keedy, who only scored two, but Hogg's departure gave the prolific Alan Richardson his second wicket of the day.

Thankfully from Lancashire's perspective, the wickets kept tumbling as Hogg, Chapple and Tom Smith all struck to put the contest back in the balance with Worcestershire 119-6, but opener James Cameron, 87 not out at the close, and wicketkeeper Ben Scott (45) shared an unbroken 90 for the seventh wicket to enable the hosts to finish on 209-6 from 58 overs, leading by 48. Cameron enjoyed his fair share of luck, most notably when a Mahmood ball squirmed back off his body and onto the stumps without disturbing the bails, and despite numerous plays and misses, the left-hander deserved his second half-century of the campaign.

All but one of the day's 16 wickets fell in the morning and afternoon sessions, until Cameron and Scott gave concrete evidence that the pitch wasn't a total minefield, even though there were distinct signs of uneven bounce.

Kyle Hogg was the only Red Rose player to come out of the Championship game at New Road with any credit after Lancashire's worst batting display of the season. He scored 46 in the first innings to prevent a complete humiliation. It was one of a number of important contributions he made with the bat in 2011

After Chapple won the toss and elected to bat, no doubt on the basis that the track wouldn't get easier for batting, Paul Horton was first to go 20 balls into the day when he was rapped on the pads playing around Richardson. Karl Brown was adjudged plumb in front five balls later, this time to Roach as he offered no shot, and Lancashire were in bother at 10-2 in the fifth.

Moore and Chilton steadied the ship by adding 41 for the third wicket in little over 10 overs, the former punishing through the off-side and the latter elegant through leg. Having taken the score beyond 50, Moore played back to a Jones delivery and was bowled for 18 on his four-day return to New Road. The Johannesburg-born opener was the first of five wickets to fall for just 16 runs in 31 balls.

Croft went the very next ball, the third man to see the finger raised from either Tim Robinson or, in this case, Peter Willey for an lbw appeal. Then came the over of Andrew's life. Chilton was struck on the pad as he played around a straight one, wicketkeeper Cross went in identical fashion for a golden duck and Chapple played on. Smith also edged Roach into the slips before lunch, although Mahmood hit five fours and a six in a 24-ball 28 to help his side to three figures.

The Boltonian fell three balls after the break when Roach, who had replaced Pakistani off-spinner Saeed Ajmal as the New Road overseas player, claimed his third wicket. But thank goodness for Hogg, who at least gave some respectability to the score. The left-hander, who spent time on loan at Worcester earlier in his career, smeared five fours and two sixes off Richardson and Roach, who was becoming more and more frustrated at the audacity of his opponent. Hogg's footwork wouldn't have been out of place on Strictly Come Dancing!

The wickets kept on tumbling when Worcestershire replied – two of them in six and a half overs to be precise. Daryl Mitchell was caught at third slip by Moore off Hogg before Vikram Solanki, a century maker in the reverse fixture at Blackpool, steered Chapple to Chilton in the gully. With the score on 43 in the 16th, Moeen Ali edged Smith to Horton

> *"We need to get those four wickets as quickly as possible. We're disappointed overall. We'd have obviously liked more than 160."*
>
> *– Kyle Hogg*

at first slip before Alexei Kervezee played on in Smith's next over. Teenager Aneesh Kapil also made the short walk back to the pavilion when he was trapped in front to hand the impressive Smith his third scalp on the stroke of tea, and then Andrew fell in identical fashion to Kervezee off Hogg's bowling.

Cameron and Scott, however, having been dropped by Smith and Horton respectively, ensured that was the last wicket of the day, even taking 23 off two Keedy overs to assert their side's authority on the game.

Hogg said: "We need to get those four wickets as quickly as possible. We're disappointed overall. We'd have obviously liked more than 160. We bowled well, and we'd got ourselves into a good position, but they had a good partnership, which can happen. They played well with a bit of luck. We created chances, but we dropped a couple of catches, which no-one means to do."

CLOSE OF PLAY DAY ONE:
Lancashire, having won the toss and decided to bat, 161 trailed Worcestershire 209-6 (JG Cameron 87no) by 48 runs

DAY TWO

FOR all but one of Lancashire's team, the second and final day at New Road was a nightmare. That person was opening batsman Stephen Moore, as it was arguably the happiest day of his life thanks to the birth of his first child, a baby daughter called Emilia. Whilst Moore was travelling back up and down the M6 and M5 to be at his wife Ruth's side, Lancashire were hurtling towards a fourth defeat of the campaign in amazing fashion. Having seen 16 wickets fall on day one, 13 more fell in little over a session and a half to really put the cat amongst the pigeons in the title race.

Worcestershire started the day on 209-6 and were bowled out for 237, which amounted to a first innings lead of 76. There was no doubting that Lancashire were firmly on the ropes, but it wasn't a disastrous situation. What followed proved to be exactly that as Alan Richardson and Kemar Roach tore them apart.

Moore had left the ground at approximately 9 o'clock on the second morning to head back up to Manchester, where Emilia was born at 11.18am. Despite heading back down to the Midlands soon afterwards, his journey was a fruitless one as wickets tumbled with regularity. Richardson, who claimed 2-32 in the first innings, took five of the first six wickets to go as Mark Chilton – opening the batting – Karl Brown, Tom Smith and Gareth Cross all fell lbw, while Paul Horton was caught behind for the innings top-score of 21.

Lancashire had gone into lunch at 37-3, by which time Moore was on his way back as a new father. Then came the real horror spell. The visitors lost five wickets for 15 runs in 26 balls to slip from 45-3 to 60-8. After Smith and Cross had gone, Steven Croft fell, also lbw to Richardson, and Glen Chapple and Sajid Mahmood were both bowled by Roach.

As he did in the first innings, Kyle Hogg briefly resisted for a quarter of an hour with a quartet of boundaries, but the game was up when he was bowled by the West Indian, leaving Lancashire all out for 80. Incredibly, it was the seventh time in 12 innings that they had been bowled out for a score of less than 200. Moore, meanwhile, had got to within 50 miles of reaching New Road. At least he didn't have to pay the fiver for the M6 Toll!

> *"We've batted poorly in both innings, so we've got no complaints. We've won some great games this season, we've won some tight games. This time we just didn't play very well."*
>
> **– Peter Moores**

Mahmood later said that he thought this fixture was the only time during the season when Lancashire panicked, while it gave a few of the journalists time to head up to Edgbaston the following day to assess Warwickshire's credentials as they faced struggling Yorkshire.

With the game finishing so early, it left the Red Rose camp in limbo for a couple of days because fixtures involving Warwickshire, Durham and Somerset, who were also on the fringes of the title race, still had two days to go. It was pretty clear that this result was damaging to their chances, but they would have to wait until the weekend to discover the full extent of the damage.

As it turned out, Somerset were beaten by Hampshire to virtually end their hopes, big rivals Warwickshire were held by Yorkshire, thanks to some welcome bad light on day four after the Bears had got themselves well placed chasing a victory target of 349, and Durham beat Sussex at Hove. It all meant that Lancashire dropped down to third, 10 points behind Durham having played one less and only three behind Warwickshire, who had also played 14 matches. Thankfully, after a demoralising couple of days, it was still very much anybody's Championship.

Peter Moores said: "We've batted poorly in both innings, so we've got no complaints. We've won some great games this season, we've won some tight games. This time we just didn't play very well. We didn't get one significant partnership in the game. If we had got a lead of 150, I think it would have been an interesting game.

"Babies take precedence over cricket matches, which should be the case. Stephen's got a little baby girl. The baby was due this coming Sunday. Most first babies come late, so we thought we'd get away with it. It's a risk you run, but he wasn't far off being back with us. He was on his way. The baby was born this morning, and that's a plus out of the day."

CLOSE OF PLAY DAY TWO:
Lancashire 161 and 80 (A Richardson 6-22) lost to Worcestershire
237 (JG Cameron 98) and 5-0 by 10 wickets

Worcestershire 20pts (Batting 1, Bowling 3)
Lancashire 3pts (Bowling 3)

LV= County Championship table September 3

	P	W	L	D	BaP	BoP	Pts
Durham	15	7	4	4	45	42	211
Warwickshire*	14	8	4	2	40	39	204
Lancashire**	**14**	**8**	**4**	**2**	**28**	**40**	**201**
Somerset	14	6	5	3	40	34	179
Nottinghamshire	14	5	4	5	31	40	166
Sussex	14	4	6	4	26	34	136
Worcestershire	14	4	9	1	28	38	133
Yorkshire+	15	2	6	7	34	34	119
Hampshire++	14	3	5	6	24	32	114

* Warwickshire deducted eight points for poor pitch and one point for slow over rate
** Lancashire deducted one point for slow over rate
+ Yorkshire deducted two points for slow over rate
++ Hampshire deducted eight points for poor pitch

SCORECARD

Lancashire first innings		Runs	Balls	Mins	4s	6s
PJ Horton	lbw b Richardson	3	21	14	-	-
SC Moore	b Jones	18	30	60	3	-
KR Brown	lbw b Roach	1	2	3	-	-
MJ Chilton	lbw b Andrew	22	51	62	4	-
SJ Croft	lbw b Jones	0	1	1	-	-
TC Smith	c Solanki b Roach	15	31	43	3	-
+GD Cross	lbw b Andrew	0	1	1	-	-
*G Chapple	b Andrew	0	2	1	-	-
SI Mahmood	b Roach	28	24	35	5	1
KW Hogg	c Kapil b Richardson	46	43	44	5	2
G Keedy	not out	2	11	27	-	-
Extras	(8 b, 7 lb, 10 nb, 1 w)	26				
Total	(all out, 35.2 overs)	161				

Fall of wickets:
1-9 (Horton, 3.2 ov), 2-10 (Brown, 4.1 ov), 3-51 (Moore, 14.4 ov), 4-51 (Croft, 14.5 ov), 5-67 (Chilton, 19.1 ov), 6-67 (Cross, 19.2 ov), 7-67 (Chapple, 19.4 ov), 8-85 (Smith, 24.3 ov), 9-113 (Mahmood, 28.3 ov), 10-161 (Hogg, 35.2 ov)

Worcestershire bowling	Overs	Mdns	Runs	Wkts	Wides	No-Balls
Roach	12	2	69	3	-	5
Richardson	11.2	3	32	2	-	-
Jones	6	2	8	2	-	-
Andrew	6	1	37	3	1	-

Worcestershire first innings		Runs	Balls	Mins	4s	6s
*DKH Mitchell	c Moore b Hogg	10	15	18	2	-
JG Cameron	b Chapple	98	207	275	13	-
VS Solanki	c Chilton b Chapple	0	7	5	-	-
MM Ali	c Horton b Smith	21	37	37	3	-
AN Kervezee	b Smith	1	6	6	-	-
A Kapil	lbw b Smith	15	24	29	2	-
GM Andrew	b Hogg	17	30	45	2	-
+BJM Scott	c Cross b Hogg	47	63	89	4	1
RA Jones	lbw b Chapple	4	16	17	-	-
KAJ Roach	b Chapple	6	23	23	1	-
A Richardson	not out	4	3	7	1	-
Extras	(2 b, 10 lb, 2 nb)	14				
Total	(all out, 71.4 overs)	237				

Fall of wickets:
1-13 (Mitchell, 5.1 ov), 2-14 (Solanki, 6.3 ov), 3-43 (Ali, 15.5 ov), 4-45 (Kervezee, 17.4 ov), 5-77 (Kapil, 25.5 ov), 6-119 (Andrew, 37.1 ov), 7-216 (Scott, 60.4 ov), 8-221 (Jones, 65.4 ov), 9-232 (Cameron, 69.3 ov), 10-237 (Roach, 71.4 ov)

Lancashire bowling	Overs	Mdns	Runs	Wkts	Wides	No-Balls
Chapple	21.5	5	58	4	-	-
Hogg	21	2	50	3	-	1
Mahmood	12.5	0	52	0	-	-
Smith	14	4	42	3	-	-
Keedy	2	0	23	0	-	-

Lancashire second innings		Runs	Balls	Mins	4s	6s
PJ Horton	c Scott b Richardson	21	29	37	5	-
MJ Chilton	lbw b Richardson	3	24	28	-	-
KR Brown	lbw b Richardson	1	13	22	-	-
TC Smith	lbw b Richardson	10	44	51	2	-
SJ Croft	lbw b Richardson	10	36	60	1	-
+GD Cross	lbw b Richardson	0	2	1	-	-
*G Chapple	b Roach	12	15	12	-	1
SI Mahmood	b Roach	0	1	1	-	-
KW Hogg	b Roach	18	15	16	4	-
G Keedy	not out	0	4	12	-	-
SC Moore	absent					
Extras	(1 lb, 4 nb)	5				
Total	(all out, 30.1 overs)	80				

Fall of wickets:
1-20 (Chilton, 7.4 ov), 2-25 (Horton, 9.5 ov), 3-36 (Brown, 13.1 ov), 4-45 (Smith, 23.1 ov), 5-45 (Cross, 23.3 ov), 6-60 (Chapple, 26.4 ov), 7-60 (Mahmood, 26.5 ov), 8-60 (Croft, 27.2 ov), 9-80 (Hogg, 30.1 ov)

Worcestershire bowling	Overs	Mdns	Runs	Wkts	Wides	No-Balls
Roach	8.1	1	44	3	-	2
Richardson	15	8	22	6	-	-
Jones	7	1	13	0	-	-

Worcestershire second innings		Runs	Balls	Mins	4s	6s
*DKH Mitchell	not out	4	3	2	1	-
JG Cameron	not out	0	0	2	-	-
VS Solanki	did not bat					
MM Ali	did not bat					
AN Kervezee	did not bat					
A Kapil	did not bat					
GM Andrew	did not bat					
+BJM Scott	did not bat					
RA Jones	did not bat					
KAJ Roach	did not bat					
A Richardson	did not bat					
Extras	(1 lb)	1				
Total	(no wicket, 0.3 overs)	5				

Lancashire bowling	Overs	Mdns	Runs	Wkts	Wides	No-Balls
Smith	0.3	0	4	0	-	-

Umpires: RT Robinson & P Willey   Scorers: ND Smith & A West

Gary Keedy

WHEN you talk to the Lancashire squad about their champagne moments, Gary Keedy's run out against Somerset at Taunton crops up regularly, along with a number of Steven Croft's catches and Farveez Maharoof's innings against Yorkshire at Liverpool, but, for the man himself, it's only a pretty hazy recollection.

Keedy finished the season as Lancashire's leading Championship wicket-taker with 61, the fourth time he has taken more than 50 in a first-class campaign, but it was his direct hit from cover point to get rid of Gemaal Hussain as the game was slipping away that caught the headlines, especially when he later revealed that it was the first of his career!

"I just can't remember another one," he said. "It was definitely my first in 17 years. I've had ones where you nick the bails off, or get a deflection at the bowler's end, but they don't count. Every morning I throw at a stump, but I never think 'today is going to be the day when I run somebody out'. As for that one, I just can't remember what was going through my head as the ball came to me because it all happened so quickly. I do remember the usual shouts of 'keeper, bowler, batter, throw it' from the lads. I was obviously delighted to see off-stump come out."

It was an incident that capped off what was a quite remarkable season and a half for the Wakefield-born player, who missed the first half of 2010 with a broken collarbone after a pre-season fielding accident. He took 31 wickets in seven matches on his return, admitting that it was the best that he'd ever bowled. He then took that form into 2011 with five wickets in the season opener against Sussex.

"I'm delighted, especially after coming back from injury last year and wondering whether I'd play again," continued Keedy, who turned down a three-year contract offer from Warwickshire in September to stay at Lancashire. "I finished last season well. To be able to maintain my form over the 16 matches with a few ups and downs along the way this year was great.

"I've said before that I don't really judge my own performance on how many wickets I get. I judge my own performance on how much influence and impact I've had on a game. The most pleasing thing is that there have been significant moments where I've turned a game around."

Keedy, who was a deserving choice to receive a benefit season in 2010, is studying for a physiotherapy degree at Salford University, completed part-time over four years, so he should have been in an ideal position to know exactly how much hard work he would have to put in to recover from his collarbone injury. Despite starting this season at peak fitness, the former England Lions man has admitted that there are still some doubts that linger in his mind.

"I put a lot of work in on the rehab side, but the only concerns I had were what the surgeon said about some nerve damage," he continued. "I still get a little bit of trouble with tightness in the region, but it's nothing that I can't manage.

"As far as being able to bowl and do what I always do, there's no real difference. I can be a little bit apprehensive when we're fielding. When I dive on it, I still get moments where I think back to the time when I did it. They're the hardest scars to try and get out of your head."

It was a bit of a running joke between Keedy and the local media in the opening weeks of the season that he kept saying the same thing in post-day interviews. Something along the lines of 'I've just never seen anything like it' was a regular line. He recalls: "I remember after the Sussex match I said 'as long as I've played, I've never seen a collapse like that, seven for 22, on a good pitch like that'. Then other things happened throughout the season that superseded what had happened the week before. I felt like I was saying it every week, which was great."

It was a slight disappointment that Keedy's run of interviews stopped ahead of the Hampshire match at the Rose Bowl when Kyle Hogg took 7-28 in his first game of the season following injury. So now, you'll not be surprised to know that it can exclusively be revealed: "I really hadn't seen anything like that. For someone to come back after injury and take 7-28 in his first game, I'd never seen anything like it. It was the type of performance that summed up our season."

CHAMPAGNE MOMENT: *"Steven Croft's catch to get last man Steve Patterson out at Liverpool set the game up for us. I don't think you can put a value on that from a fielder who is the best in the country".*

MATCH 15

Lancashire v Hampshire

(Aigburth, Liverpool) September 7-10

DAY ONE

AFTER the New Road horror show, Lancashire knew they couldn't afford another slip-up against bottom-of-the-table Hampshire if they were to have any chance of winning the title. Some fans had already given up hope. Message boards and Twitter were full of doubters believing that once again the Red Rose had blown their chances of ending their Championship drought. The people who mattered, however – the players – hadn't given up hope.

Just days earlier they had watched a video of highlights from their previous eight Championship wins during the season put together by performance analyst Emma Allsop. Coach Peter Moores is big on players being reminded of the good things they have done and the Red Rose dressing room, both at home and for away games, is plastered with pictures of magic moments from earlier in the season. Centuries celebrated, five-wicket hauls, terrific catches. They are all there just to remind the team of how good they are.

It seemed to have an effect, especially on captain Glen Chapple. The 37-year-old knew more than anyone in the side how it feels to be in contention for so long only to fail at the final hurdle. In the previous 13 seasons, he had finished runner-up five times with Lancashire. On top of that, he was part of the 2007 side which finished an agonising 25 runs short of the title in a dramatic finale at the Oval which saw the Championship eventually go to Sussex. Now, as skipper, he was determined this time the biggest prize in the county game wasn't going to slip through his fingers again.

Hampshire are no strangers to Aigburth, having also played there in the previous two seasons. Then, they were confronted with seaming tracks. However, having seen the same wicket take plenty of spin on the final day against Warwickshire a couple of weeks earlier, the Red Rose were confident this one was going to turn and dropped Sajid Mahmood in favour of a second spinner, Simon Kerrigan. What a move it proved to be!

After losing their seventh toss in eight home games, Lancashire were in trouble at 125-5. By close of play Chapple was 76 not out, having shared an unbeaten 99-run partnership with Kyle Hogg, and dragged Lancashire back into the game on 337-7.

Lancashire had battled to 78-2 at lunch, with Stephen Moore and Karl Brown, who was run out after being turned back by Paul Horton while going for a second, the men dismissed. After the interval, Sean Ervine produced a bit of extra bounce to surprise Horton, who edged behind for 35, ending a 57-run stand with Luke Procter, and then

Karl Brown and Steven Croft move to shake hands, quietly contemplating the enormity of what they have achieved, while (below) their team-mates rush on to the field and celebrate. Some of those players had been rooted to their seats for many hours, unable to move for fear of jinxing Lancashire's chances as the drama unfolded both here at Taunton and at the Rose Bowl.

The players turn to the travelling supporters and begin a rousing rendition
of 'Lanky! Lanky! Lanky! Lanky! Lancashire!', gathering together (below)
in front of the 200-plus visiting crowd as their achievement begins to sink in.

Tom Smith embraces skipper Glen Chapple as the look of delight and relief is clear in their faces.

Although not selected for the game at Taunton, both Sajid Mahmood and Farveez Maharoof played important roles in the team's success and rejoiced in the moment.

It's just utter relief for cricket director Mike Watkinson and Luke Procter as the side crossed the line after an enthralling summer.

Glen Chapple receives the coveted LV= County Championship trophy from former England captain Mike Gatting. The look of joy on his face is readily apparent and was magnified by the photo that was to appear in the newspapers the next day. The champagne corks begin to fly (below) after the presentation ceremony as most of the team (right) took their turns to hold the trophy aloft.

As the rest of the team mingle with the backroom staff and crowd (below), Chapple is interviewed on Sky Sports by former Kent skipper David Fulton. So sure were Sky that Warwickshire would clinch the Championship, most of their resources had gone to the Rose Bowl. For much of the exciting conclusion, the thousands of Lancashire fans at home watched pictures of Brown and Croft surging towards the target initially with no commentary, but later described by Lancashire committee member Paul Allott from the studio at the Rose Bowl.

While Chapple is being interviewed, the team once again pose for photographs with Mark Chilton, who did not play at Taunton. Chilton stood in as captain several times during the season when Chapple was absent injured. He is holding the trophy with Simon Kerrigan, flanked by Stephen Moore, Paul Horton and Steven Croft.

Despite the noise, only around 200 Red Rose supporters made it to Taunton for the final day, a measure of how much the title battle swung during those final hours.

Having made their way up to the dressing room, the party begins for the delighted Lancashire players and staff. Far left is Ken Grime, one of the club's unsung heroes.

The players spill out on to the balcony for further renditions of 'Lanky! Lanky! Lanky! Lanky! Lancashire', led by Oldham-born Luke Procter.

Karl Brown hasn't even had time to take his pads off as he explains to the
dressing room how he and Crofty did it, while the photograph below captures
both the joy and the sense of camaraderie of a Lancashire outfit which
had proved themselves to be the best in the country.

Assistant coach Gary Yates looks on as Luke Procter dances for the camera.

Below: Members of the backroom staff celebrate the victory. Left to right: Ashley Spires (dressing room attendant), Emma Allsop (analyst), Sam Byrne (physio) and Mark Nunn (head dressing room attendant).

It's all change now for the new county champions as the festivities in the changing room and on the pitch wind down.

Steven Croft, trophy in hand, waves goodbye to the Taunton dressing room as the players finally leave a ground that is sure to bring back fond memories in the future.

It's time for a moment of quiet contemplation for Peter Moores and Glen Chapple on the balcony of the dressing room at Taunton with the satisfaction of a job well done.

The whole squad and backroom staff pose for a photo in the dressing room. On the right is Alan West (scorer), another of the club's unsung heroes.

After arriving back from Taunton the following day, the players began celebrating again outside the Old Trafford pavilion. Despite the fact that their arrival in Manchester was delayed by two and a half hours, a large crowd had gathered for the opportunity to see the returning heroes.

On Thursday, October 13, the players and their families, along with staff from Old Trafford and the local media, made their way to Buckingham Palace for the presentation of the **LV=** County Championship trophy and medals.

The players and staff take their places in the South Drawing Room at Buckingham Palace in front of the men's and women's **LV=** County Championship trophies.

The team pose with Prince Philip, the Duke of Edinburgh, and the trophy (above). Despite being a cricket fanatic, many of the Lancashire players would have been unfamiliar to him, but not Jimmy Anderson (left). Anderson played just two Championship games in 2011, but the Burnley-born fast bowler's contribution to the club has been immense. He is currently Lancashire's only full England international. How long before that situation changes?

Head coach Peter Moores is presented with his Championship medal (below) by the Duke and (right) compares it with that of skipper Glen Chapple. The events at the Palace would have brought back memories to Moores, who was in charge at Sussex when they won the Championship for the first time in their history in 2003. His success with Lancashire marks him out as one of the game's top coaches.

A few days after the trip to the Palace, the club held its Player of the Year awards night at The Point in front of 750 guests. Above sees the Lancashire squad welcomed at the start of the event by a ticker-tape reception.

Glen Chapple is presented with the Player of the Year trophy by Brian Jenkins, sales director of club sponsors Thwaites. Chapple is the first player to have won it on three separate occasions, a fitting reward for his contribution in 2011.

bowled Steven Croft off his next delivery. It was the second time in three innings the Lancashire batsman had been out first ball. When Procter, given his chance ahead of Mark Chilton and overseas player Farveez Maharoof, went for an impressive 45, bowled by James Tomlinson, Lancashire were in real trouble.

Fears that they were beginning to run out of gas at the most crucial stage of the campaign were blown out of the water as the Red Rose went on the attack. Gareth Cross and Tom Smith led the fightback, putting on 58 in quick time before Cross, who had done his bit to get Lancashire back on track, edged Chris Wood to wicketkeeper Michael Bates for 34 off just 47 balls. Smith, who had been getting better and better as the season progressed with both bat and ball, then shared a blistering 55-run stand in just 10 overs with Chapple as the Red Rose began to get on top.

> *"We're desperate to win the Championship. We're never going to stop trying."*
>
> **– Glen Chapple**

Smith's knock ended when he top-edged Ervine – the Hampshire bowler's third wicket of the day – but not before he had made a crucial 63, which included 12 boundaries. That's when the fireworks really started as Hogg and Chapple laid siege to the Hampshire bowlers, putting on 145 runs in an enthralling and entertaining final 25 overs of the day to ensure Lancashire claimed three batting bonus points.

"I've been due some runs," said Chapple after reaching his highest score in more than two years. "I felt like I owed the team. We got hammered last week, but it happens now and again. If you have any sense you throw that away and look on all the good performances we have had previously. That is what we have tried to do. It was important for us to clear our minds and get our heads right. We're desperate to win the Championship. We're never going to stop trying."

CLOSE OF PLAY DAY ONE:
Lancashire, having lost the toss and been invited to bat, 337-7 (G Chapple 76no, TC Smith 63)

DAY TWO

LANCASHIRE'S decision to play two left-arm spinners started to pay dividends mid-way through the second day. At different ends of their careers, Simon Kerrigan and Gary Keedy had teamed up just twice previously in the Championship during the campaign – with differing outcomes. They tore title rivals Warwickshire apart at Edgbaston in early May as Kerrigan claimed 5-7 and Keedy 3-2 to bowl out a home side which included England Ashes heroes Ian Bell and Jonathan Trott. Two months later, however, they claimed just two wickets between them as Lancashire slumped to only their third defeat of the season when they lost to Nottinghamshire at Southport.

Glen Chapple crashes a four on his way to 97

Despite both being left-arm spinners, they provide enough variety to pose batsmen different questions and showed once again as they sent down 55 overs between them on day two that they can work together in tandem. They both out-bowled Hampshire's left-arm spinner Danny Briggs, who ended the season in the England set-up.

Lancashire added 51 to their overnight score before they were bowled out for 388 in their first innings. Kyle Hogg reached his second half-century of the campaign before he was given out lbw off the bowling of Dimitri Mascarenhas. He and Chapple had done enough to go down in the Red Rose record books by beating Paul Allott and Warren Hegg's eighth-wicket stand of 116 against Hampshire in Southampton in 1987. Agonisingly, Chapple then fell three runs short of what would have been his first century in seven years when he top-edged a Mascarenhas delivery and was caught by Chris Wood. His innings included eleven boundaries and two sixes, and the skipper deserved to reach three figures, having rescued Lancashire from a spot of bother on day one.

Kerrigan, who made a career-best 18 not out, and Keedy then gave a glimpse of the team-work that was to come as they frustrated Hampshire with the bat, guiding Lancashire to their highest score since April. Even that target looked below par at first as Jimmy Adams and Liam Dawson saw off the new ball and posted a century opening stand. It was Kerrigan who made the breakthrough by bowling Dawson for 54, while Keedy accounted for the dangerous Michael Carberry, who earlier in the season had scored 300 in an innings, for just two by bowling him with the last ball before tea as Hampshire ended the session on 118-2.

They say catches win matches, and Paul Horton produced two stunners as the game swung back Lancashire's way. First Kerrigan deceived Adams and he went for 54 as Horton clung on to a difficult chance at slip, and then Keedy got the better of James Vince in the next over as Horton pounced once again. When South African Test player Neil McKenzie was caught by Gareth Cross as Keedy claimed his third wicket, Hampshire had slumped to 186-5. Things could have been even better for Lancs had Cross been able to take a difficult chance off Sean Ervine, who ended the day unbeaten on 52 as the visitors closed 159 runs behind on 229-5.

"I was pleased to get the wickets," said Kerrigan. "Adams nicked it to slip and then Dawson cut one that didn't spin. That's the magic delivery. Shane Warne bowled one to Ian Bell once and that was called a zooter. It was just a leg-spinner that didn't spin!

"It was nice to get a personal best with the bat too. It must have been a batter-friendly pitch for me to get 18. I was pleased the PA announcer mentioned it to the crowd when I walked off too.

"Keeds is a good bowler to work with and we showed here we can work well in tandem if we get the right wicket. He is a great bowler to have around and has had a big influence on my career.

"It is down to me and Keeds to turn it on in the rest of the game now. If you were the only spinner on the staff the temptation may be to slacken off. But there's no room for that in this squad."

> *"If you were the only spinner on the staff the temptation may be to slacken off, but there's no room for that in this squad."*
>
> **– Simon Kerrigan**

CLOSE OF PLAY DAY TWO:
Lancashire 388 (G Chapple 97, TC Smith 63, KW Hogg 51) led Hampshire 229-5 (JHK Adams 54, LA Dawson 54, SM Ervine 52no) by 159 runs

DAY THREE

YOU wonder if Paul Horton and Stephen Moore had watched Dead Poets' Society at the end of day two. In the film, the character played by Robin Williams tells his students: "*Carpe diem*. Seize the day, boys. Make your lives extraordinary." That is exactly what the Lancashire openers did. After Hampshire all but matched the home side's first-innings total as they batted until mid-way through the third day, the Red Rose knew they were running out of time to try and force the victory they desperately needed to stay in the title race, especially with rivals Warwickshire on the verge of victory in their match against Nottinghamshire.

So Horton and Moore took the game by the scruff of the neck, pummelling the visiting attack in the final 50 overs of the day, and setting the platform for Lancashire to launch a victory bid on the final day. It was enthralling stuff as they put on 168 for the first wicket in just 44 overs, their highest partnership of the season.

At lunch, all hopes of a win looked to be over. Hoping to gain a first-innings lead, Lancashire had only managed to prise out three Hampshire batsmen in the opening session as the visitors reached the interval on 323-8. A brilliant catch by Karl Brown at short extra cover in Gary Keedy's first over of the day accounted for Michael Bates, but only after he had made 43 and put on 88 with Sean Ervine. Simon Kerrigan then claimed his third wicket of the innings as Dimitri Mascarenhas edged to Tom Smith at second slip and Keedy completed his 32nd five-wicket haul in first-class cricket when Kerrigan took the catch at mid-off to dismiss Chris Wood just before lunch.

Ervine continued to punish Lancashire for the chance they gave him on day two as he notched his century in 169 balls. He also shared a frustrating 59-run stand with Danny Briggs as Hampshire closed in on Lancashire's first innings 388. Skipper Glen Chapple returned, however, to break the partnership as Briggs went for 29, and in the next over Ervine finally went for 128 as Steven Croft claimed the ninth Hampshire wicket to fall to spin in the innings. However, Hampshire had made 381, giving Lancashire a paltry seven-run first-innings lead.

The feeling around Aigburth was that, with Hampshire also desperate for a win to ease their battle against the drop, the two sides would set up a final day run chase. Nobody had told the two teams, especially not Horton and Moore. They flew out of the blocks, racing to 63 without loss off just 18 overs before tea, and the onslaught continued in the final session as they both posted half-centuries with some blistering stroke play.

Three times previously during the campaign, Horton had been dismissed while in the nineties and, just as frustrating, he had twice been left stranded just a few runs short of his century in CB40 games. So, as he closed in on three figures again, you could feel the nervous tension around the ground. Surely this time he would make it? As he went down on one knee to sweep Briggs for what Horton hoped would be the boundary which would take him to his hundred, he got a top edge and Mascarenhas took the catch at deep square leg. He was out for 96!

Lancashire showed their intent by sending Chapple in at three to continue the quick-fire scoring, with Moore continuing to lead the onslaught. The skipper fell just before close having added 13 off 10 balls, while Moore ended the day on 77 not out as Lancashire finished on 195-2, a lead of 202. The decision now was when to declare.

> *"I would prefer to have six scores in the nineties than six ducks. It's a team game at the end of the day."*
>
> ## – Paul Horton

"We are going to be positive," said Horton. "If we lose to Hampshire in trying to win the Championship, then so be it. In terms of declaring, it depends how quickly we score. I don't think we would set them anything less than a target of 300. We don't want to be too generous and the more runs we have in hand, the more fielders we can have around the bat to create pressure.

"If we hadn't played that positively in the afternoon, the game would've petered out into a draw. I would prefer to have six scores in the nineties than six ducks. It's a team game at the end of the day. We're trying to win a Championship. If we win this game and the next one we have a chance of becoming the first side in 77 years to do it and that is something special."

CLOSE OF PLAY DAY THREE:
Lancashire 388 (G Chapple 97, TC Smith 63, KW Hogg 51) and 195-2 (PJ Horton 96, SC Moore 77no) led Hampshire 381 (SM Ervine 128, JHK Adams 54, LA Dawson 54) by 202 runs

DAY FOUR

THERE are times in a season when it seems a team is destined to win the title, when you know their name is on the trophy. For Lancashire, the 2011 campaign was littered with them. The win over Yorkshire at Aigburth in the final over, the stunning victory over Warwickshire at Edgbaston, coming back from the dead to beat Yorkshire again at Headingley. Then there were the freak results, with Warwickshire, Durham and Somerset all losing games they looked certain to win – even the weather was in their favour.

The time when you knew without doubt that the engravers were already booked to scratch '2011 Lancashire' on the LV= County Championship trophy came with four minutes left on the final day of the game against Hampshire. That's the moment Tom Smith claimed the catch to dismiss Neil McKenzie and secure a win which, just two hours earlier, looked impossible. It was the moment which sent Lancashire down to Taunton to face Somerset in their final

Stephen Moore leaves the field after making Lancashire's highest individual score of the summer and setting the stage for a dazzling finale

match of the season knowing they were still right in the title race. And it was the moment 22-year-old Simon Kerrigan wrote his name in the Lancashire record books as he claimed a remarkable 9-51 to produce the most amazing win in a season of amazing wins.

Lancashire's big dilemma going into the final day was when to declare. They wanted to set a big enough target in order to avoid defeat, but one low enough for Hampshire – still in need of victory to help their fight against relegation – to want to chase on a wicket which, as Lancashire had shown in their second innings, was easy to score on. While others were debating, Stephen Moore just carried on where he left off the previous night as he continued to punish the Hampshire attack. He reached his second century of the season in 184 deliveries, then took just 33 more balls to add another 50 as he scored Lancashire's highest individual total of the campaign.

Karl Brown joined in the fun too, reaching his half-century in 80 balls as the pair put on a blistering 158 in just 27 overs, and when Brown went for 54 to Liam Dawson, Glen Chapple waved Moore, who was unbeaten on 169, in as Lancashire declared on 353-3. It left Hampshire needing 361 to win in a minimum of 67 overs. It was a tough ask at just over five an over, but Lancashire had scored close to six an over throughout the first part of the day and the visiting batting line-up had the potential to score heavily and quickly.

Hampshire, however, never really looked interested in the chase, and it proved to be their downfall as Lancashire went on the attack in the field knowing defeat wasn't an option. With Kerrigan and Gary Keedy bowling in tandem from the 12th over of the innings onwards, the Red Rose were always going to bowl more than the minimum 67 overs allotted, and, crucially as it turned out, more than the minimum of 16 overs they had to send down in the last hour.

Kerrigan made the early breakthroughs as Dawson was stumped by Cross and Jimmy Adams trapped lbw, and although Keedy claimed the key wicket of Michael Carberry to leave Hampshire 69-3, time was running out for Lancashire as tea approached.

Kerrigan, who had been bowling all his overs from the Pavilion End, got word to Chapple that he fancied his chances from the River End. So, backing his bowler, the skipper swapped him and Keedy. Kerrigan rewarded him with his first ball as he trapped James Vince lbw as Hampshire went in at tea on 91-4 with a minimum of 26 overs left.

A Red Rose victory still looked far-fetched, especially with a batsman of Neil McKenzie's quality at the crease, but Kerrigan had other ideas. He produced a world-class display of spin bowling, claiming five wickets in a devastating seven-over spell as Hampshire slumped from 107-4 to 119-9. Sean Ervine and Michael Bates went within three deliveries, Dimitri Mascarenhas followed in his next over before Chris Wood was caught behind. Then Aigburth went berserk when Kerrigan claimed the scalp of Danny Briggs to leave Lancashire needing just one wicket to win with still over an hour to go.

The drama and agony wasn't over, however. Despite every fielder being around the batsmen, McKenzie and James Tomlinson somehow batted out 21 overs. Time after time, defensive prods fell just short of a Lancashire player, with groans from the enthralled crowd as each chance went a-begging. All eyes were on the clock as the last hour of play drew to a close and the Hampshire batsmen saw off delivery after delivery with barely a run scored.

Then, with just minutes left, McKenzie prodded forward to Kerrigan and Smith grasped the ball in his hand. He was out. The place went mad. Hampshire were all out

**Simon Kerrigan on his way to becoming the first Lancashire player
since Roy Tattersall in 1953 to take nine wickets in an innings**

for 138 and Lancashire had won by 222 runs, but that barely told the story. Kerrigan had become the first Red Rose player to take nine wickets in an innings since Roy Tattersall in 1953. He ended the game with figures of 12-192.

The Aigburth crowd ran onto the field to salute their heroes as Kerrigan, proudly sporting the biggest smile you have ever seen, was ushered to the front by this team-mates to lead them off the field. Players and fans alike celebrated as if they had already won the Championship, and, in hindsight, maybe they had. It was a fitting way to end Lancashire's home campaign at Liverpool.

"They were crazy scenes towards the end," said Kerrigan. "There was a bit of panic setting in when we only had four minutes left to get that last wicket. We were bowling at them for 45 minutes with them at nine down, but thankfully we got it. When Tomlinson came in, we thought we'd get him every ball. When he started finding his rhythm, we got a bit worried. Time starts ticking by, and all of a sudden we've only got four minutes left. The lads are going into that last game believing that anything's possible after today.

"I don't think I'll beat those figures during the rest of my career. It's a really great moment, and I'll remember stuff like this when I retire. When I get into a rhythm, and this is a bit of arrogance from myself, I feel that I can bowl as well as anyone in the world."

Peter Moores said: "What a game! Simon's performance was stunning, for a young bloke to take nine on a wicket like that was great. He has the ability to put pace on the ball, he's got two or three different deliveries, and in the second innings his bowling was the quality of an international spinner. That's the highest compliment I can pay. He got good players out with fairly unplayable balls on a pitch that became quite sub-continental."

> *"When I get into a rhythm, and this is a bit of arrogance from myself, I feel that I can bowl as well as anyone in the world."*
>
> **– Simon Kerrigan**

CLOSE OF PLAY DAY FOUR:
Lancashire 388 (G Chapple 97, TC Smith 63, KW Hogg 51) and 353-3dec (SC Moore 169no, PJ Horton 96, KR Brown 54) beat Hampshire 381 (SM Ervine 128, JHK Adams 54, LA Dawson 54) and 138 (SC Kerrigan 9-51) by 222 runs

Lancashire 22pts (Batting 4, Bowling 2)
Hampshire 6pts (Batting 3, Bowling 3)

LV= County Championship table September 10

	P	W	L	D	BaP	BoP	Pts
Warwickshire*	15	9	4	2	43	42	226
Lancashire**	**15**	**9**	**4**	**2**	**32**	**42**	**223**
Durham	15	7	4	4	45	42	211
Somerset	15	6	6	3	42	37	184
Nottinghamshire	15	5	5	5	32	41	168
Sussex	15	5	6	4	30	37	159
Yorkshire+	16	3	6	7	34	37	138
Worcestershire	15	4	10	1	29	41	137
Hampshire++	15	3	6	6	27	35	120

* Warwickshire deducted eight points for poor pitch and one point for slow over rate
** Lancashire deducted one point for slow over rate
+ Yorkshire deducted two points for slow over rate
++ Hampshire deducted eight points for poor pitch

SCORECARD

Lancashire first innings		Runs	Balls	Mins	4s	6s
PJ Horton	c Bates b Ervine	35	102	142	4	-
SC Moore	c Bates b Wood	5	27	35	-	-
KR Brown	run out	16	19	24	2	-
LA Procter	b Tomlinson	45	103	122	4	-
SJ Croft	b Ervine	0	1	1	-	-
TC Smith	c Mascarenhas b Ervine	63	98	126	12	-
+GD Cross	c Bates b Wood	34	47	47	4	-
*G Chapple	c Wood b Mascarenhas	97	117	171	11	2
KW Hogg	lbw b Mascarenhas	51	79	93	5	-
SC Kerrigan	not out	18	45	50	2	-
G Keedy	c McKenzie b Briggs	8	11	15	2	-
Extras	(4 b, 4 lb, 8 nb)	16				
Total	(all out, 107.3 overs)	388				

Fall of wickets:
1-21 (Moore, 8.3 ov), 2-41 (Brown, 15 ov), 3-98 (Horton, 36.5 ov), 4-98 (Croft, 37 ov), 5-125 (Procter, 46.2 ov), 6-183 (Cross, 60.1 ov), 7-238 (Smith, 70.5 ov), 8-354 (Hogg, 95.2 ov), 9-369 (Chapple, 103.5 ov), 10-388 (Keedy, 107.3 ov)

Hampshire bowling	Overs	Mdns	Runs	Wkts	Wides	No-Balls
Wood	21	2	111	2	-	3
Tomlinson	26	4	88	1	-	-
Mascarenhas	30	13	76	2	-	-
Ervine	14	1	66	3	-	1
Briggs	13.3	4	34	1	-	-
Carberry	3	1	5	0	-	-

Hampshire first innings		Runs	Balls	Mins	4s	6s
*JHK Adams	c Horton b Kerrigan	54	139	204	5	-
LA Dawson	b Kerrigan	54	119	166	5	-
MA Carberry	b Keedy	10	28	17	-	-
ND McKenzie	c Cross b Keedy	29	82	78	3	-
JM Vince	c Horton b Keedy	1	7	3	-	-
SM Ervine	c Procter b Croft	128	212	268	6	1
+MD Bates	c Brown b Keedy	43	105	108	3	-
AD Mascarenhas	c Smith b Kerrigan	13	29	36	-	1
CP Wood	c Kerrigan b Keedy	4	4	9	1	-
DR Briggs	c Croft b Chapple	29	50	50	4	-
JA Tomlinson	not out	0	0	1	-	-
Extras	(5 lb, 6 nb, 5 pen)	16				
Total	(all out, 128.4 overs)	381				

Fall of wickets:
1-103 (Dawson, 37 ov), 2-118 (Carberry, 44 ov), 3-142 (Adams, 50.2 ov), 4-143 (Vince, 51.3 ov), 5-186 (McKenzie, 69.5 ov), 6-274 (Bates, 100 ov), 7-311 (Mascarenhas, 111 ov), 8-318 (Wood, 113.2 ov), 9-377 (Briggs, 128 ov), 10-381 (Ervine, 128.4 ov)

Lancashire bowling	Overs	Mdns	Runs	Wkts	Wides	No-Balls
Chapple	20	2	48	1	-	-
Hogg	13	4	42	0	-	-
Kerrigan	45	3	141	3	-	-
Smith	5	0	20	0	-	2
Procter	4	1	13	0	-	1
Keedy	37	6	93	5	-	-
Croft	4.4	1	14	1	-	-

Lancashire second innings		Runs	Balls	Mins	4s	6s
PJ Horton	c Mascarenhas b Briggs	96	137	167	10	1
SC Moore	not out	169	230	290	17	-
*G Chapple	c Ervine b Briggs	13	11	15	1	-
KR Brown	c McKenzie b Dawson	54	88	105	4	-
SJ Croft	did not bat					
TC Smith	did not bat					
+GD Cross	did not bat					
LA Procter	did not bat					
SC Kerrigan	did not bat					
KW Hogg	did not bat					
G Keedy	did not bat					
Extras	(4 b, 3 lb, 8 nb, 6 w)	21				
Total	(3 wickets, dec 77 overs)	353				

Fall of wickets:
1-168 (Horton, 44.5 ov), 2-192 (Chapple, 48.1 ov), 3-353 (Brown, 77 ov)

Hampshire bowling	Overs	Mdns	Runs	Wkts	Wides	No-Balls
Tomlinson	15	3	60	0	-	-
Wood	9	0	76	0	2	4
Ervine	3	0	18	0	-	-
Briggs	28	3	125	2	-	-
Carberry	1	1	0	0	-	-
Mascarenhas	17	5	44	0	-	-
Dawson	4	0	23	1	-	-

Hampshire second innings		Runs	Balls	Mins	4s	6s
*JHK Adams	lbw b Kerrigan	21	74	72	1	-
LA Dawson	st Cross b Kerrigan	10	26	40	-	-
MA Carberry	c Brown b Keedy	29	61	54	2	-
ND McKenzie	c Smith b Kerrigan	38	186	168	6	-
JM Vince	lbw b Kerrigan	8	23	16	-	-
SM Ervine	c Horton b Kerrigan	16	35	32	1	1
+MD Bates	b Kerrigan	0	2	1	-	-
AD Mascarenhas	c Horton b Kerrigan	0	5	5	-	-
CP Wood	c Cross b Kerrigan	4	28	19	-	-
DR Briggs	c Procter b Kerrigan	0	15	10	-	-
JA Tomlinson	not out	1	51	53	-	-
Extras	(11 b)	11				
Total	(all out, 84.2 overs)	138				

Fall of wickets:
1-26 (Dawson, 11.3 ov), 2-53 (Adams, 22 ov), 3-69 (Carberry, 30.1 ov), 4-77 (Vince, 36.1 ov), 5-107 (Ervine, 48.3 ov), 6-107 (Bates, 48.5 ov), 7-107 (Mascarenhas, 50.4 ov), 8-115 (Wood, 58.3 ov), 9-119 (Briggs, 63 ov), 10-138 (McKenzie, 84.2 ov)

Lancashire bowling	Overs	Mdns	Runs	Wkts	Wides	No-Balls
Chapple	5	2	12	0	-	-
Hogg	4	2	5	0	-	-
Keedy	33	16	38	1	-	-
Kerrigan	37.2	14	51	9	-	-
Croft	5	1	21	0	-	-

Umpires: PJ Hartley & JF Steele Scorers: A West & AE Weld

Simon Kerrigan

AS far as winners go in the Lancashire dressing room at Taunton, Simon Kerrigan could argue that he was top of the list. Not only had he become part of history in winning the County Championship title, but he had also gained a new bat and a bottle of Jägermeister liqueur from two of his team-mates. To top it all off, the left-arm spinner had also managed to hold onto his iPad following a daring dressing room challenge.

Initially, wicketkeeper Gareth Cross told Kerrigan that he would buy him a meal if he could bat for 50 balls in the first innings of the match against Hampshire at Liverpool in early September, which he failed to do by five balls because Gary Keedy's dismissal left him stranded on 18 not out. So this started a trend. Cross gave Keggsy, as he is otherwise known, another challenge: a free meal if he could get five wickets in the second innings of the match. And, with 9-51 his final figures as the crucial win was achieved in heart-stopping fashion, the rest is history as they say!

"It went into Somerset as a dressing room joke that I need incentives," explained the former Fulwood and Broughton youngster, who had taken 5-7 against Warwickshire at Edgbaston in May. "So that's when Roofy came up and offered a bat. He said that if I got 35 runs in the first innings, I could have the pick of the bats in his bag. Crofty also said that he'd throw in a bottle of Jägermeister. To even things up, I said to Crossy, 'If you get 200 runs in the match, you can have my iPad'. He never got close, so I was pretty lucky there."

All of the above added to what was a pretty strange and memorable year for Kerrigan. Despite only playing four Championship matches, he finished with an impressive 24 wickets, which led to him being picked for the England Lions during the summer and the elite group of England Performance Programme players for their busy winter training schedule.

He continued: "It has been a strange year. It started off by getting picked at Warwickshire when it looked like being a seamer-friendly wicket, but me and Keeds bowled them out in the second innings. Then I got picked against Notts at Southport when we thought it was going to spin, but it was a green seamer. Then, when I got another chance later in the season, luckily I performed."

Kerrigan played two one-day matches for the Lions against Sri Lanka A in mid-August, taking 3-21 at Northampton in the latter. He recalled: "It was really good playing for the Lions because most of the guys were ones who I'd played against before, so I knew them quite well. It was really good watching them perform for the full side in the two series at the end of the summer against India and the West Indies because it makes me think that if I keep performing, I'll be with them one day."

Performances like his nine-for against Hampshire during the final day will certainly help him achieve that goal. They were the best figures by any Lancashire bowler since Roy Tattersall's 9-40 against Notts in 1953, and led coach Peter Moores to say: "The way Simon bowled was the quality of an international spinner."

"When you think back about all the memories of the day and look at all the pictures, it was a great day for me and, in particular, the team," said Kerrigan. "When you play league cricket, it can be quite a similar feeling when it comes down to the last hour because teams regularly try to bat out for the draw.

"You start off quite calm when you get to the last hour needing just one wicket, as we did. Then the clock ticks closer and closer towards the end, everybody starts getting more anxious. I know that Chappie was even saying that he was stood at mid-off doing all these calming routines. Lee Richardson, our sports psychologist, has got all these calming techniques that he tries to get people to do, and Chappie said that he'd never even contemplated doing them, but there he was tapping his hands on his shoulders and clicking his fingers.

"Winning the Championship means a lot to me, but you can only imagine what it means to people like Chappie, who has put in so much hard work down the years and never got the rewards like this. It has undoubtedly been a season to remember."

CHAMPAGNE MOMENT: *"I remember the Yorkshire game at Liverpool. Our celebrations on the balcony after winning that show our unity as a team. Our celebrations when we've won the close games or got the vital wickets are things that really stand out."*

MATCH 16

Somerset v Lancashire

(County Ground, Taunton) September 12-15

DAY ONE

SO, after 15 gruelling matches, five months of blood, sweat and tears, just three points separated Lancashire and Warwickshire at the top of the LV= County Championship going into the final round of games. Somerset were out of the title battle, and Durham were hanging on by their fingernails, but really it was a two-horse race between the Red Rose and Warwickshire, who faced a trip to the Rose Bowl to play relegation-threatened Hampshire in their final match.

The equation was easy. Lancashire needed to collect three more points than leaders Warwickshire in order to win their first outright title in 77 years. If the two teams finished level on points, the crown would go to the Red Rose because they had a better head-to-head record against the Bears this season having beaten them at Edgbaston. The maths may have been easy, but achieving the desired result wasn't, as Lancashire found out on the opening day. In fact, it was probably as bad an opening day as they could have imagined.

After Simon Kerrigan's heroics against Hampshire at Liverpool in the previous match, Lancashire named an unchanged side for the title decider, meaning there was no place for the experienced trio Sajid Mahmood, Mark Chilton and Farveez Maharoof in the line-up as skipper Glen Chapple went for two spinners.

If you had to pick a ground to win a match on to claim the Championship, Taunton would probably be bottom of the pile. Although this year had seen more results at the venue than in previous years, the pitch was still a batsman's paradise. It was a point proved by James Hildreth after Lancashire had lost their 13th toss out of 16 in the Championship this season, Somerset piling on 314-5 by the end of the opening day thanks to a century from the England Lions player. Worse still for the Red Rose, skipper Chapple sustained a suspected hamstring tear, which twice forced him off the field and meant he bowled most of his 14 overs off a shortened run-up.

Lancashire did make an encouraging start, thanks to Chapple, as Alex Barrow was caught behind in the seventh over for just eight. Somerset were in trouble on 20-2 when Chris Jones was caught in the gully by Steven Croft off the bowling of Tom Smith. Smith then had the chance to end Hildreth's knock early, but he failed to take a difficult low chance while diving at second slip off Luke Procter's bowling. He was made to pay as Hildreth dominated the rest of the day. First, he and opener Arul Suppiah shared a 69-run stand for the third wicket before Chapple put his injury pains behind him to bowl Suppiah for 29 just before lunch.

That led to a difficult session for the Red Rose, who conceded 142 runs without taking a wicket as Hildreth and Jos Buttler, who was celebrating being called up to the England Twenty20 side, piled on the runs. Hildreth brought up only his second century of the season with a six over mid-wicket off Gary Keedy as he and Buttler added 170 for the fourth wicket. Just as frustrating for Lancashire was the news that Warwickshire had made an impressive start to their game with Varun Chopra and former Red Rose batsman Shivnarine Chanderpaul both making centuries as the Bears closed day one on 296-3.

> *"We've got to remember what we're playing for. No-one's going to lie down. Whatever it takes, whether it's until the last ball, we'll be scrapping."*
> – Gary Keedy

Lancashire, however, continued to plug away, with Hildreth and Buttler failing to hit a boundary in 41 overs during the late afternoon and evening session, and the Red Rose were eventually rewarded as Keedy finally broke the stand by catching Buttler off his own full toss for 68. Five overs later, he struck again as Peter Trego was caught at cover by Smith. Hildreth was still there at the close, unbeaten on 161, with Craig Meschede 24 not out. Lancashire had plenty of work to do.

Keedy said: "To lose the toss at Taunton, they're always going to bat. The wicket over the years has proved to be a good one, so we were expecting a tough day. We came off at lunch quite happy with 90-3, we dropped a catch, but they played well in the middle session. Towards the end of the day, to keep them down to three an over on that wicket and with a lightning fast outfield, we've done a reasonable job. It would have just been nice to have them one or two more wickets down.

"We're going to have to roll our sleeves up and get stuck in. We've got to remember what we're playing for. No-one's going to lie down. Whatever it takes, whether it's until the last ball, we'll be scrapping. The way Chappie was hobbling around, it doesn't look too good, but if we can get a few more overs and wickets out of him, that might be good enough."

CLOSE OF PLAY DAY ONE:
Somerset, having won the toss and decided to bat,
314-5 (JC Hildreth 161no, JC Buttler 68)

DAY TWO

LANCASHIRE showed all season they don't go down without a fight, and they were not about to start now with the title so close. If day one hadn't gone to plan at both Taunton and the Rose Bowl as far as the Championship race was concerned, the Red Rose were determined to make sure day two would be better. It started as early as the fourth over of the day with a stunning delivery by Kyle Hogg – some would say the best of his career – which Craig Meschede could do nothing but edge and Gareth Cross pounced to begin a tumble of wickets which saw Somerset lose their last five batsmen for just 66 runs.

Tom Smith finally got some revenge for having dropped James Hildreth on day one by claiming his wicket thanks to a brilliant catch at slip by Paul Horton, but not before he had made a dazzling 186. Gary Keedy then struck twice in three overs as first Murali Kartik – who five years earlier had been named in the Lancashire side ahead of Keedy for the 2006 C&G Trophy final at Lord's – was out lbw for 12 and Alfonso Thomas followed, again lbw, for 20. It left the spinner with 4-57.

The two wickets, however, had come too late for Lancashire to pick up maximum bowling points within the 110 overs, and they therefore had to be content with two. Simon Kerrigan wrapped up the Somerset innings with the fifth ball after lunch by trapping Steve Kirby, who started his career at Central Lancashire League side Heywood, lbw as the home side were bowled out for 380. It was an impressive morning's work from Peter Moores's side, especially considering skipper Glen Chapple was unable to bowl a ball.

Paul Horton and Stephen Moore then continued the good work they had started in the previous match against Hampshire as they posted their second consecutive century opening partnership, proving once again the pitch was a belter if you had a bat in your hand. Horton became the first Lancashire player to reach 1,000 first-class runs without scoring a century since Trevor Jesty in 1989 as he moved on to his seventh half-century of the campaign. However, just five balls later, he was caught behind by Jos Buttler while playing back to Kartik as Lancashire went in at tea on 133-1.

Karl Brown continued where Horton left off, taking the lead as he and Moore put on 102 for the second wicket before Moore was caught by Chris Jones pulling Kartik for 68. Brown followed six overs later when he was caught by Peter Trego in the slips for 60, although there was some doubt over whether the ball carried, and although he stopped walking off following a signal from the dressing room, he was waved away by the umpires. Steven Croft and Luke Procter saw Lancashire to the close at 247-3 and on the verge of a second batting point. At the Rose Bowl, Warwickshire had piled on 493 in their first innings at the Rose Bowl, but missed out on maximum batting points, so Lancashire were still only three behind the leaders.

Moore said: "It's a lovely pitch, I've been hoping for one of those all year! We're in a good mood, and in a good position. We have to win this game to give ourselves a chance of winning the title, we can't control what is going on elsewhere, so we are doing what we have done all season – playing our cricket in a positive manner.

> *"We turn up at every game prepared to go to the very last ball of the last day."*
>
> – Stephen Moore

"We turn up at every game prepared to go to the very last ball of the last day. We felt if we could get them out for less than 400 we would be giving ourselves a good chance of winning, and we did that. It's a good wicket, but with two spinners in our side in Simon Kerrigan and Gary Keedy, who can turn it on any track, we can put pressure on them in the second innings.

"Chappie's hamstring isn't in great condition, but over the years he has played through injuries and he will give it a good crack over the next two days. You will do well to keep Chappie off the field, especially in the last game of the season!"

CLOSE OF PLAY DAY TWO:
Somerset 380 (JC Hildreth 186, JC Buttler 68) led Lancashire 247-3 (SC Moore 68, KR Brown 60, PJ Horton 58) by 133 runs

DAY THREE

YOU just can't keep a good man down, as Glen Chapple showed on the third day at Taunton. Suffering with a suspected torn hamstring and having been unable to bowl on day two, the inspirational Red Rose skipper strapped himself up with the help of physio Sam Byrne, dosed himself up to the eyeballs with pain killers and led his troops into a winning position against Somerset. He played a crucial role in claiming maximum batting bonus points for the first time in the campaign, before starting a Somerset collapse which put Lancashire firmly in control of their match.

The Red Rose innings was a perfect example of the team ethic which characterised their season as – for the first time in 54 years and for only the second time in the club's history – every batsman reached double figures in their total of 480, a first-innings lead of exactly 100.

Luke Procter made 35 before he was bowled by Murali Kartik, while Tom Smith was trapped lbw by Alfonso Thomas for 28, but not before he and Steven Croft had added another batting point to Lancashire's tally. Croft, however, followed in the next over as he was caught by Peter Trego for 54, his fifth half-century of an impressive season, and as Lancashire went in at lunch on 356-6, they needed 44 more runs in nine overs to claim what could be a crucial final batting point.

That task got even more difficult when Gareth Cross went for 20 after a good catch

Despite suffering a suspected torn hamstring on day one, Glen Chapple played a key role in securing the Championship at Taunton

> *"Whatever happens, if we do win this game, we'll have had a great year."*
>
> **– Glen Chapple**

from Alex Barrow just after the interval, but captain Chapple came to the rescue as he and Kyle Hogg – who played his part in some crucial partnerships during the season – passed the magic 400 mark with just three balls to spare. With Hampshire's Liam Dawson – whose parents are from Bury – frustrating Warwickshire's bid for bowling points by making an unbeaten 152 at the Rose Bowl, Lancashire moved enticingly to the top of the table with just over four sessions of the season to go. All in all, the lead changed hands four times in a matter of hours.

Hogg and Chapple didn't survive much longer as they were both victims of Gemaal Hussain, Hogg for 46 and Chapple for 23 from just 26 balls. However, the Red Rose weren't finished. Buoyed by the promise of a new bat from Farveez Maharoof if he made more than 35, Simon Kerrigan shattered his previous first-class best of 18, set in the previous match, by reaching 40 from 41 balls before he was stumped by Buttler off Kartik, who claimed his fifth wicket.

Lancashire then turned the screw on the home side with the ball. Despite being in obvious pain, Chapple opened the bowling and amazingly took the wicket of Arul Suppiah in the seventh over. Kyle Hogg had Barrow caught by Paul Horton – his 31st catch of the campaign – and then took 50 wickets in the season for the first time in his career as Chris Jones was caught behind. Gary Keedy and Kerrigan then claimed the key scalps of James Hildreth and Buttler, who had put on 67 for the fourth wicket, to leave Somerset reeling on 105-5 at the close.

Lancashire's problem was at the Rose Bowl. Despite Dawson's resistance, Hampshire – whose relegation had been confirmed during the day – trailed Warwickshire by 126 runs, and within minutes of the close at Taunton, they lost two more wickets to leave themselves three down at stumps following-on in their second innings. Warwickshire were well and truly on top in the match and, moreover, in the title race.

"If we win this match it will be 10 wins this season, and if someone offered you that at the start of the season, you'd bite their hand off," said Chapple. "We would take that next season as well. Whatever happens, if we do win this game, we'll have had a great year.

"Hampshire are a good batting side, and it's a good pitch at the Rose Bowl, but we've just got to get on with our stuff and hope that's enough. We can't affect games going on 100 miles away."

CLOSE OF PLAY DAY THREE:
Somerset 380 (JC Hildreth 186, JC Buttler 68) and 105-5 led Lancashire 480 (SC Moore 68, KR Brown 60, SJ Croft 54, PJ Horton 58; M Kartik 5-137) by five runs

DAY FOUR

Peter Moores gives a final pep talk to the players on the morning of the final day

THERE was a glum mood around Lancashire's fans up and down the country at the beginning of the final day of the season. The Red Rose looked certain to end the campaign with a victory over Somerset, but Warwickshire were also on the verge of victory against Hampshire. There was talk that the visiting players, who were expected to wrap up the game sometime just after lunch, were planning to head straight back up the motorway to Manchester even before Warwickshire's match at Hampshire had finished. Christopher Martin-Jenkins and former Lancashire opener Michael Atherton were among those in the Taunton press box, although it looked like being the same old story of Lancashire once again falling short in the title race.

Having seen the scores at the end of the third day, hundreds of Red Rose supporters – along with a number of committee members including legend Jack Simmons – shelved plans to travel down to Taunton for the final day, assuming the title had gone. Amongst the doom and gloom, however, a group of players were laughing and joking as they warmed up. The only thing they were interested in was winning the match. They could do little else about what was happening at the Rose Bowl. Whatever will be will be was their attitude. Little did those Lancashire players know that they were on the verge of making history.

Glen Chapple, still struggling with his hamstring injury, put them on their way by claiming two early wickets. First, Steve Kirby went lbw and then Craig Meschede followed quickly afterwards, caught behind by Gareth Cross, as Somerset were reduced to 130-7, a lead of just 30. Although Somerset had the CB40 final at Lord's two days later,

> *"It's unbelievable. It's what I dreamed of when I joined the club seven years ago. Over the last 77 years we've had some world-class players at the club. To win the Championship now with this team is just amazing."*
>
> **– Steven Croft**

followed immediately by a trip to India to play in the Champions League, Peter Trego wasn't about to let his side's Championship season end with a whimper. He put on 75 with Alfonso Thomas and then 95 with, of all people, former Red Rose spinner Murali Kartik to frustrate Lancashire.

There was good news from the Rose Bowl. Hampshire's Michael Carberry and Neil McKenzie had batted through the whole of the morning session as they put on a stunning 182-run fourth-wicket partnership, which was beginning to scupper Warwickshire's hopes of a victory. All of a sudden, Lancashire's title hopes were alive again, but they needed to bowl Somerset out and leave themselves enough time to knock off any lead the home side built. Simon Kerrigan and Gary Keedy sent down 65 overs between them in the innings, but struggled to make the breakthrough. Out of the blue, a draw in both games seemed likely as the title hung in the balance.

Kerrigan finally ended Thomas's resistance when he was caught at slip by Tom Smith, but Lancashire used up another precious 23 overs before they finally dismissed Trego, who was also caught by Smith off Kerrigan's bowling, for 120. There was light at the end of the tunnel at last, although Kartik was still there on 65.

In 17 seasons of playing professional cricket, Keedy hadn't run anyone out with a direct hit. Season after season he had thrown thousands of balls at the stumps in practice. Now, all that work was about to pay off at the most crucial of times as he broke the stumps with a throw from backward point to dismiss Gemaal Hussain. Somerset were all out for 310.

Although Carberry had fallen for 111 at the Rose Bowl, McKenzie was still going as he reached three figures. Amazingly, the duo had put the game out of Warwickshire's reach. There were 140 minutes left with 16 overs minimum to be bowled in the last hour. It meant Lancashire had 34 overs to get the 211 they needed to win their first outright Championship in 77 years.

The pitch was ideal to bat on, but it was still a big ask to score at more than six an over considering what was at stake. Paul Horton and Stephen Moore, as they had done in the previous match against Hampshire at Aigburth, got Lancashire off to a flier, knocking 32 off the first five overs going into tea, setting up the biggest session of the season. Horton smashed his way to his eighth half-century of the campaign, while Moore joined him in the 1,000-run club in the Championship as he brought up his 50 with a straight six. The duo were well up with the run rate, and Lancashire fans were beginning to dream that this could be the moment.

But it wouldn't be Lancashire if there was no late twist. The openers smashed 131 for the first wicket in just 17 overs before Horton was out lbw to Meschede as he made 55 off 49 balls. Moore followed him two deliveries later for 71, which came off just 55 balls, as he was caught by James Hildreth off the bowling of Trego. Lancashire still needed 74 to win from 16 overs. Now was not the time for a case of the jitters!

Steven Croft and Karl Brown, however, didn't panic and continued where Horton and Moore had left off. As they closed in on their target, word spread that Warwickshire had shaken hands on a draw at the Rose Bowl, sending the Lancashire fans at Taunton into raptures. Fourteen minutes later Croft wrote his name into the Red Rose record books as he hit the historic runs which secured the title Lancashire had been waiting 77 years for.

As Croft and Brown embraced in the middle, the rest of the squad charged onto the outfield to mob the duo. They had won the game with 29 balls left in the season. The fact two Lancashire lads – Brown from Bolton and Croft from Blackpool – who came through the ranks at Old Trafford guided the side home was a fitting way for a side made up largely of home-grown players to secure the trophy.

In the end, Lancashire finished the season with 10 wins and 11 points clear of second-placed Warwickshire. Chants of 'Are you watching Yorkshire?' and 'We love you Hampshire, we do' filled the Taunton air as players and fans alike were drenched in celebratory beer and champagne.

It was then left to Chapple, who for 20 seasons put his all into reaching this very moment, to lift the trophy. In a season of unbelievable performances, tight finishes and dramatic results, Lancashire had pulled off the biggest victory of them all. It may have taken 77 years, but it was worth the wait.

Croft said: "It's unbelievable. It's what I dreamed of when I joined the club seven years ago. Over the last 77 years we've had some world-class players at the club. To win the Championship now with this team is just amazing. There have been no stars, no high-profile overseas players. We put in the hard yards from November onwards and it has been an awesome team effort all round. Browny and I are Lanky lads, so it was nice we were there at the end. It is an indescribable feeling. Hopefully, it's the first of many trophies."

Chapple said: "This couldn't be any sweeter. It makes it even better that this group of lads were dismissed as being unable to win the title at the start of the season. People didn't think we were good enough to turn over more highly-rated teams, and I didn't blame them for that, but they couldn't see into the character of these players. They have been amazing, they have had the belief that they could win it and fought to the end."

CLOSE OF PLAY DAY FOUR:
Somerset 380 (JC Hildreth 186, JC Buttler 68) and 310 (PD Trego 120, M Kartik 65no) lost to Lancashire 480 (SC Moore 68, KR Brown 60, SJ Croft 54, PJ Horton 58; M Kartik 5-137) and 213-2 (SC Moore 71, PJ Horton 55) by eight wickets

Lancashire 23pts (Batting 5, Bowling 2)
Somerset 5pts (Batting 3, Bowling 2)

Final LV= County Championship table

	P	W	L	D	BaP	BoP	Pts
Lancashire**	**16**	**10**	**4**	**2**	**37**	**44**	**246**
Warwickshire*	16	9	4	3	46	45	235
Durham	16	8	4	4	47	45	232
Somerset	16	6	7	3	45	39	189
Sussex	16	6	6	4	34	40	182
Nottinghamshire	16	5	6	5	35	43	173
Worcestershire	16	4	11	1	31	44	142
Yorkshire+	16	3	6	7	34	37	138
Hampshire++	16	3	6	7	30	36	127

* Warwickshire deducted eight points for poor pitch and one point for slow over rate
** Lancashire deducted one point for slow over rate
+ Yorkshire deducted two points for slow over rate
++ Hampshire deducted eight points for poor pitch

SCORECARD

Somerset first innings		Runs	Balls	Mins	4s	6s
AWR Barrow	c Cross b Chapple	8	19	26	1	-
AV Suppiah	b Chapple	29	99	117	5	-
CR Jones	c Croft b Smith	1	17	25	-	-
JC Hildreth	c Horton b Smith	186	307	346	20	1
+JC Buttler	c and b Keedy	68	137	157	9	-
PD Trego	c Smith b Keedy	1	22	15	-	-
CAJ Meschede	c Cross b Hogg	27	72	76	2	-
*AC Thomas	lbw b Keedy	20	52	64	3	-
M Kartik	lbw b Keedy	12	18	23	2	-
GM Hussain	not out	5	13	13	1	-
SP Kirby	lbw b Kerrigan	0	3	2	-	-
Extras	(8 b, 5 lb, 10 nb)	23				
Total	(all out, 125.4 overs)	380				

Fall of wickets:
1-18 (Barrow, 6.3 ov), 2-20 (Jones, 13 ov), 3-89 (Suppiah, 30.1 ov), 4-259 (Buttler, 81 ov), 5-265 (Trego, 86.4 ov), 6-320 (Meschede, 107.5 ov), 7-352 (Hildreth, 114.4 ov), 8-372 (Kartik, 120.4 ov), 9-379 (Thomas, 124.5 ov), 10-380 (Kirby, 125.4 ov).

Lancashire bowling	Overs	Mdns	Runs	Wkts	Wides	No-Balls
Chapple	14	2	43	2	-	-
Hogg	21	6	78	1	-	4
Smith	18	2	67	2	-	-
Procter	10	0	46	0	-	1
Kerrigan	34.4	6	76	1	-	-
Keedy	28	6	57	4	-	-

Somerset second innings		Runs	Balls	Mins	4s	6s
AWR Barrow	c Horton b Hogg	8	27	40	1	-
AV Suppiah	lbw b Chapple	12	23	26	2	-
CR Jones	c Cross b Hogg	4	16	17	-	-
JC Hildreth	st Cross b Keedy	39	59	73	5	-
+JC Buttler	c Horton b Kerrigan	27	86	84	3	-
PD Trego	c Smith b Kerrigan	120	217	222	9	1
SP Kirby	lbw b Chapple	4	16	21	1	-
CAJ Meschede	c Cross b Chapple	1	11	21	-	-
*AC Thomas	c Smith b Kerrigan	18	73	78	1	-
M Kartik	not out	65	100	90	6	2
GM Hussain	run out	0	12	10	-	-
Extras	(4 b, 6 lb, 2 nb)	12				
Total	(all out, 106.4 overs)	310				

Fall of wickets:
1-20 (Suppiah, 7.1 ov), 2-24 (Barrow, 10.3 ov), 3-25 (Jones, 12.2 ov), 4-92 (Hildreth, 32.2 ov), 5-104 (Buttler, 39.4 ov), 6-116 (Kirby, 45.4 ov), 7-130 (Meschede, 51.1 ov), 8-205 (Thomas, 79 ov), 9-300 (Trego, 102.5 ov), 10-310 (Hussain, 106.4 ov)

Lancashire bowling	Overs	Mdns	Runs	Wkts	Wides	No-Balls
Hogg	13	1	52	2	-	-
Chapple	19	4	53	3	-	1
Smith	4	0	15	0	-	-
Kerrigan	35.4	6	109	4	-	-
Keedy	30	8	55	1	-	-
Croft	5	0	16	0	-	-

Lancashire first innings		Runs	Balls	Mins	4s	6s
PJ Horton	c Buttler b Kartik	50	80	93	9	-
SC Moore	c Jones b Kartik	68	147	207	11	-
KR Brown	c Trego b Kartik	60	138	131	10	-
LA Procter	c Trego b Kartik	29	76	75	5	-
SJ Croft	c Trego b Kirby	54	98	124	6	1
TC Smith	lbw b Thomas	28	46	57	1	-
+GD Cross	c Barrow b Thomas	20	28	39	2	-
KW Hogg	c Kartik b Hussain	46	61	68	6	-
*G Chapple	c Kirby b Hussain	23	26	43	2	-
SC Kerrigan	st Buttler b Kartik	40	41	44	5	1
G Keedy	not out	13	28	38	-	-
Extras	(14 b, 8 lb, 22 nb, 5 w)	49				
Total	(all out, 126.2 overs)	480				

Fall of wickets:
1-104 (Horton, 24.5 ov), 2-206 (Moore, 56.2 ov), 3-219 (Brown, 63 ov), 4-272 (Procter, 81 ov), 5-325 (Smith, 95.2 ov), 6-331 (Croft, 96.5 ov), 7-371 (Cross, 103.3 ov), 8-418 (Hogg, 114 ov), 9-423 (Chapple, 115.1 ov), 10-480 (Kerrigan, 126.2 ov)

Somerset bowling	Overs	Mdns	Runs	Wkts	Wides	No-Balls
Kirby	17	4	51	1	-	1
Hussain	21	2	99	2	-	1
Thomas	21	1	97	2	-	3
Kartik	45.2	11	137	5	1	6
Trego	7	0	25	0	-	-
Meschede	4	1	13	0	-	-
Suppiah	11	3	36	0	-	-

Lancashire second innings		Runs	Balls	Mins	4s	6s
PJ Horton	lbw b Meschede	55	49	76	5	1
SC Moore	c Hildreth b Trego	71	55	79	6	1
SJ Croft	not out	40	33	45	5	-
KR Brown	not out	33	39	41	4	-
LA Procter	did not bat					
TC Smith	did not bat					
+GD Cross	did not bat					
*G Chapple	did not bat					
SC Kerrigan	did not bat					
KW Hogg	did not bat					
G Keedy	did not bat					
Extras	(3 b, 7 lb, 2 nb, 2 w)	14				
Total	(2 wickets, 29.1 overs)	213				

Fall of wickets:
1-131 (Horton, 17 ov), 2-135 (Moore, 17.2 ov)

Somerset bowling	Overs	Mdns	Runs	Wkts	Wides	No-Balls
Kirby	3	0	22	0	-	-
Thomas	7	0	51	0	-	-
Kartik	5	0	40	0	1	-
Trego	7	0	43	1	-	1
Meschede	3.1	0	24	1	-	-
Suppiah	4	0	23	0	-	-

Umpires: G Sharp & P Willey Scorers: GA Stickley & A West

Glen Chapple

OUTWARDLY Glen Chapple seemed cool, calm and confident as Lancashire headed into the final match of the County Championship season at Somerset knowing they were on the verge of history. Inside, however, the enormity of the moment was dawning on the Red Rose skipper.

"Going into the game I was thinking 'shit, this is it!' After 20 years of playing, it comes down to one game and this is it," revealed Chapple, who had finished second five times in 13 years. "I was thinking it with four games to go to be honest. In public I was saying we will take one game at a time, but secretly at Taunton I was saying 'shit, one more game!' It was such a big deal.

"But I did think we were going to win it. The worry after the first couple of days was at the Rose Bowl where Warwickshire were playing Hampshire. Again, in public we were saying we were paying no attention to what was going on there. You say it to keep your focus on the game you are playing, but I was checking the score every five minutes on my phone when I was in the dressing room!"

At the start of the final day, the title looked lost, with Lancashire and Warwickshire both seemingly certain to win their matches, meaning the Championship was bound for Edgbaston, but Chapple saw it differently. "I thought Hampshire would save the game, I promise you, I thought they would get a draw," he said. "I also thought we were far from certain to win our game. Somerset were five down with a lead of just five runs at the start of the final day. But both the Rose Bowl and Taunton pitches were flat. I thought two draws were on the cards.

"I was telling the lads we couldn't take our foot off the gas because 5-5 could quickly become 150-5, and it bloomin' well did! So I knew we had to work hard to win our game, but was convinced if we did, we would win the title. Scores from Hampshire were getting to us on the field, but I was paying absolutely no attention to them because our game was becoming too twitchy. We got to the stage where we were looking unlikely to win the match.

"Keedy's run out changed everything. It changed my thinking from 'we're screwed' to 'we have won the title'! I was thinking about the game and only half-noticed they had gone for a quick single, all of a sudden I saw Keeds let go of the ball and it's not missing! At that instant I thought 'we've won it!' Even though we still needed over 200 runs, the pitch was just so flat.

"When I got in the dressing room, I realised it was still a hell of a chase. But there was hope and belief again after that run out. Before it, I didn't know where that wicket was going to come from. That run out is the moment I will remember most from the whole season. The feeling in the dressing room during the run chase was weird. We were still twitching when we needed just 16 off 10 overs with eight wickets left! We were so nervous because of the seriousness of the situation. In

any other game we would be shaking hands in the dressing room at that stage, Saj would be singing and high-fiving, game over. But nobody moved until we needed about five runs! It just showed how important it was to everyone. It was a tough day. A brilliant day, but a tough day.

"I've spent 20 years trying to win the title. It is brilliant, but there wasn't this great outpouring of emotion from me. I was more thinking 'that's a relief!' I felt like it was a weight off my shoulders."

The title race went right down to the last session of the season, but Chapple could see signs that the squad could challenge as early as the second match of the campaign. "We always think the side can win the Championship at the start of each season," he said. "But if I'm honest, I didn't think we had more of a chance than in any other previous year. Although the attitude of the players was superb, there wasn't the weight of runs and wickets behind them. Everybody needed to step up and that doesn't normally happen.

"The first game against Sussex was an outstanding team performance. I was injured for the next one against Somerset and when I watched the lads play I was thinking 'wow, we've scored over 400 twice in two games and demolished two really strong teams.' The character was there, and now all of a sudden we had outplayed two teams who thought they could win the league. That is probably the time when I thought something special could be happening."

Chapple, who was born in Yorkshire but is Lancashire through and through, took over the captaincy in 2009 following Stuart Law's departure. Just a few months after he took the job, Peter Moores came in as the new coach having just been sacked from England after problems with the skipper Kevin Pietersen.

"Because Jimmy Anderson and Andrew Flintoff knew him so well, I had a chat with them and they both said he would be brilliant for Lancashire," revealed Chapple. "If it wasn't for what they said, maybe I would have been wary because with any new coach there is a bedding-in period.

"It was my first year as captain. It's an honour to do the job, but if I am perfectly honest I wasn't bothered who was captain of our team. It wasn't a case of 'I need to hang on to this job'. I just wanted to impress Mooresy to be honest. He has worked with some top cricketers in the past, so I wanted to make sure I was up to scratch! I felt like I needed to prove myself to him. Peter has made a huge difference. He's the complete package. He has technical and tactical skills and also people skills like nobody who has ever worked with us.

"In theory I would like to stay as captain until I retire, but I don't necessarily think that should happen if there's a good candidate there. I really enjoy doing it, and it's not a case of me being glad when it's over, although it might be nice to have a year at the end of my career back in the ranks. There are massive plusses to being captain of Lancashire. I've had so much praise on the back of what the team has achieved that I'm getting the credit for."

Chapple's performances in 2011 earned him the Player of the Year award for a record third time and also the Championship Player of the Year for the third successive time, and although the accolades are well received, they don't sit comfortably with him. "I don't like being praised," said Chapple. "I don't know why. I just don't. I would rather just blend into the background. I don't think I necessarily deserved the trophy this year."

Chapple may be 37 and have more overs under his belt than he cares to think about. In fact, with his five-year-old son always in the back garden with cricket bat in hand as soon as daddy comes home from work ready to play, he has bowled even more overs than most people realise! But he has no plans to retire any time soon. "I think realistically I've got two or three more years left," he said, "but that doesn't mean it couldn't be four because then I would only be 41. Some bowlers lose their pace earlier than the age I'm at now, and I haven't done. I would love to play when I'm in my forties.

"The new stadium, playing with this group of lads, working with a great coach, wanting your kids to remember you play – they all keep me hungry to keep going. At the end of the day it's a great job, a really great job. I want to be a coach when I finish. I might have to go somewhere else to get a chance, but the best job would be at Lancashire."

Having scored over 7,000 runs and taken more than 800 wickets in first-class cricket, he is seen as the best player never to have won an England Test cap. "I think I should have played for England, although it doesn't bug me because I tried my best and it didn't work out," admitted Chapple. "At 29, I got in the Test squad and was left out of the game. That annoyed me at the time, and I still think it was the wrong decision.

"I had the right attitude but I don't think I showed enough determination to get into the England team. I just thought it would happen and I trusted it would happen. But, to be fair, even though England weren't that successful at the time, there were some great cricketers playing. I was competing for places with Darren Gough and Andrew Caddick. They were really good bowlers!

"Not playing for England would be my one regret when I retire, but only a mild one. It really doesn't bother me. I find it quite entertaining how people go on about it. It seems to bug other people more than it bugs me. If I'd played for England I would've been hugely satisfied and proud. But I haven't. Every now and again I will see someone playing and I will think they shouldn't be. There is a bit of sourness there, but it doesn't spoil my day."

Over recent years, Chapple has regularly suffered with injuries, so it was no surprise when he tore his hamstring on the first day at Somerset, but he battled on, and was steaming in at full pace on the final day. It summed him up as a player and a person.

"I had strapping on and was drugged up with pain killers, and Sam Byrne the physio was brilliant," said Chapple. "I didn't have a scan on it after the game because I didn't want to risk there being nothing there! It would have shattered the illusion!"

CHAMPAGNE MOMENT: *"Gary Keedy's run out at Somerset. I knew then we had won the title."*

LV= County Championship Averages

BATTING AND FIELDING:

	Ms	Inns	NO	Runs	HS	Ave	Balls	R/100	4s	6s	100s	50s	C/St
LA PROCTER	7	10	1	366	89	40.67	725	50.5	33	5		2	2
SC MOORE	16	28	3	1013	169*	40.52	1795	56.4	135	5	2	5	8
MF MAHAROOF	5	7	1	241	102	40.17	369	65.3	24	3	1		4
PJ HORTON	16	29	1	1040	99	37.14	2196	47.4	145	2		8	32
KR BROWN	16	28	2	888	114	34.15	1763	50.4	128		1	6	7
SJ CROFT	16	27	1	825	122	31.73	1521	54.2	96	9	2	5	20
JM ANDERSON	2	3	2	28	18*	28.00	55	50.9	2				3
TC SMITH	12	19	1	459	89	25.50	1055	43.5	69			4	22
OJ NEWBY	3	3	2	23	14	23.00	66	34.8	4				
MA CHILTON	13	21	0	478	87	22.76	1242	38.5	62			2	8
GD CROSS	16	25	0	557	125	22.28	977	57.0	70	6	1	2	46/10
KW HOGG	11	18	1	365	52	21.47	510	71.6	51	3		2	2
G CHAPPLE	12	20	1	365	97	19.21	499	73.1	42	7		1	2
SI MAHMOOD	10	15	0	256	50	17.07	333	76.9	37	3		1	3
SC KERRIGAN	4	6	2	66	40	16.50	138	47.8	8	1			1
G KEEDY	16	24	15	111	20	12.33	322	34.5	12				5
JUNAID KHAN	1	2	0	16	16	8.00	15	106.7	1	2			
TOTAL	176	285	33	7097	169*	28.16	13581	52.26	919	46	7	38	165/10

BOWLING:

	Ovs	Mds	Runs	Wkts	BB	Ave	SR	R/O	NB	Wds	5wl	10wM
SC KERRIGAN	183	38	437	24	9-51	18.2	45.8	2.4			2	1
KW HOGG	309	68	940	50	7-28	18.8	37.1	3.0	17	1	3	1
G CHAPPLE	412.3	94	1090	55	6-70	19.8	45.0	2.6	2		3	
G KEEDY	562.4	110	1442	61	6-133	23.6	55.3	2.6	1		3	1
SI MAHMOOD	250.1	30	1045	35	5-74	29.9	42.9	4.2	55	1	2	1
TC SMITH	226.3	44	747	25	4-32	29.9	54.3	3.3	11	4		
SJ CROFT	68	16	193	6	2-10	32.2	68.0	2.8				
OJ NEWBY	62	14	260	8	2-26	32.5	46.5	4.2	6			
JM ANDERSON	71.3	20	165	5	3-57	33.0	85.6	2.3	1			
LA PROCTER	83	8	332	9	3-33	36.9	55.3	4.0	5	4		
MF MAHAROOF	112.5	18	397	9	4-35	44.1	75.0	3.5	25			
JUNAID KHAN	27	4	90	1	1-44	90.0	162.0	3.3				
TOTAL	2368.1	464	7138	288	9-51	24.8	46.2	3.0	123	10	13	4

Peter Moores

WHEN Peter Moores drove through the Old Trafford gates on February 11, 2009, there were question marks surrounding the former Sussex coach, who had hit the headlines just five weeks earlier following his departure as England's coach as a result of a breakdown in his relationship with national captain Kevin Pietersen. Maybe not from himself, but Lancashire's fans, players and even the Red Rose hierarchy would have no doubt wondered how the former King's School, Macclesfield student would cope with the public nature of his dismissal.

On September 16, 2011, he drove through the Old Trafford gates on the Lancashire team coach after his side had won the County Championship at Taunton just 24 hours earlier with all those questions answered in the best way possible. He was a champion!

To be fair to Moores, those answers came pretty quickly. It was clear from the outside looking in that Lancashire were moving forward within months of him taking the job, and, from the inside, those answers came even quicker.

Red Rose seamer Kyle Hogg explains: "I remember training in the Indoor Centre, and he was watching us from the balcony having just taken over. I'd never met him before, but I felt like I'd known him for ages as soon as he introduced himself. It says everything about him.

"When he finished with England, he could have come and just had three years on auto pilot, but he took this job on with the same enthusiasm as he must have done with England. In fact, it was almost as if it was his first ever job. I've never met anybody who's on the same level with regards to his

enthusiasm. His knowledge is also different class. Some say he's the best coach in county cricket, but I'd say world cricket. There's not a lot of other international coaches who would have done that."

Moores was contacted by cricket director Mike Watkinson almost immediately after being sacked by England, and the ex-wicketkeeper was actually unsure whether he wanted the job, even though he applied just to be on the safe side.

"When that job came up, of all the jobs, you're thinking 'that's my home club, it would be great'," said Moores. "But, if you can imagine, things happened from an England point of view very quickly. I was in a job and then out of one. It was literally within two or three days that I was asked to put in an application, but I didn't know whether I wanted to jump straight back into county cricket, forgetting what club it was for a second. Then I got offered the interview, so I thought that I might as well go for it and see what happened.

"The interview process was really tough, but fair. I presented for 15 minutes, was questioned for an hour, went away, came back and did it again. As I went through the process, I started to look into the club deeply again because I'd not been following it too closely because I'd been busy with England.

"I've always loved the club, and that's never changed. As a kid, I came along to nets run by Jack Bond at Old Trafford, and I remember playing in an under-13 tournament on the Nursery ground. We went into the players' dining room, which is the Trafford Suite now, and I've still got a menu signed by Farokh Engineer and Peter Lever. I took all those memories with me to the interview, but I had to look at where the club was at again.

"The fact that they'd lost a few senior players and maybe been struggling a bit, and there was a new captain as well. It really got my juices flowing all of a sudden, and I was keen to get stuck in. I really liked the fact that they were making the process hard, and I realised it was just what I needed by the time I'd done the interview. Once you want it, you're then panicking that you might not get it."

There were no worries on that score for the coach who had won the Championship with Sussex in 2003, and he and new skipper Glen Chapple soon had Lancashire moving in the right direction. Having escaped a relegation battle in 2008, 2009 brought a fourth-place finish in the Championship as well as semi-final and quarter-final spots in the two one-day competitions. Another fourth-place finish followed in 2010 along with another Twenty20 quarter-final.

"The main thing when we started – me and Glen – was to win the Championship," continued Moores. "We'd obviously had a tough year the year before I came to the club. Although we didn't say it out loud to anybody, we were going to play to win it, even though it just didn't seem quite right. By the time we started our second year, 2010, Glen sat the players down and made it clear that winning the Championship was our goal. It didn't happen, but we were in the mix. Then we lost a couple of players ahead of this season, but our goal was still pretty clear.

"It always means a lot more when you achieve something that you set out to do. People ask me whether I had a point to prove, which I didn't in that respect, but it's nice to get something that you crave. We've become the best side in the country in this form of the game. No-one will ever take that away from us.

"What was lovely about this season was that there were a lot of things that happened that said we shouldn't. But we did. There was a pretty strong belief within the squad, both from the players and the coaching staff, that we'd got a good side. The thing was though, it was untried and untested.

"The batting was always going to be less experienced than the bowling, and there were going to be players who you didn't quite know how they were going to do. People like Karl Brown hadn't played a run of games, so you don't know. People like Luke Procter hadn't played a run of games, so you don't know. We just saw the season as a land of opportunity. I certainly did as a coach. It was a great opportunity for some players to stamp their mark and for others that were already in to step up and become proper senior players. Horton, Moore, Smith come to mind."

All those players did step up and more to make this an epic season in every sense. There wasn't a Mushtaq Ahmed to lead the way with 103 wickets, or a Murray Goodwin with 1,496 runs as there had been at Sussex. Instead, there were three players taking 50 wickets or more and two players scoring 1,000 runs or more with others chipping in here and there. Karl Brown, Steven Croft and Simon Kerrigan are the perfect examples.

"This was a team in the true essence of the word," stated Moores. "Absolutely everything from on the field to off the field, the whole thing. If you write everybody's name down, you've got a match winning performance from pretty much every player. You can't win a Championship with one person. If that was the case, Hampshire would have won it when Shane Warne was there. Batting-wise, we found a way of getting one more run than the opposition. Moore and Horton got three 100-run partnerships in the last three innings. That's what I loved about the whole thing. It's been great fun."

What next for this group of players? Moores gave a fairly big indication at the club's Player of the Year dinner in October when he admitted on stage that he had spoken to some of his players' parents and asked them to make sure the lads keep their feet on the ground because winning it again in 2012 is the aim.

"We're trying to win on winning and create something that lasts, something that has foundations to it," he added. "We want to have the right culture for producing and attracting players. We've seen sides win, but it's almost a cancer that destroys the club. The ingredient needed to win on winning is humility. The age of the team means it will mature, so it should be in good shape. But there's no guarantee."

CHAMPAGNE MOMENT: *"There's loads, absolutely loads. Catches were significant. The obvious ones are Croft's at Liverpool to get Patterson and Horton's at Somerset to get Buttler. He had no right to catch that. Kyle and Saj put on a hundred stand for the last wicket at Yorkshire plus I don't think you can get away from nine-for for Keggsy either. You could go on for ever. But Keedy's run out stands out for me. We'd been throwing at a stump all winter and all summer, and you say to somebody 'there'll be a moment that splits the game that could win you the Championship'. There it was."*

Mike Watkinson

AS champagne and beer was being sprayed and a chorus of "Oh Lanky, Lanky" filled the Taunton air, Mike Watkinson could finally relax and enjoy the feeling of satisfaction. First as a player, captain, then coach and now cricket director, Winker had been chasing the dream of winning the County Championship with Lancashire for 29 years.

"It's a magic moment in the club's history," said Watkinson, who made his debut as a player in 1982. "Different people react to winning in different ways. Some people go mental and crazy with excitement. For others it is more of a 'thank God for that!' Avoiding failure is something people play for. Did I play to win? Probably. Did I play to not lose? Definitely. I am not going to be beaten by you and if a by-product of that is winning then so be it. That's how I approach things.

"So when we knocked the winning runs off I was feeling elated, but instead of throwing champagne over everybody's heads, I was more reflective and had an unbelievable feeling of satisfaction. It was the next morning I started behaving a bit giddy! It was the relief and relaxed feeling that comes through. I, more than most in the group, know how long this has hung on our backs for. It is an unbelievable amount of time."

The satisfaction wasn't just down to finally ending the title drought, but also because the Championship victory justified a major change in the way the club was run, a move initiated by Watkinson three years previously. At the end of the 2008 season, after seven years as cricket manager, Watkinson realised the pressure of his workload meant his time with the players was being sacrificed and that something needed to be done to change that. After much lobbying, the club agreed and he was made cricket director and one of his first jobs was to appoint Peter Moores as coach. With Watkinson now focusing on a wide range of off-field issues, such as players' contracts, the cricket budget, the club's links with the Lancashire Cricket Board and local leagues, it leaves Moores to concentrate solely on the senior squad.

Watkinson - who played four Test matches for England, captained Lancashire for four seasons and who is one of only two Red Rose players to score over 10,000 runs and take more than 700 wickets for the club - was also able to play a key role in the successful bid to bring an Ashes Test back to Old Trafford. Moving to a new role was a much-needed and crucial change, and now the whole club is truly feeling the benefit.

"It was something we had to sell as the right way to go," said Watkinson. "The way the club's business has gone over the last couple of years, and the demands of the modern game, for a club like Lancashire it was impossible to do what I was doing. It wasn't working, something had to give with everything I had on my plate, and it was my time with the players, which wasn't right. That's when I put my hand up and said we need to change something.

"There is a lifespan with working with particular groups of people. There are one or two exceptional individuals like Sir Alex Ferguson down the road who become the centre of the club, but other than that you need to freshen things up and make sure you are using your skills in the right areas.

"I enjoy being with the group, coaching and using my tactical observations to help Peter Moores. But I also enjoy being away and distancing myself from the group, planning and making their life easier.

"Initially at the club there were one or two wondering what we were doing. Now, they can see how it works. We're a more diverse business than any other county, I would suggest, and we need a structure to reflect how we do our business. This works really well. We've moved with the times. If we hadn't made the change I don't think we would be holding a 2013 Ashes Test and we probably wouldn't be looking at the Championship. It is a working model now."

As cricket director, Winker is also charged with the task of finding overseas players, a job made even more difficult this year with the lack of money at the club. There would be no Muttiah Muralitharan,

no VVS Laxman and no Shivnarine Chanderpaul, but he pulled two rabbits out of the hat by bringing in Sri Lankan Farveez Maharoof and Pakistan youngster Junaid Khan, both of whom became cult Red Rose heroes during the season.

"You have to do a lot of homework and, although people said taking on Maharoof was a gamble, he had played 95 one-day internationals and 25 Tests, so we knew he wasn't a donkey," said Watkinson.

"We have a good relationship with players around the world. Maharoof plays in the same team in Sri Lanka as Kumar Sangakkara, who we had spoken to in 2010 about joining Lancashire. I left a message on Kumar's phone saying we were thinking about signing Maharoof. A little while later I am at the top of a mountain in Austria on holiday, the phone rings and it's Sangakkara telling me Farveez is a good lad, filling me in on what his bowling is like and talking about what a great attitude he has.

"It is great to get endorsements like that through friendships you make over the years around the cricketing world. It was the same with Junaid. When we thought about taking a punt on him, it was nice to get the decision endorsed by Wasim Akram, which we did. At the end of the day, if both signings hadn't worked, it wouldn't have cost us very much. It was a shot to nothing really."

Not usually one to show his emotions, Winker came close to a moment of madness at Taunton, having watched Steven Croft hit the winning runs – but Sajid Mahmood got in his way!

"I was sat in the dug-out at Taunton when we hit the winning runs and, although it is not my style, I felt like running on the field to get hold of Browny and Crofty," explained Watkinson. "But I had a slight calf injury and was worried that if I sprinted off, it would go half-way and I would have to be carried off! As I was still debating what to do, Saj passed me, left tyre tracks on the outfield and left me for dead! The moment had passed.

"Every season, the Championship throws up surprises, things you don't think are going to happen. You have favourites who go down, sides who were less fancied who do well. There are a few factors which influence that on the way. A good start gives you belief and momentum and you start looking at the top which is what happened to us.

"This season we have had our eyes taken off the ultimate goal because of the issues we have had to deal with off the pitch. However, I think we react best when we have things to deal with. The club as a whole has been put under the pump in all departments and we have come through really well. But to have our budgets cut, to off-load players who we didn't really replace, and to focus on our own youngsters to see us through, has created something which feels a bit special.

"Support is fickle, we know that. If you put young players in and they do well they say 'brilliant, but why have you not done it before?' And if it doesn't work they say 'why have we not got Muralitharan back?'

"People have mentioned playing at outgrounds was the key, but it was more the freshness that caused which made it a bit of a special season.

"I think people have enjoyed watching us play this season. England are doing well with young, energetic, high-tempo cricketers. We are doing a similar thing and people like that, especially when they are Lancastrians who are playing that way. That is why it was so fitting Karl Brown and Steven Croft were there at the end in Taunton.

"What happened this season really does inspire young players. They see people like Crofty go back to Blackpool and there are pictures of him all over the wall. Browny pops back at Atherton, and a kid starting out there will think 'I am 14 now, in six years that could be me'. It's a great story all round."

CHAMPAGNE MOMENT: *"Farveez Maharoof hitting the winning runs to beat Yorkshire at Liverpool. This bloke has come from Sri Lanka, has been with us for just a couple of weeks so doesn't really know us from a bar of soap, and we are paying him buttons. He has just won a game of cricket and he is throwing his helmet in the air, dropping his bat and skipping around like a little kid. That was brilliant and showed how much we meant to him. It was humbling in many ways."*

Jim Cumbes

2011 has been a roller-coaster year for Lancashire in every sense, and nobody will have felt it more than long-serving Red Rose chief executive Jim Cumbes. From legal battles to international match bidding, to missing the final day of the season and celebrating the title win with a giraffe, the 67-year-old former football goalkeeper has been through it all. The man who also forged a successful career as a fast bowler with Lancashire, Worcestershire, Surrey and Warwickshire has lived to tell the tale of what he believes is one of the greatest 12 months in the Red Rose county's illustrious history.

"People will definitely talk about the 2011 season in the terms of it being a very special campaign, without any doubt," he stated. "You could better it cricket-wise next year if you won two or three competitions. But on and off the field combined, I don't think you could have a better period.

"Winning the Championship was definitely the culmination because we'd fought this legal battle over the redevelopment for nearly two years. We were always thinking we'd get over the line, but just not sure when. We were starting to run out of time with that, so it was a huge relief when we got that sorted.

"Then we went down to Lord's to make our presentation for the international matches in early August, and I was convinced that no other club could have done a better pitch. I felt we were going to get the Ashes back in 2013, which we did the following month. Then came the Championship win. That was the icing on the cake."

In many senses, Lancashire's victories off the field were more important to the club's future than winning the Championship as finances were running out fast due to legal fees and lost grants.

"We weren't quite hand-to-mouth, but we weren't far off," continued Cumbes. "What Peter Moores, Mike Watkinson and the players did so well was to cast aside all the off-field problems. We said to them in January, 'look there's no more money for players'. Peter wanted two experienced players, a middle order batsman and a seam bowler, as cover because our squad was only 17 plus Jimmy Anderson."

Despite the financial issues, money was found to fund the capture of two overseas players in Farveez Maharoof and Junaid Khan, although it was well documented that they had come on modest terms.

Cumbes explained: "That was absolutely amazing. When Mike came to me with the figures, I actually questioned it, especially the Maharoof one. It was a case of him bringing his family, and I was seriously concerned that he wouldn't be able to live on that kind of wage. I told Mike that we may have to tweak it if the guy was struggling whilst over here. But it worked for both of them, although it wasn't so bad with Junaid because he was single and getting his car and accommodation paid for."

It was always planned that Cumbes, who took the job in 1998, would retire at the end of the year, but the hectic nature of the last 12 months means there has been little time to confirm that plan. And now that decision may be delayed.

"I'm convinced there is a time when a club has to move on and when new blood has to come in. I don't know whether now's the right time, but that's not really for me to say," he said. "The club is moving into a different era. There is going to be a time for somebody new at the top. Whether that is immediately or a little way down the line, I don't know. I've not got anything further planned, although I'm sure I will do something else when the time comes. It might be something that I really want to look at and do. I've got various ideas. It might be something like driving a tram. I've always fancied working in a zoo you know, working with animals. It's funny isn't it?"

And that brings us to Lanky the Giraffe, who was part of the celebrations in the club's offices at Old Trafford after Cumbes realised that he had no chance of making it down to Taunton on the final day after promising to attend an awards ceremony at The Point the night before.

"Myself and Lee Morgan (finance director) sat down after the third day and decided that we were going to beat Somerset and that Warwickshire would beat Hampshire. To our mind, we'd miss out by three or four points.

"At lunchtime, I still thought that it had to be Warwickshire's. But then things started to build in our favour when we got Somerset out. Only then did I think 'we're going to win this'. For a split second, I went onto the website and looked at flights to Exeter, but they'd all gone.

"It was on TV in the offices, and there must have been 25 people and one giraffe watching at about 4pm. There were two cases of champagne there, which the president had bought to give to the team, but we couldn't resist opening three or four bottles. We replaced them the next morning."

CHAMPAGNE MOMENT: *"There's one statistic that I'm glad to be rid of. It has been said for years that there's one person in the club who won a Championship medal as a player. It was me with Worcester in 1974. Now we've got 18 of the buggers!"*

Fight For Survival

WHILE their players were battling to win the LV= County Championship, off the field Lancashire were facing an even bigger fight – for their very survival. A crippling 18-month legal battle with Derwent Holdings over the redevelopment of Old Trafford had cost them £4m and left them in severe financial trouble.

That is a huge amount of money for anybody, but for a county cricket club who had no guarantee of Test cricket, it was a potentially fatal amount. Ironically, it helped them on the field as, with no funds available for big-name imports, they put their faith in the home-grown players and won the title.

There were times during the 2011 season, however, that the club came close to not being able to pay their staff, and chief executive Jim Cumbes warned that if they hadn't eventually triumphed in their battle with Derwent, the very existence of Lancashire would have been in doubt. "We were within a week of running out of money," he admitted. "There's been two occasions this year when we were wondering how to pay the payroll."

In 2006 Lancashire received the stunning news they had been out-bid for a 2009 Ashes Test by Glamorgan, who were backed financially by the Welsh Assembly. It was a devastating blow, considering just 12 months earlier around 20,000 people had been locked out of Old Trafford for the final day of the Ashes Test.

Worse was to come as the increasingly decaying Old Trafford was stripped of Test status altogether. Something had to be done. Despite having discussions with Wigan Metropolitan Borough Council and Manchester City Council about moving to new, purpose-built stadiums, tradition held sway as Lancashire decided to stay at their historic home, but it needed vital redevelopment, and that needed to be paid for.

They struck a unique deal with Trafford Council, Ask developers, Stretford High School and Tesco which would see the supermarket pay £21m to the council for a patch of land not far away from the ground, and that money would be given to Lancashire to put towards a major facelift of Old Trafford. In the meantime, Lancashire borrowed £10m from the bank to build The Point, an impressive and eye-catching new 1,000-seat conference suite which would, they hoped, underpin the financial security of the club.

At a planning meeting in March 2010, attended by Lanky the Giraffe as well as club staff and supporters, their joint application for a £32m redevelopment of the ground and the 100,000sq ft superstore were approved. At the same meeting, Derwent had their application to build a food store on their nearby White City retail park refused.

It led to a fierce legal battle as Derwent fought the decision all the way. The Secretary of State called the scheme in three times, and in December 2010 Derwent were granted a judicial review of Trafford's decision, which was rejected in March 2011. But they didn't go away. Just two months later Derwent, owned by Albert Gubay, won leave to appeal that ruling, setting up what was the biggest day in the club's history at the Court of Appeal in London on July 4.

**Lancashire chairman
Michael Cairns**

After just four minutes of deliberation, the judge dismissed the appeal and, the following month, Derwent officially admitted defeat by revealing they would not take the battle to the House of Lords. Lancashire could finally start work on transforming Old Trafford into one of the best Test grounds in the world. "It was a crucial day," said Cumbes, "the most important in the club's 147-year history."

The victory didn't come cheap. It cost the club around £2m in legal and planning fees and the delay in starting work not only cost them a further £2m in lost grants from the North West Regional Development Authority, but at one point looked to have jeopardised the ground being ready in time for an Ashes Test in 2013. However, exactly seven days after they won the County Championship, all of Lancashire's dreams came true when – following an impressive presentation to the ECB – they were awarded a 2013 Ashes Test and were ensured Test cricket for years to come.

"This process started 10 years ago when we took a good look at the state of the club," said chairman Michael Cairns. "We had some problems so we went off with the then committee for an away day and had a hard look in the mirror. We agreed there was a significant level of dilapidation and the ground was desperately in need of tender loving care. We developed a vision as to what we thought should happen, but then we lost Test cricket. That was a real kick up the pants, but, in retrospect, helped. We then started to take some massive risks.

"The first was, having realised the finances of the club were quite fragile and that we needed to protect what income stream we had, taking on £10m of debt to build The Point. It has been a great success. The second was to invest £2m in planning for the major phase of the redevelopment. That was rewarded when we were given the green light by Trafford Council.

"However, Derwent made sure we made more appearances in court than Ken Dodd has made at the Palladium! We have all got free law degrees out of the process, but we won every court case. While it was very satisfying, it was very expensive. Things were very tough financially because the project was delayed so much, but we just kept our head above water. Lancashire are now back on the Test match scene.

"We have also tried to change the governance of the club because it is no longer amateur week. Running a cricket club of this magnitude requires a good group of commercial experts on one hand and the best cricket management on the other.

"During the legal battle one day we were in front, the next day we had a kick in the teeth. We rolled up our sleeves and started again. That 'we will not be beaten' ethos on the cricket side has now developed through the rest of the club. Now all our dreams really have come true."

For One Summer Only

Outground Cricket in 2011

by Paul Edwards

I only went out for a walk, and finally concluded to stay out till sundown, for going out, I found, was really going in.

John Muir, naturalist

PLAYING Championship cricket at outgrounds is one of the English game's more charming and useful customs: taking a match away from headquarters can help a county prepare for a lucrative event like a Test match or a pop concert; but it also offers local supporters a precious opportunity to watch their team without the inconveniences of a longish journey. It gives players a chance to display their skills in relatively unfamiliar surroundings, yet on grounds where the attendance is swelled by spectators making the most of the cricketers' one visit of the year.

In the late summer of 2010, though, Lancashire's officials found that an occasional tradition was soon to be a season-long necessity. Rotating the Old Trafford square through 90 degrees meant that Manchester would be out of commission for seven of the following summer's eight first-class games. (In late July it was announced that even the one match pencilled in at Old Trafford would have to be moved too.)

Faced with the prospect of a season as four-day nomads, Lancashire were fortunate that they had available to them three venues, all of which were eager to provide the county with a temporary resting place. Liverpool, already regarded by many as the Red Rose's second home, was originally allotted five games, eventually hosted six, but had been keen to stage all eight; Southport would have been happy to welcome Glen Chapple's players on two occasions, but was rewarded for its courteous lobbying with the visit of the 2010 county champions Nottinghamshire, thus ensuring that first-class cricket returned to Trafalgar Road for the first time since 1999; while Blackpool was given the Worcestershire match in mid-August, thereby giving officials at Stanley Park the chance to erase memories of their 2008 washout against Surrey and attract a holiday crowd to their home on the Fylde.

"Scarborough at Festival time is first-class cricket on holiday," wrote J.M. Kilburn, and that fine writer's crisp judgement catches something of the mood in which outground games on the western side of the Pennines were played in 2011. While the cricket was almost always hard-fought, there was often a certain gaiety among the crowds at the three venues, as if the punters were determined to relish every moment of a summer in which a glance at Lancashire's fixture-list made them feel as though they had won some sort of prize.

Nowhere was the ambience more buoyant than at Liverpool, although few spectators went to the lengths of the streaker who sprinted across Aigburth on the very chilly third evening of the Roses match. While this adventuresome soul was not – how can we put this? – grabbed by the stewards, he still risked confronting doctors on Merseyside with one of their more unusual cases of frostbite.

Twenty-four hours later, though, the world and his wife were on the outfield after Lancashire had won one of the most dramatic Roses matches in history, and even those celebrations were dwarfed by the scenes of delight which followed the conclusion of Kerrigan's match in September.

Playing at outgrounds clearly makes such behaviour rather more tolerable: the cheering spectators who danced and sang on Liverpool's outfield last September were hailed as good-humoured supporters, their own conduct almost a complement to the hugs and high fives being exchanged on the balcony of the great old pavilion; however, had the fans cavorted in a similar fashion at Old Trafford, they would have probably found themselves £1,000 poorer the next morning after having had their coffee with a magistrate.

If anything, the festival atmosphere was even more apparent at Southport, where Lancashire enjoyed their best four-day crowds of the season, and at Blackpool, where Steven Croft's century and Gary Keedy's bowling wrested victory from a resolute Worcestershire side. At both venues spectators combined with the players to produce occasions worthy of special recollection, even in this most memorable of summers.

But a sense of occasion, however powerful, is not by itself sufficient reason for Lancashire continuing to take games to other venues once Old Trafford is redeveloped. Playing out-ground cricket is only justified if a wicket capable of lasting four days can be provided and this requirement is a *sine qua non* of a club getting the gig. If that condition is satisfied, though, counties like Lancashire should play a game or two away from their geographical comfort zones because to do so constitutes an acknowledgement that a first-class county has allegiances and connections beyond its headquarters. To watch Blackpool's Croft bat in his own backyard in August, or Paul Horton make two of his nineties at Aigburth, just down the road from his old school and only a mile or so from the club where he still plays, was to be reminded of the symbiosis between the county and its clubs.

The Lancashire Cricket Board has over 400 clubs affiliated to it, and junior coaching takes place at the vast majority of them. When Glen Chapple's players went on the road in the summer of 2011, they gave more young cricketers easier access to four-day county matches than had been possible in previous years, or will be practicable in the future. Some of those spectators, perhaps, were encouraged in their efforts to emulate their new heroes.

If 2011 is already enshrined as the year when the outright Championship returned to Old Trafford, it may also come to be seen as a time when the next but one generation of the county's cricketers were fired with the enthusiasm to tread the same paths as Tom Smith and Karl Brown. Viewed from that perspective, Lancashire's summer on the road appears an even more vital experience, not only for Chapple's players, but also for the youngsters who were inspired to realise their lovely dreams.

Four Blokes at a Cricket Match

The Team behind the Team

by Paul Edwards

AS might have been expected, *The Cricketer* went big on Lancashire's Championship success. The "world's No.1 cricket magazine" devoted most of six pages in its November 2011 issue to reports and interviews, and page 28 is dominated by a photograph of the title-winning squad in all its celebratory pomp. Mouths agape, the players and coaches are thrusting cans of lager at the camera and are clearly in the middle of an almighty cheer, chant or song.

But wait a moment…what's this? On the extreme right of the snap is a distinguished silver-haired figure, immaculately turned out in navy-blue blazer and tie. He is obviously pleased with events, but the tube of Foster's looks a little incongruous in his hand; one suspects he would prefer a pint of Thwaites' bitter, or possibly a decent Merlot. Also, while most of the Lancashire squad are clearly on the far side of ecstasy and preparing to party "big style", our subject seems intent on savouring a moment for which he has, in fact, been waiting for all of the 61 years since he first visited Old Trafford. None of these impressions are wide of the mark. "I'm not an emotional chap," concedes the Lancashire scorer Alan West. "I'm pretty phlegmatic and I don't leap up and down or get very excited. I just feel very contented inside."

Now let us rewind to that Steven Croft shot which, if it didn't ring around the world, certainly resounded down the Rossendale Valley. Ken Grime was sitting in the away dressing room at Taunton tweeting characters of joy to LCCC's followers at the moment the title was won; he was also managing the Lancashire website. Such multi-tasking is all part of a summer day for a man who joined the staff at Old Trafford 30 years ago last August. "It was the week of Botham's Test," he remembered. "I was the accounts department, lock, stock and one smoking barrel. When I started we had an office staff of nine and four ground staff and that was it. The staff now numbers over a hundred." Grime is also the county's Marketing Services Manager and the Match Manager for home games. Like West, he comes from a family which was deeply involved in league cricket and he is a Lancashire supporter to his marrow.

So when Croft cut Craig Meschede for four to clinch the title, the club's longest serving employee could have been forgiven for losing it a little? The reality was rather different. "I make a conscious effort to separate supporting the team and working at Lancashire," he explained. "When we get games that go down to the last ball or the final over, part of me insists that I've got to be professional about it all. When we won the title you can see me on the TV grabbing the camera that I've got next to the laptop and taking photographs. I could easily have downed tools and gone leaping around with everyone else but I had to take photographs to see if I got anything worthwhile. I knew I had a job to do rather than running out on the pitch and going mad."

Over in Somerset's committee room another Lancashire supporter was careful to keep his emotions in check, albeit that he was almost bursting with pride. Keith Hayhurst has been on the committee at Old Trafford for 25 years and he now sits on the board, which makes most of the key decisions at the club. He is secretary of the Players Association and curator of the museum. At his own expense, he publishes and circulates "the green book" which gives the names and contact details of every other committee member in the country. Since taking early retirement from his job as an Education Inspector 25 years ago - he had also been a Primary School headmaster – Hayhurst has only missed a handful of Lancashire games. Dapper, enthusiastic and possessed of exquisite manners, he likes nothing more than to sit with fellow cricket lovers and watch Lancashire play well. In the best sense, he is a supporter of old school: being offered a high five by Hayhurst would be about as surprising as discovering that Tinchy Stryder had landed a part in *Downton Abbey*.

Scorer Alan West holds the trophy aloft at Taunton

"During the season a lot of people from other counties told me that this was Lancashire's year," said Hayhurst, "After we won it, I was contacted by at least one committee member from each county to offer their congratulations. I've always had a tremendous passion for Lancashire cricket and the nice thing is that these players share that. They have a youthful, infectious confidence, which has been inculcated by Peter Moores, who is a very skilful coach. They also have a naïve enthusiasm, they're wonderful to be with and they put on a spirited exhibition of cricket in the way I like it to be played."

Spirit, however, is only of limited use without fitness, especially in the 2011 English season when Lancashire's cricketers were scheduled to play on 92 of the 161 days between April 8 and September 15. The physical condition of the Old Trafford players is the responsibility of Sam Byrne, who, paradoxically, is one of the key men on the Old Trafford staff and also one of the least recognisable. (Perhaps it is fitting that his face is half-hidden on that *Cricketer* photograph.)

"An hour before a game, when they are wondering if a player will be able to last four days, they are all staring at Sam," said the ex-England physio and current Old Trafford Head of Medical Services Dave Roberts. Such comments give a vivid insight into the importance of Byrne's work and they cast light on a side of professional cricket not seen by anyone but the players and coaches themselves.

"Cricket puts huge demands on the players' bodies and on those of the bowlers in particular," said Byrne. "We had periods this year when we played almost every day for

Ken Grime celebrates at Taunton with Sajid Mahmood and Karl Brown

three weeks, and in between we had days when we were travelling. It's incredibly hard but you can't approach that in a negative way, you have to see it as a challenge and our players have certainly done that. At the beginning of the year we looked at the fixtures on a big white board, accepted what we had to do and got on with it. We like to think the team is one of the fittest in the country."

Lancashire's "staff" at Taunton numbered many more than the four men we have considered. There was, for example, David Sleight, a supporter who regards a drive from his home in Glasgow to his other home at the Old Trafford Lodge as casually as if he were popping out to Spar for a pint of milk. Strength and conditioning coach Alex Horn, analyst Emma Allsop and psychologist Lee Richardson contributed to the win enormously, while there were others, like the club's former analyst and fielding coach Jason Swift, who played a huge part but couldn't be there to see the title secured. What unites them is not just a fondness for the club but a quite unforced liking for the mostly young players on the staff.

"I'm old enough to be the grandfather of some of them but they're a great set of lads and they're very good to me," said West, whose quiet demeanour does not hide his deep-rooted affections. Grime took up the theme. "Along with the 1990s side, this is the Lancashire team to which I feel closest," he admitted. "This is just a fantastic bunch and I can't speak too highly of them. We get on well and they're very helpful to me in what I do and I do my best to support them in any way I can. I think that is appreciated." But it is perhaps Hayhurst who sums up the supporters' view best: "These players went out and gave joy to us," he said.

For Glen Chapple's men, the autumn of 2011 was taken up with dinners and interviews, a visit to the Palace and yet more interviews. Yet when all the ballyhoo had died down, one of the most pleasant things to be said about Lancashire's cricketers was that they and their backroom staff deserved each other.

Nobody Wants to Make the Tea

John Stanworth and the Lancashire Academy

by Paul Edwards

CRITICS wishing to put the mockers on a group of young sportsmen could do far worse than label it "a golden generation". All too often a lack of discipline, heart or gumption can put paid to exciting potential, even as the first bloom of youth rests gentle upon it. So the person who is charged with developing raw talent at a first-class county has one of the most vital jobs on the staff. Please step forward John Stanworth, one of the principal architects of Lancashire's 2011 County Championship triumph.

Stanworth is steeped in Lancashire cricket. A player from 1983 until 1994, he has since held a number of important posts at Old Trafford, including that of Player Development Manager. But it is as director of the Lancashire Academy that he has made his most lasting contribution to the county. The 51-year-old former wicketkeeper celebrates 10 years in the job next summer and of the 53 cricketers who have attended the Academy since its opening, 17 have played county cricket, 10 of them in Lancashire's first team. Of the side that beat Somerset, eight have come through an Old Trafford youth system developed and managed by Stanworth and his skilled colleagues Gary Yates and Steve Titchard.

Behind the statistics lies a structure designed to identify talent and develop it as fully as possible: the Emerging Players Programme ensures that the fundamentals are in place; the Academy allows Stanworth to develop young cricketers and prepare them to play competitively; the Scholarship programme is a much-valued bridge between the Academy and a possible professional contract. "Academy and Scholarship places are not determined by age," said Stanworth. "Players must possess the necessary skill to have any chance of playing professionally, but after that, it's the character of a player that can determine whether he is kept on or not. The Scholarship system helps us to make that decision."

Examining a cricketer's character invariably entails challenges, although sometimes it is the coach himself who needs to review his methods: Stanworth admits that working in an elite environment with the England Under-19 squad in 2009/10 elevated his horizons. Then the arrival of Peter Moores in 2009 came at just the right time for him. The two men sang from the same flip-chart. "I found myself working with an elite coach who had been working in an elite environment," said Stanworth.

Helped by the other Old Trafford staff, the pair sought to test the players who would soon be mounting an assault on the title. "We had performance nets and challenge days when there was a consequence to finishing last, and that was often a menial task, like making everyone a brew," said Stanworth. "The person who finished bottom didn't feel that good but it was all done in a supportive way. I don't think it's a coincidence that Karl Brown performed as he did in 2011, because last winter he was challenged to bat for half an hour against an 85 mph bowling machine with the ball swinging away quite dramatically. He was one of the few players who survived that test and the other batters wanted to match him. There was a challenge for every individual."

The Lancashire players warmed to the demanding regime, even when it exposed their deficiencies. "John can be pretty blunt but he knows what makes you tick as a player," said Simon Kerrigan. "He'll tell you if you're not fit enough or if your fielding needs to improve. He makes Academy players experience professional situations."

"It was when I was at the Academy that I first started to believe I could be a professional cricketer," added Steven Croft. "There was a definite element of challenge, but John also got me to look at my technique and encouraged me to go back to playing my natural game. He was highly respected and we all wanted to do our best for him."

The effectiveness of these long apprenticeships was itself put to the test on September 1, 2011 when Glen Chapple's players returned to the pavilion at New Road having lost to Worcestershire by 10 wickets in little over a day and a half. In their dressing room the visiting players sat and listened to Daryl Mitchell's men banging their bats in celebration. Suddenly, everyone was doubting Lancashire's title credentials.

Well, perhaps not everyone. "The Worcestershire players were stronger than us mentally and I don't think we were prepared for them to be at us as they were," Stanworth reflected. "There was a little time for the players to dust themselves off, but then they just worked their tails off. There's always been something about Gareth Cross's character which has spoken to me, but I've never seen him work with any greater intensity in all the time I've known him than after that defeat. He'd bagged a pair and he was determined that wasn't going to happen to him again. He wasn't going to be making the tea again. As coaches we didn't need to say anything. Peter has a calmness which doesn't make too much of a victory or a loss. As a quality coach he went about sowing the seed of the next challenge and players came back with a renewed desire."

Precisely a fortnight later that collective desire was in evidence again as the Lancashire players responded to their final challenge of the season. Stanworth couldn't be at Taunton for the final day of the first-class season, but, perhaps appropriately enough, he watched the final overs of the game on TV in the Academy. "I couldn't believe we were going to win it and I wasn't there," he said, "but then I saw Browny and Crofty hug and I was emotional… and I still am…it couldn't have been any better…to see two of our initial Academy intake hugging each other just after winning the title with that group of players was brilliant."

John Stanworth was at Taunton all right. Great coaches are present on every ground where their graduates perform. They influence players without impairing their essential talent. And amid their revelry in Somerset, more than a few former members of the Lancashire Academy contacted their former coach; perhaps they recalled cold winter mornings and hard practice sessions with the man whose quiet dedication helped them become professional cricketers. Meanwhile, over at the Rose Bowl, Warwickshire's players were making the tea.

Will the Eliminator

Twenty20 Finals Day 2011

by Paul Edwards

THE most stinging memories of failure which Lancashire's cricketers sought to expunge in 2011 stretched back to the eras of Al Bowlly and Buddy Holly. Their disappointments at Twenty20 Finals Day, though, recalled nothing more distant than the rarely remembered heyday of Atomic Kitten. Three times in four years the Old Trafford side had attended English cricket's twelve-hour festival of admirable invention and regrettable kitsch, only to return home with nothing more substantial than victory in the Mascots' Race.

2011 saw no improvement in the Red Rose's fortunes at Edgbaston, but at least Glen Chapple's players took part in the English professional game's first ever one-over match after their semi-final against Leicestershire had ended in a tie. Dubbed 'The Eliminator', the title of this affair reminded some spectators of the brutal robot played by Arnold Schwarzenegger in one of his more thoughtful films; so perhaps it was fitting that the ultra-short form of the game was settled by a giant of a man, 6ft 10ins Will Jefferson pulling Gary Keedy high into the Hollies Stand to overhaul Lancashire's total of 13 with one ball to spare – which, in a one-over thrash, comes rather near to showing off.

What made this defeat all the more annoying was that Lancashire's prospects in the Friends Life t20 had looked bright: successive victories in their final six group games secured an increasingly impressive Old Trafford team a quarter-final tie at Hove, where a tightly-controlled bowling and fielding performance helped them defeat Sussex by 20 runs.

However, hopes for success at Birmingham in late August were dampened by the unavailability of the Pakistani fast bowler Junaid Khan, whose ability to bowl swinging 90mph yorkers had caught the approving attention of his country's selectors, who promptly summoned him home to prepare for the tour of Zimbabwe. James Anderson was also unavailable for the Birmingham jamboree, but Chapple had made the best of a mid-season lay-off caused by a muscle pull and seemed as fit as he might have expected to be in April. The Lancashire skipper proclaimed his readiness for battle by having Josh Cobb caught behind off the first ball of Finals Day.

Stephen Parry and Gary Keedy built on this breakthrough by bowling their eight overs for 40 runs and Leicestershire's total of 132-6 in 18 overs – there had been a 45-minute break for rain – seemed little better than par. At 53-1 after 8.1 overs Lancashire's batsmen were well placed to book their place in the final and, thereby, in the lucrative Champions League, but yet more rain caused the target to be reduced to 80 in 11 overs. The headlong dash for 27 runs in 17 balls saw five wickets lost in 14 deliveries and it needed Gareth Cross to whack Wayne White's last ball over long-on for six to trigger that one-over showdown.

"Well, it rained," said Chapple pithily, as he identified one factor in his team's defeat. "It's entertainment," he added later, and, yes, that was a crucial factor too: the semi-final had been reduced to an 11-over contest to make sure the Final started at 7pm, and in order to accommodate other elements of the Finals Day experience, such as the Mascots' Race. Even there, though, misery awaited the Lancastrian faithful as the pre-race favourite Lanky the Giraffe entered the ball pond and didn't re-emerge until his rivals were cantering away in the distance. "It comes to something when you can't even rely on a felt mammal to cheer you up," said one Red Rose fan. "I had hoof issues," mourned the inconsolable giraffe.

Epilogue

...about bloomin' time!

1934 is a life-time away (most members don't count the shared Championship in 1950) and it seems in a different age: Pre-war, although Hitler was making mischief in Germany, Bonnie & Clyde and John Dillinger creating mayhem in the USA. In Manchester spectators (mostly male) in grey overcoats, flat caps or trilbies were making their way to Old Trafford from the mighty engineering works and factories in Trafford Park.

There is at least one member, Ken Thomas (The Lancashire & Cheshire Cricket Society Chairman) who remembers the Championship victory. He was only ten and his father was a keen Lancashire member. One of his first cricket memories was listening to the Bodyline series in 1932-33 from Australia with Eddie Paynter (his hero) being summoned from his hospital bed to help win the Test series.

In 1934 Len Hopwood took the first of his two doubles of 1,000 runs and 100 wickets, the only Lancashire player to do this twice. Jack Iddon was in that team too, with his straight, lofted drives over the bowler's head, and, of course, Ernest Tyldesley, who played in five Championship-winning teams. Cyril Washbrook made his first appearances for the county and there was, of course, the flamboyant Lancashire wicket-keeper George Duckworth, whose appeal could be heard at the other Old Trafford!

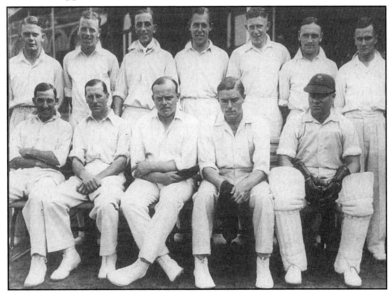

Back: Cyril Washbrook, Len Hopwood, Jack Iddon, Frank Booth, Dick Pollard, Len Parkinson, Buddy Oldfield. Seated: Eddie Paynter, Ernest Tyldesley, Peter Eckersley (capt.), Lionel Lister, George Duckworth.

Copyright Lancashire CCC

The expectation was different then. Lancashire were expected to win the Championship after all they had done it in 1926, '27, '28 and '30. Four years was like a drought. How little did they realise that it would be another 77 years before the Championship pennant could once again fly on the Pavilion.

Lancashire had won the Championship so many times that the committee were stuck as to what to give the players. They had already given them a silver cigarette case, silver lighter, silver plate and tankard. In 1934 the players had to settle for a clock!

The season did not begin well, with only two wins from their first eight matches. There was a revival with victories at Bristol, Southampton and Worcester. Then the titanic battle at Trent Bridge against Notts' feared fast bowlers, Harold Larwood and Bill Voce, with Lionel Lister scoring a fighting 86 helping to secure a crucial victory.

Lancashire finished with 13 wins out of 30 matches, but they were virtually impossible to beat and harvested vital points from draws and first innings leads. They drew their last four games, clinching the title at the Oval with Surrey following on.

They had a very lucky captain in Peter Eckersley, who won the toss 24 times out of 30. He also piloted a plane the following year with the team in it to an away game. Later he became an MP for Manchester (pause for thought Glen!).

Perhaps one of the greatest similarities between 2011 and 1934 is that most of the team in 1934 were born in Lancashire. The Lancashire team this year have come up together through the Academy, with most having played in the county all of their lives.

Maybe it was written in the heavens that Lancashire would win the Championship in 2011. Earlier in the year Manchester City won the FA Cup – and when did they also win it? Why, 1934 of course! It only happens once in a blue moon and this was the year!

Rev Malcolm Lorimer,
Lancashire Chaplain